WATERCOLOR
made simple

techniques, projects, and
encouragement to get started
painting and creating

NICKI TRAIKOS
of life i design

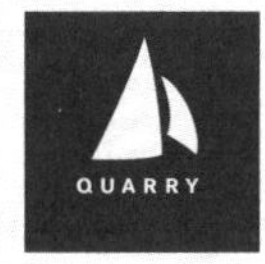

Quarto.com

© 2023 Quarto Publishing Group USA Inc.
Text, Photos, Illustrations © 2023 Antroniki Traikos

First published in 2023 by Walter Foster Publishing, an imprint of The Quarto Group,
100 Cummings Center, Suite 265D, Beverly, MA 01915, USA.
T (978) 282-9590 F (978) 283-2742

Quarry Books titles are also available at discount for retail, wholesale, promotional,
and bulk purchase. For details, contact the Special Sales Manager by email at
specialsales@quarto.com or by mail at The Quarto Group, Attn: Special Sales Manager,
100 Cummings Center, Suite 265-D, Beverly, MA 01915, USA.

27 26 25 24   4 5

ISBN: 978-0-7603-8319-3

Digital edition published in 2023
eISBN: 978-0-7603-8320-9

Library of Congress Cataloging-in-Publication Data

Names: Traikos, Nicki, author.
Title: Watercolor made simple : techniques, projects, and encouragement to
  get started painting and creating / Nicki Traikos of life design.
Description: Beverly, MA : Quarry Books, 2023. | Includes index. | Summary:
  "Watercolor Made Simple gently guides aspiring artists to develop their
  watercolor skills and create beautiful paintings in a relaxing and
  enjoyable way"-- Provided by publisher.
Identifiers: LCCN 2023011657 (print) | LCCN 2023011658 (ebook) | ISBN
  9780760383193 (trade paperback) | ISBN 9780760383209 (ebook)
Subjects: LCSH: Watercolor painting--Technique.
Classification: LCC ND2420.T73 2023 (print) | LCC ND2420 (ebook) | DDC
  751.42/2--dc23/eng/20230411
LC record available at https://lccn.loc.gov/2023011657
LC ebook record available at https://lccn.loc.gov/2023011658

Cover and page design: Stacy Wakefield Forte
Cover artwork and photo styling: Nicki Traikos
Photography: Lisa Brygidyr
Page layout: Cindy Samargia Laun

Printed in China

ACKNOWLEDGMENTS

Planning, designing, and writing this book has been a dream come true for me and has come to life with the help and support of a few people whom I want to personally thank and celebrate!

First, thank you to my editor Michelle at Quarry, whose email arrived in my inbox at just the perfect moment. Thank you for being open to me creating and designing a book that shares my passion and personal approach to art and watercolor and for supporting me through the entire process. Also, thank you to the amazing team at Quarto—Hailey, Karen, Lydia, to name a few—for making this project fun to work on and for creating a beautiful book with all the extra touches that make it special.

Thank you to my friend Lisa for the many photography sessions and for working with me to bring my ideas for this book to life.

Thank you to John and Nate, whose partnership has resulted in connecting and helping thousands of people all over the world learn and fall in love with watercolor painting through my online classes.

Thank you to one of my dearest friends, Rosa, for always celebrating and supporting me and for the endless chats, coffee dates, and text messages through this entire process.

Thank you to my parents, who may not always understand my creative path but always support and encourage me.

Finally, to my loves: John, Marcus, and Sabrina—you are where my inspiration comes from and the reason why I do all that I do.

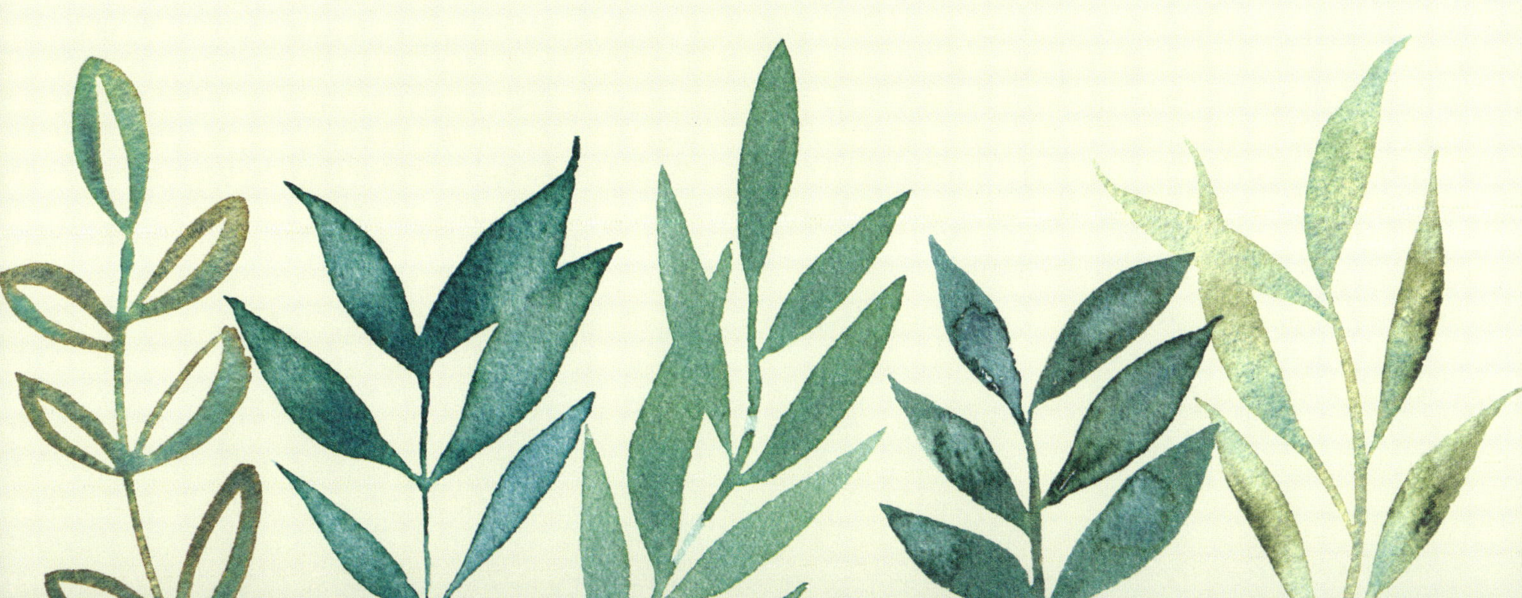

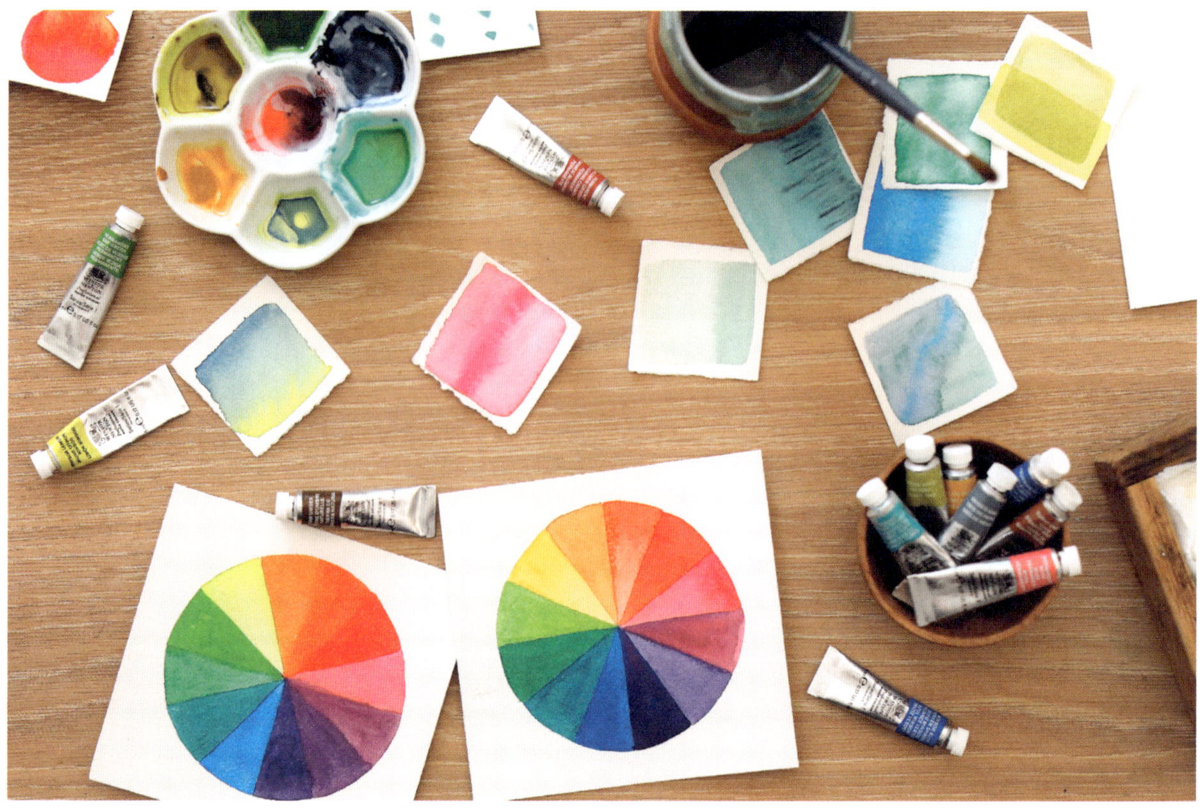

1 FOUNDATIONS

2 PRACTICE AND PLAY

3 FUNDAMENTALS

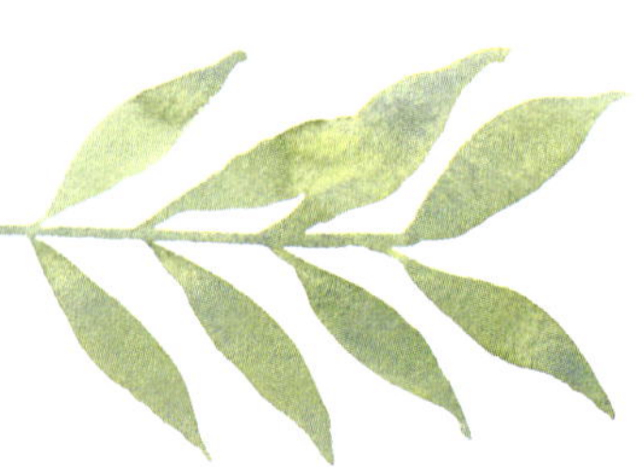

CONTENTS

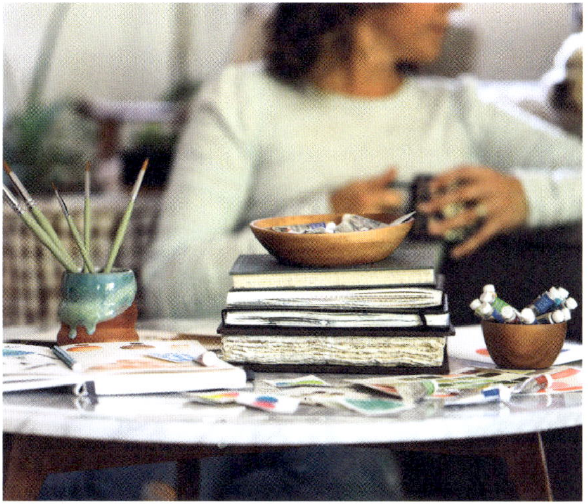
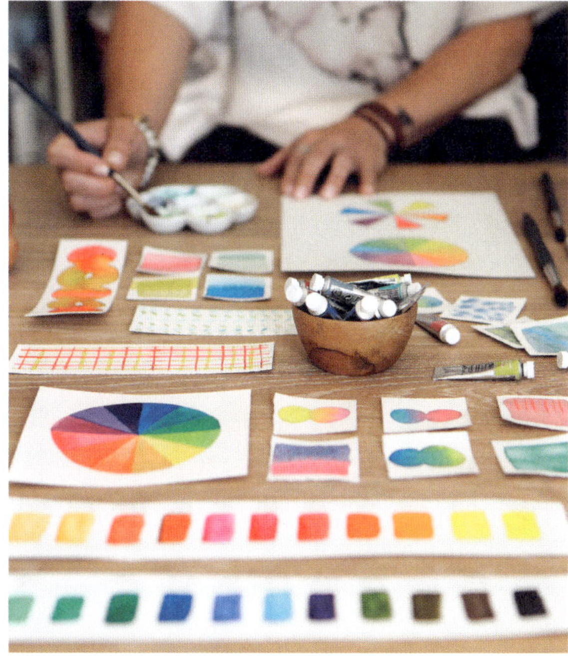
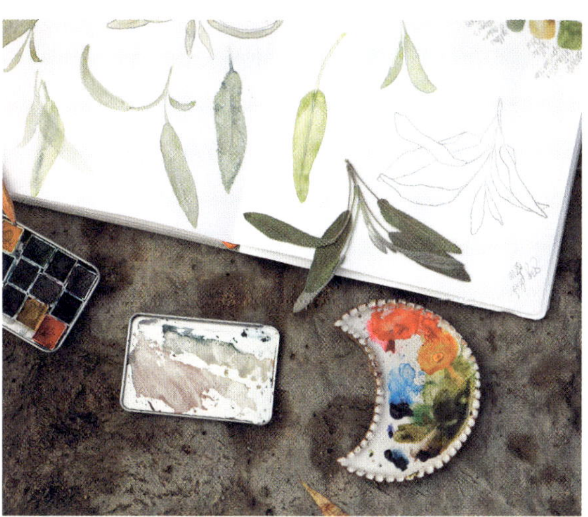

INTRODUCTION

Growing up, I always dreamed of being an artist but had no idea how to become one, never mind being too intimidated to even try. It wasn't until my early forties that I had the courage and the time to allow myself room to explore making art. With determination, I picked up a paintbrush again and again and allowed myself freedom to paint whatever needed to come out that day. I learned how to work with watercolor, not against it. When it all finally started coming together, I truly understood what it was like to actually be an artist. It's not about making gallery-worthy art, it's simply about following your artistic calling as you make art and enjoy the process along the way. That to me is what being an artist is all about.

A few years ago, I went on a mission to help others have similar breakthroughs. My goal was to create online classes to help fellow artists on their creative journey. I wanted to offer simple tools and techniques that would help encourage them not only to try but also to have success. Many of my online art students had always wanted to try watercolor painting but never had the time or the opportunity to learn. Through sharing my personal, casual approach to painting using watercolors, and with specific techniques and exercises in my online class, Watercolors Made Simple, students are now enjoying doing something special for themselves and, for many, fulfilling a lifelong dream of finally learning how to paint.

This book, *Watercolor Made Simple*, is a wonderful companion on your watercolor journey as I share with you my simplified and most important tips, techniques, and projects, guiding you through your personal watercolor art practice. I encourage you to spend time doing something for you, that you love, and that will hopefully lead to hours spent in a relaxed and joy-filled state as you make watercolor art.

I've designed this book to take you through an enjoyable journey of learning how to use watercolors with confidence and ease. Through painting simple projects, your confidence and experience with watercolor paints will grow, and I suspect you'll want to paint multiple versions of the painting projects. With the guidance in this book and with practice, you will ease into watercolor painting and enjoy what you paint. I even include line drawings of all the projects that you can trace onto your watercolor paper to make it a little easier to get started painting.

Before we get started, I'd like to share my biggest tip or piece of advice with you. I know it's easy to skip pages or, maybe if you're pressed for time, skip an entire exercise, but I encourage you to read every bit of text, try each exercise at least once, and allow yourself some grace as you go. Each time you sit down to paint, even if it's just painting color swatches or a page of leaves, you are building muscle memory, creating a habit, and connecting to your creative spirit. Don't rob yourself of those simple moments, because in those moments, there is opportunity for growth and joy. I want you to fall in love with watercolor painting, but also to be happy with the results you get from practical experience. So read the text and enjoy the images, but then put the book down, pick up your brush, and get painting.

n o t e ······ I'd love to see your paintings from this book. Share your work with me on Instagram by tagging me at @lifeidesign.

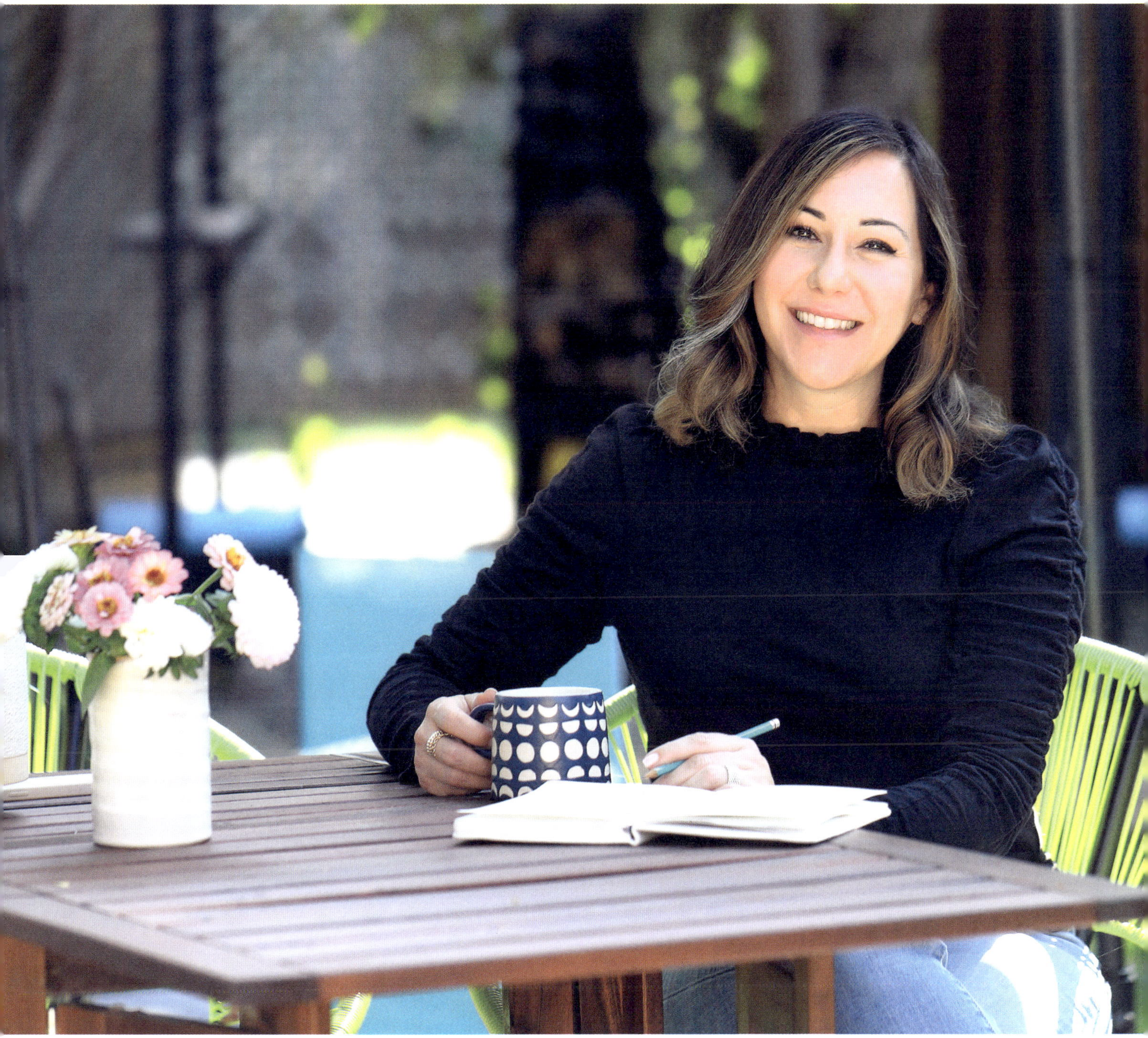

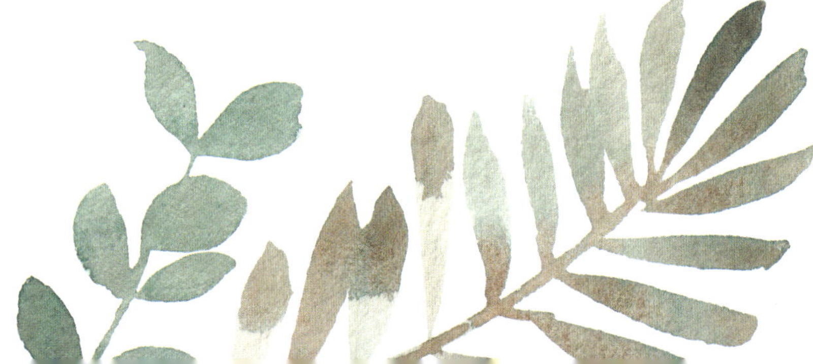

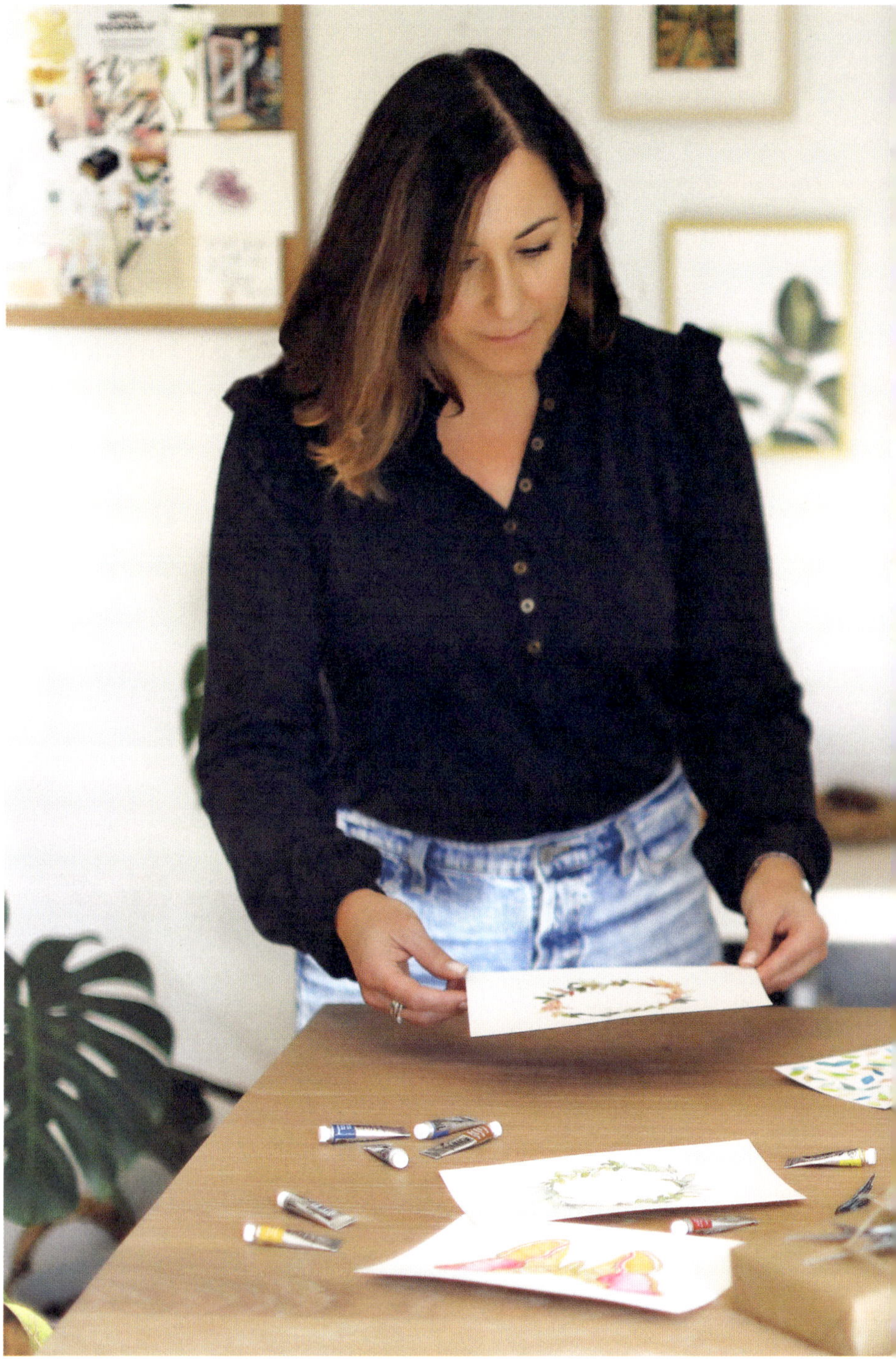

1

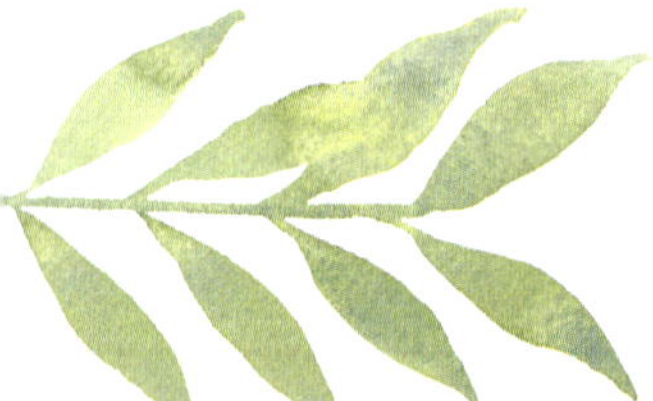

FOUNDATIONS

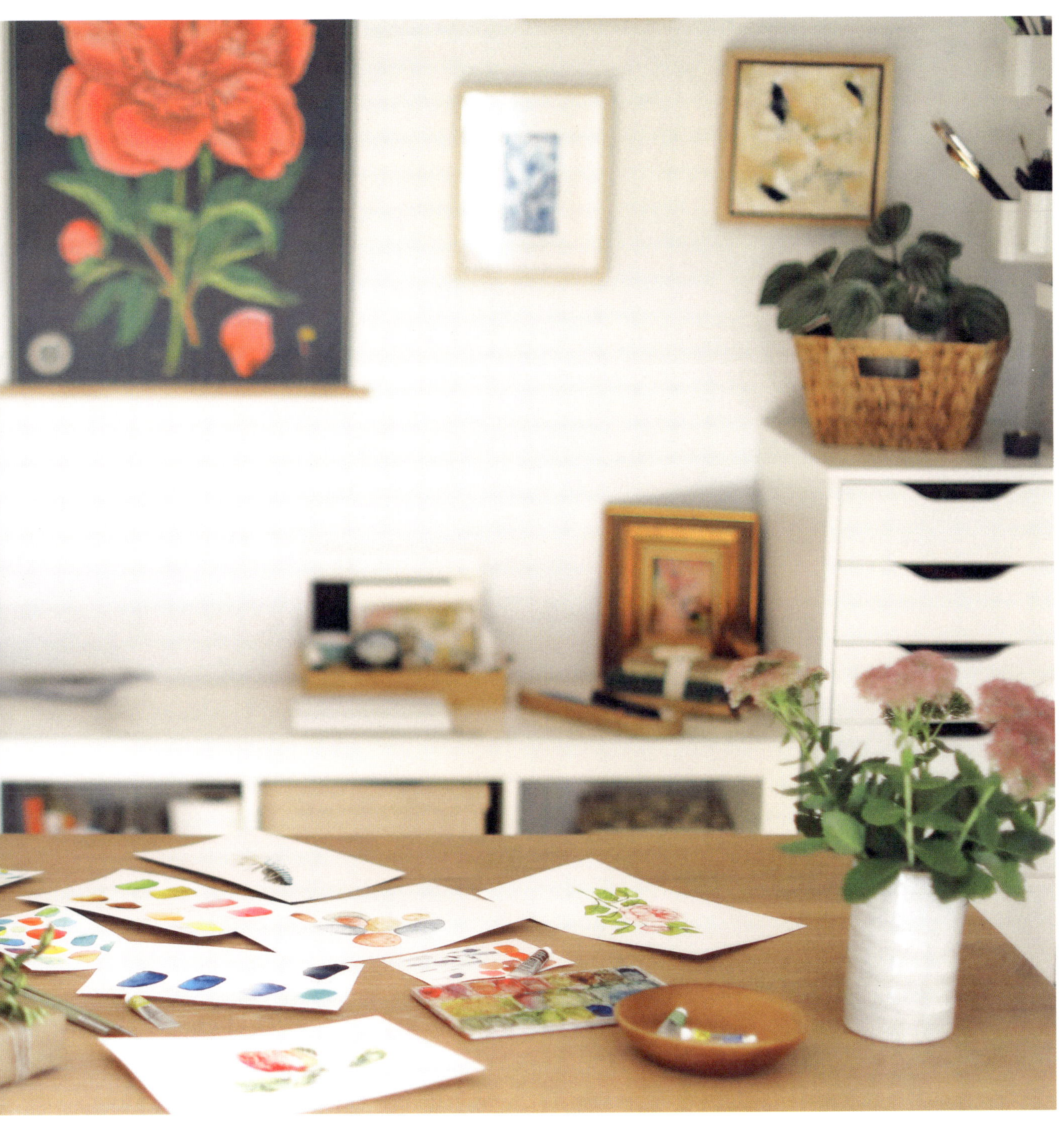

My love affair with watercolors started in 2015 when I was looking for ways to enhance my calligraphy art. I'd never painted with watercolor, but I was immediately mesmerized as I saw the effortless color variation possible within a single stroke. I fell hard and fast and soon upgraded my craft-level dry palette to tubes of beautiful watercolor paint. I looked for watercolor-specific brushes and experimented with papers. I spent many hours and probably a lot of money finding what worked best for me. In this chapter, I will share what I have learned about watercolor supplies and everything else you need to know to get started so you can begin painting with confidence.

BUILDING YOUR WATERCOLOR KIT

The questions I am most often asked are about supplies. I recommend to my students that they buy the best-quality supplies they can afford. If you start out using good-quality supplies, you will be happier with your results; however, it doesn't mean that you can't begin experimenting using student-grade supplies. The goal is simply to get started.

When I started watercolor painting, I used a craft-level dry palette and painted on cellulose paper and I just practiced and practiced and practiced. As soon as I could afford better tools, I upgraded, and it was like magic. My finished paintings were suddenly incredibly rich with color and the overall look and feel made me happier, making me even more excited to paint and practice.

Keep in mind, you may not have access to the same products and brands that I use in this book, and you may have a different budget to work with as you begin to fill your watercolor kit—and that's okay. If you can visit a local art supply shop, I urge you to shop in person and really enjoy the experience of seeing colors and materials firsthand as you begin stocking your watercolor kit.

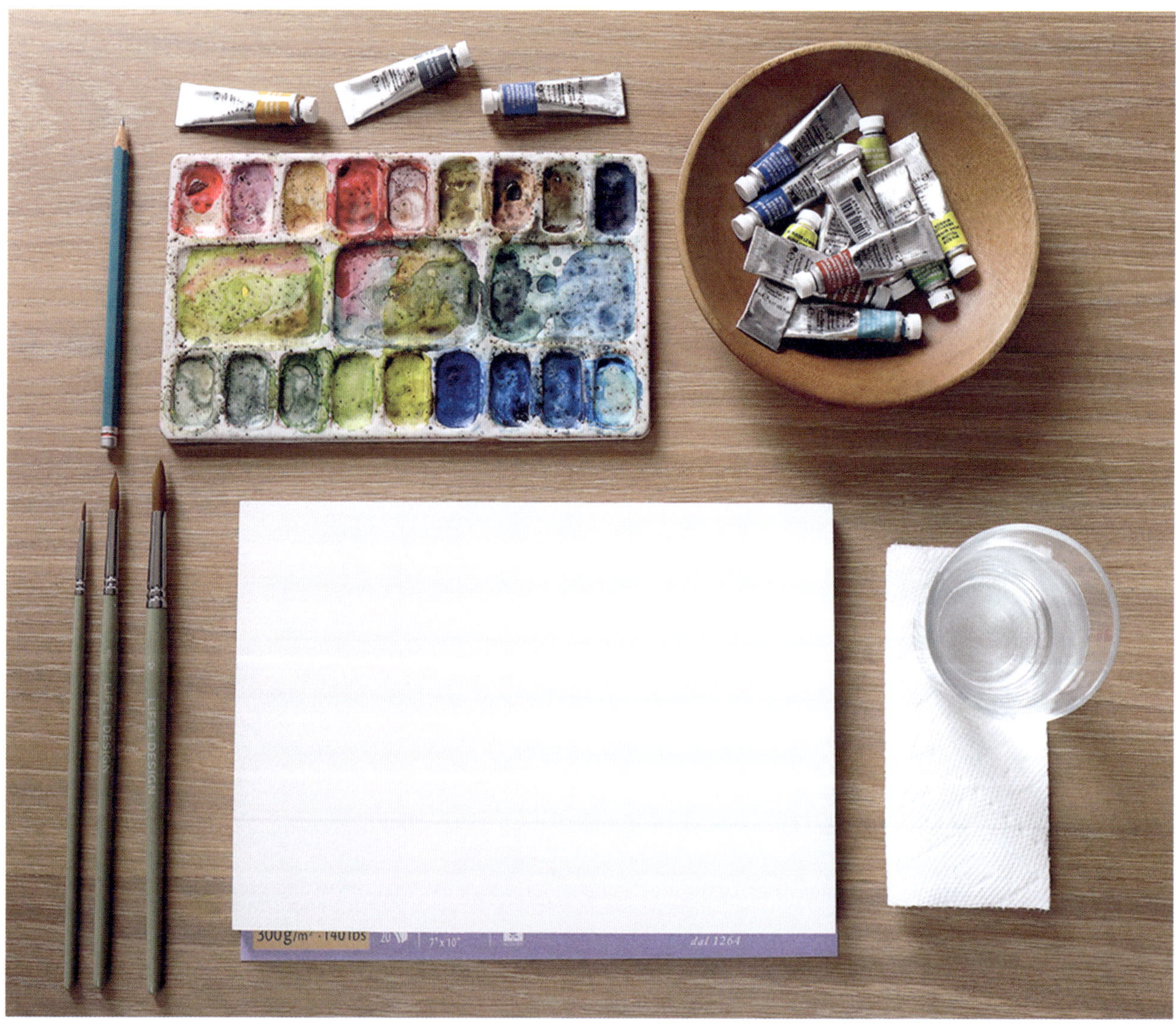

You don't need many supplies to get started exploring and painting with watercolors!

WATERCOLOR PAINT

What is watercolor paint anyway? Watercolor is a paint medium that offers such beauty and personality when you allow it to move, puddle, and dry as it likes. It is a water-based medium that is traditionally made using finely ground pigments, which are then added to a binder called gum arabic. The paint is activated using water and can be reactivated with water even when dried. Once you get the hang of painting with it, I'm hoping you will embrace all the texture and character that only watercolor paint offers.

Watercolor paint most often comes in two forms: dry palettes and tubes. What's the difference? Really, it comes down to how quickly you want to get started painting.

My preference is to use tubes of professional-quality watercolor. I can easily squeeze a pea-size amount of paint onto my mixing palette and know that the color will be intense with just a tiny bit of water mixed in. If I want to dilute the paint and create a more transparent mix, I just have to add more water to the paint. That's it.

With a dry palette, you need to "wake up" the paint by adding drops of water to the dry pan. You then have to use a mixing palette to start mixing your perfect watercolor puddle before you start painting. This requires a bit more time and patience. But watercolor painting requires lots of patience anyway, so for some, this is the meditative start to their painting session.

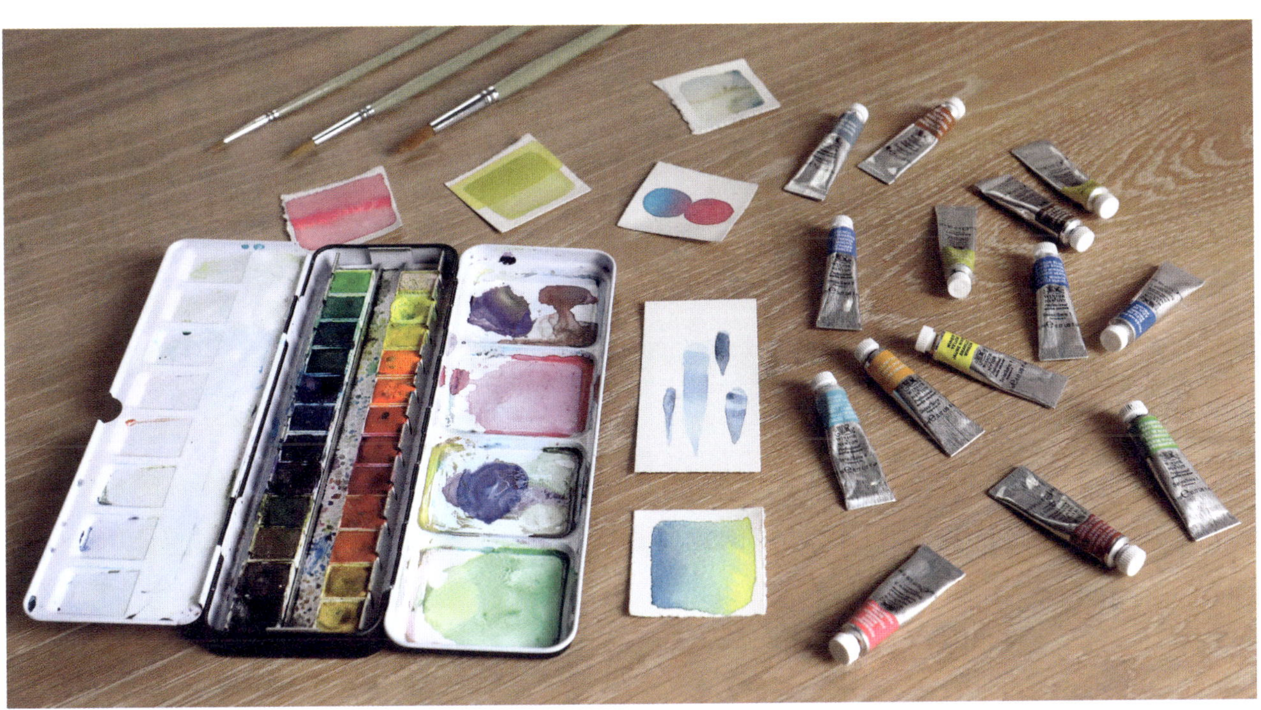

I prefer to work with tubes of paint, but a pan set can be very convenient.

t i p ······ I like the ready, set, paint approach to my watercolor practice, so I stick to watercolor tubes, but dry palettes do travel really easily, so I have a few dry pan sets that I love to use for travel.

BRUSHES

I paint using mostly round brushes. Round, pointed brushes offer the ability to paint thin fine lines as well as full, robust brushstrokes. For the projects in this book, I recommend that you have three different round brushes on hand: a large one for laying down washes of color, a medium one with a fine tip that spreads out really well to allow you to paint thin and thick strokes, and a small, fine, detail brush. This is the brush that you will use to add details to your piece as well as some fine lettering if you choose. Keep in mind what size paintings you'll be working on before you invest in brushes. I normally paint pieces that are about 9 by 12 inches (23 by 30 cm), so I don't need huge brushes.

Look for brushes that are made and designed specifically for watercolor paints. Watercolor-specific brushes are designed to hold lots of water and, as you place the brush onto watercolor paper, it should easily dispense the watery paint mix onto your paper.

As for brush hair type, there really are only two options: synthetic or animal hair. I have dozens of watercolor brushes and only three are real (animal) hair rather than synthetic. They are not my favorite to paint with, and I wouldn't recommend them because they are expensive. A good-quality nylon or synthetic hair brush can offer you years and years of painting without having to spend a small fortune.

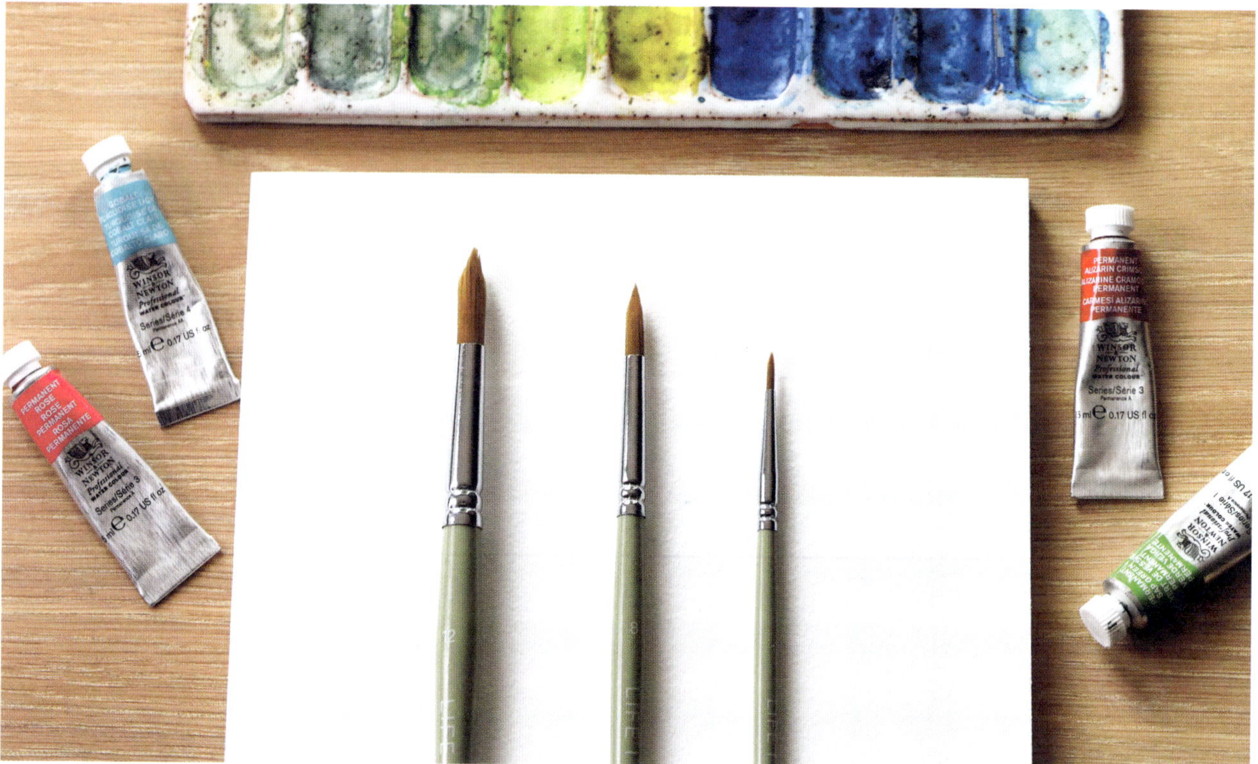

A few sizes of round brushes are all you need to paint more subjects.

WATERCOLOR PAPER

When I first started teaching, I had my students work on pulp, not cotton, paper. I did this for a few reasons, but mostly because it's very common for people to feel like they're wasting pricey paper with simple warm-up brushstrokes. This fear will often stop beginners from practicing. That is not the goal here. You need to warm up and practice your beginning strokes, feel the brush move on the paper, and observe the watercolor as it flows. I can describe it to you in as much detail as possible, but the only way to truly understand watercolor and how it behaves is by DOING.

Sorry to shout there. I want you to know that if you are feeling like you're wasting expensive paper by practicing, have a pad of pulp-based watercolor paper for practice and a pad of cotton-based paper for painting projects. When you paint on cotton paper, you will be able to use lots of water without the paper buckling, you will be able to lift color off the paper without ruining your piece, and when your paint is dry, you will be very happy with the finish because your colors will be more intense and vibrant.

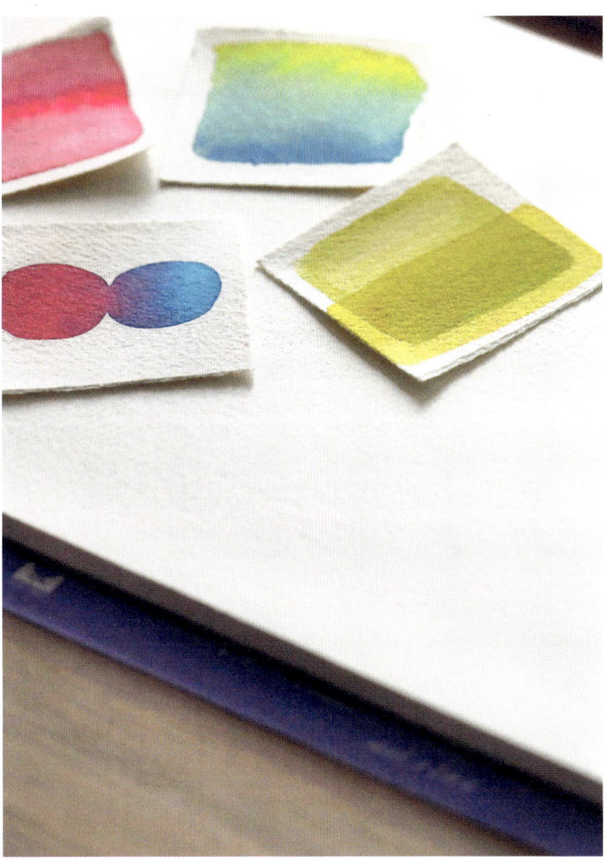

Look for watercolor paper made from cotton vs. pulp for the best painting experience.

MISCELLANEOUS SUPPLIES

Here are a few other items I suggest you have handy before you get started painting.

- Mixing palette: Preferably ceramic, because it allows you to easily mix watercolor on it. An old dish works great.
- Two water jars: Keep them clean and freshen with new water when the water begins to look muddy.
- Spray bottle or eyedropper to wake up a dry palette.
- Kitchen towels/clean cloths for wiping your brush.
- Pencil for tracing and sketching before you paint.
- Eraser: Kneadable erasers don't leave behind dust or residue.
- Tissues for dabbing off any excess water or to use for clouds.

EXTRAS

These supplies are recommended but not a must for you to get started painting.

- A watercolor sketchbook is a great place to work on your practice.
- White gouache (opaque watercolor) or white ink for adding a bit of highlight to your piece.
- Spray varnish to seal paintings. (See page 121 for more on varnish.)

tip ······ Cold press paper has texture, while hot press is smooth. My preference is cold press, as I love the texture it offers.

CHOOSING COLORS

Another popular question I get asked often is which colors to buy. I started out as a modern calligraphy artist and primarily worked in black. I shied away from colors because I didn't understand color theory well enough. As someone who doesn't wear a lot of color or use a lot of color in my home decorating, it's hard for me to think beyond white, black, and gray.

Working with colors and learning color theory is something that I suggest you spend some time on as you grow your watercolor skills. In an upcoming section, I'll show you how to use primary colors (yellow, magenta, blue) to mix a variety of colors. In the meantime, I'll share some of my personal favorites that you may consider stocking in your own watercolor kit, too.

If you've taken any classes with me, you know I always share the following: **"Paint what you love, using colors that you love, and you will love what you paint."**

So if colors that I use or suggest don't speak to you, please feel free to use colors that make YOU happy and want to paint more.

As you continue to grow your watercolor practice and paint, you will notice that you reach for the same colors again and again. This is how you begin to develop your artistic style and personal preference for what colors speak to you and make you excited to paint. I have a strong love affair with a few colors that can be found not only in my watercolor paint kit but also in my acrylic paints, my mark-making tools, and my tubes of gouache.

On the opposite page are swatches of all the colors I use in the painting projects in this book. You can also use yellow, magenta, and blue from any paint line as your primary colors.

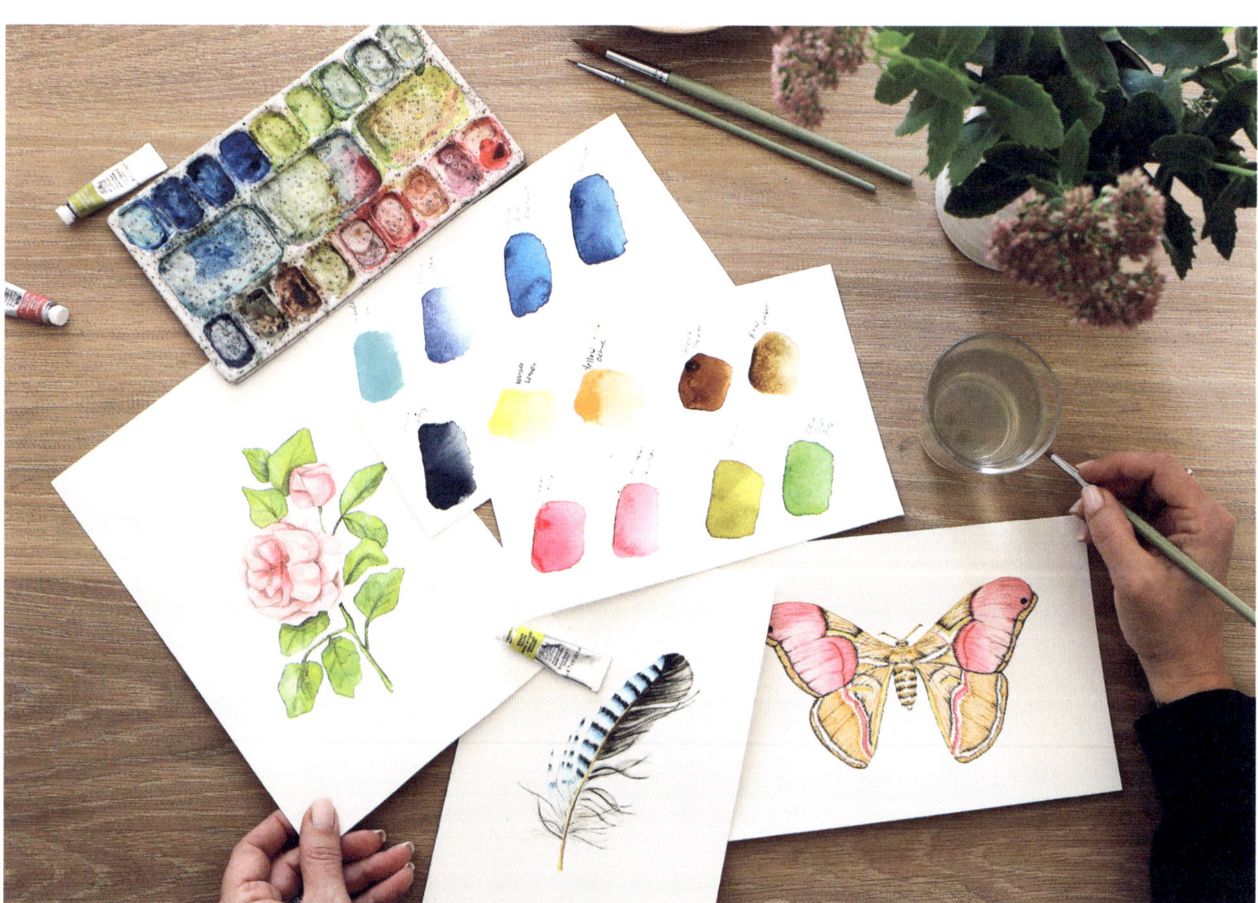

If you paint with your favorite colors, you will enjoy the process more.

COLORS USED IN THIS BOOK:

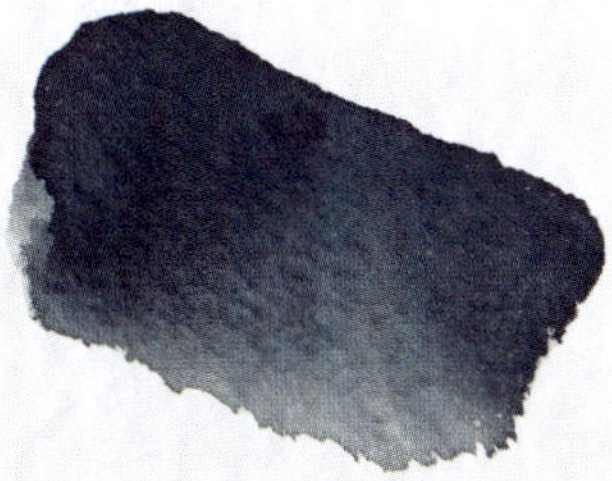

Payne's gray

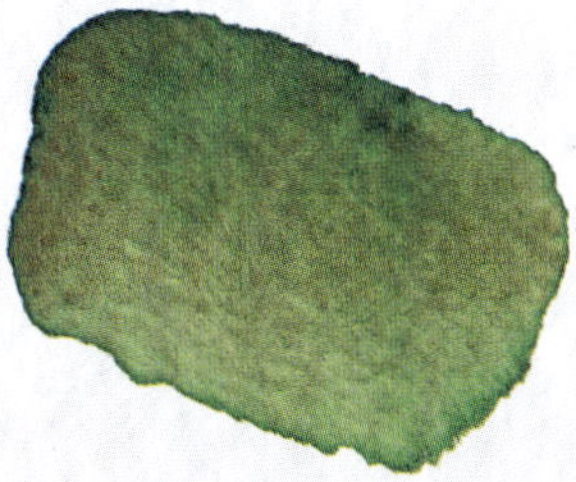

Sap green

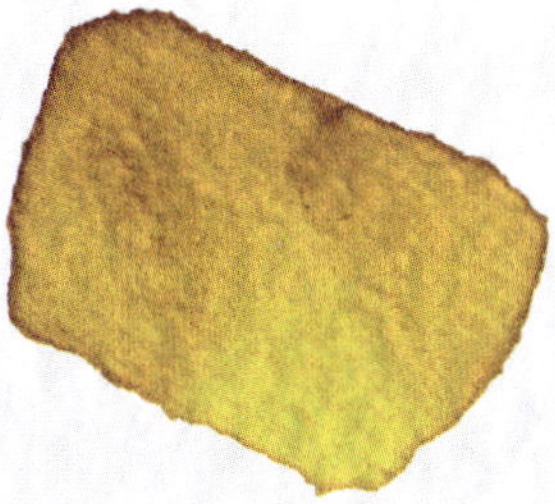

Green gold

Yellow ochre

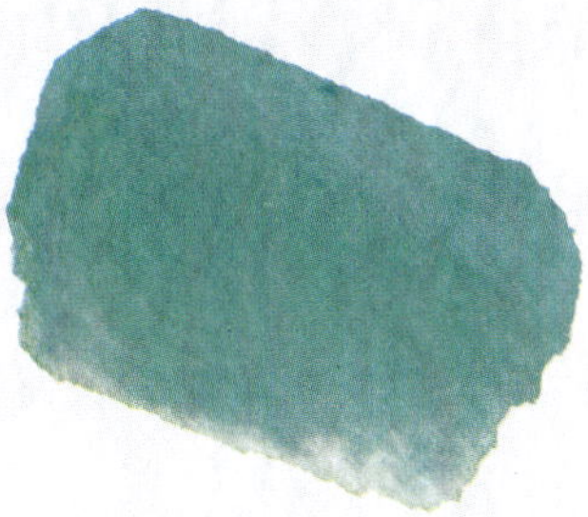

*Cobalt turquoise light
(any turquoise is fine)*

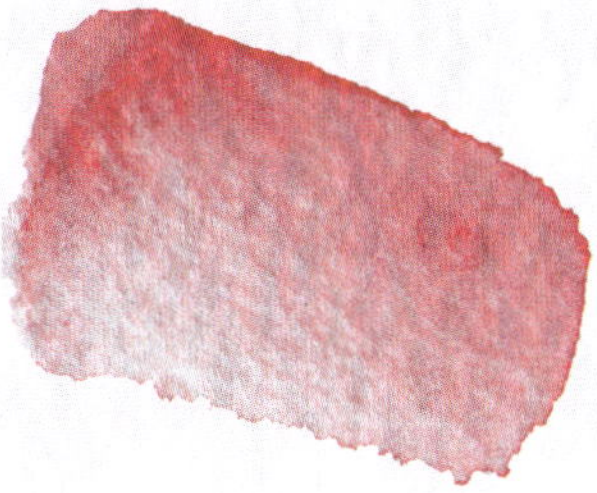

Alizarin crimson

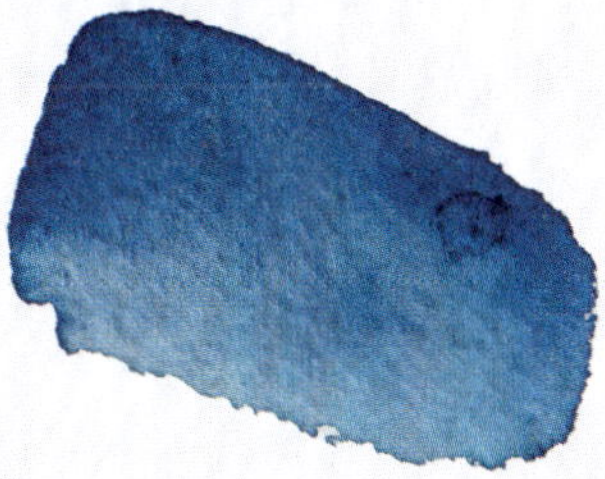

Prussian blue

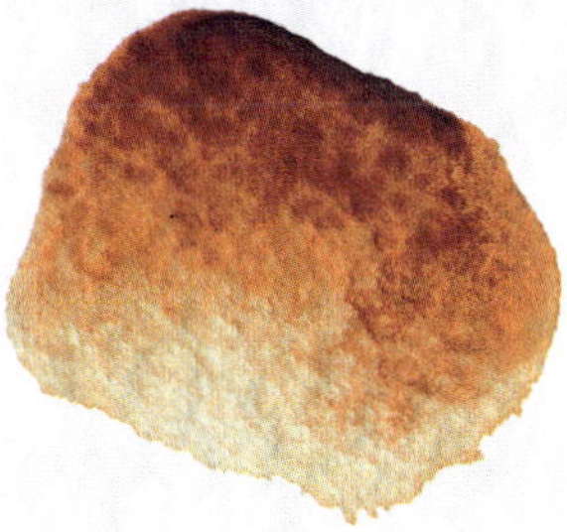

Raw umber

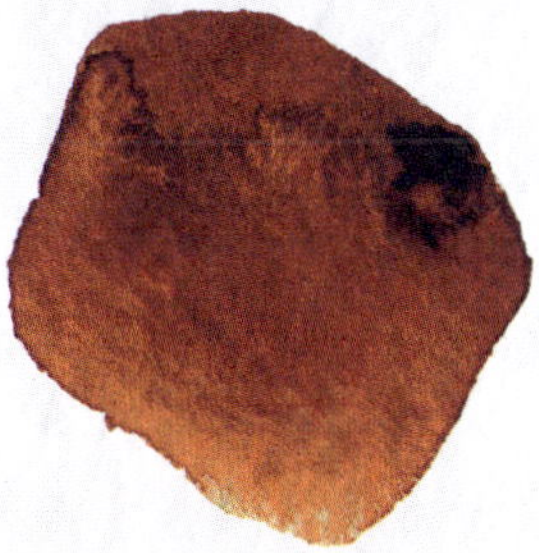

Burnt umber

ALONG WITH THE THREE PRIMARY COLORS:

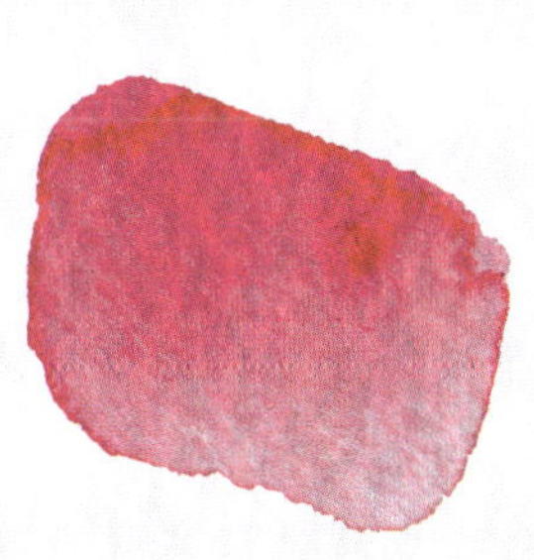

Permanent rose

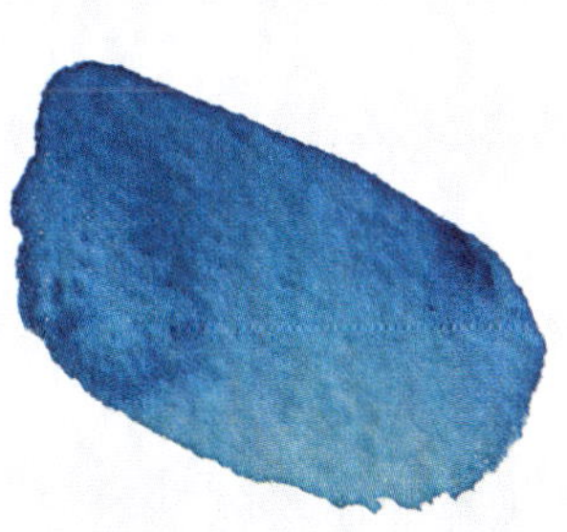

Winsor blue (green shade)

*Winsor yellow (from the
Winsor & Newton paint line)*

FINDING TIME TO PAINT

You may not be able to spend all your waking hours painting and creating (as dreamy as that sounds), but even twenty minutes a few times a week can make a big difference in your watercolor skills and confidence. Even if my desk is a mess, or the dishes are piling up, or I'm exhausted from the day, I make sure that I pick up a brush and move paint around. When the kids were little and I had to get them out of bed and off to school and tidy up after everyone was gone, I had very little time to myself. I realized that quiet mornings were my ideal time to paint. So I set my alarm clock thirty minutes earlier, brewed a hot cup of coffee, and painted before anyone else was awake.

Make sure you honor your art practice and feed your artistic passions by finding a way to create art. Paint because it makes you happy, excited, fills you up… whatever your goal is, paint for you. Decide that art is just as important as brushing your teeth. Decide that you WILL paint and practice and don't let anything change your mind. Let your inner talk tell you something like *"I am painting for me. I am painting because it makes me happy. I am painting and it's important."* Put that brush to paint and paint to paper and let the movement of the watercolor relax you, inspire you, and make you want to do it more.

When you express your creative side, it's like opening a tap. At first it trickles out slowly, and in time, when the habit is formed, it flows freely with ease and sometimes with amazing force. I recommend you work on your inner space and commit to painting and paint often, at a time that is best for you, in the time that you have available—and just do it.

Let's move on to the outer workspace.

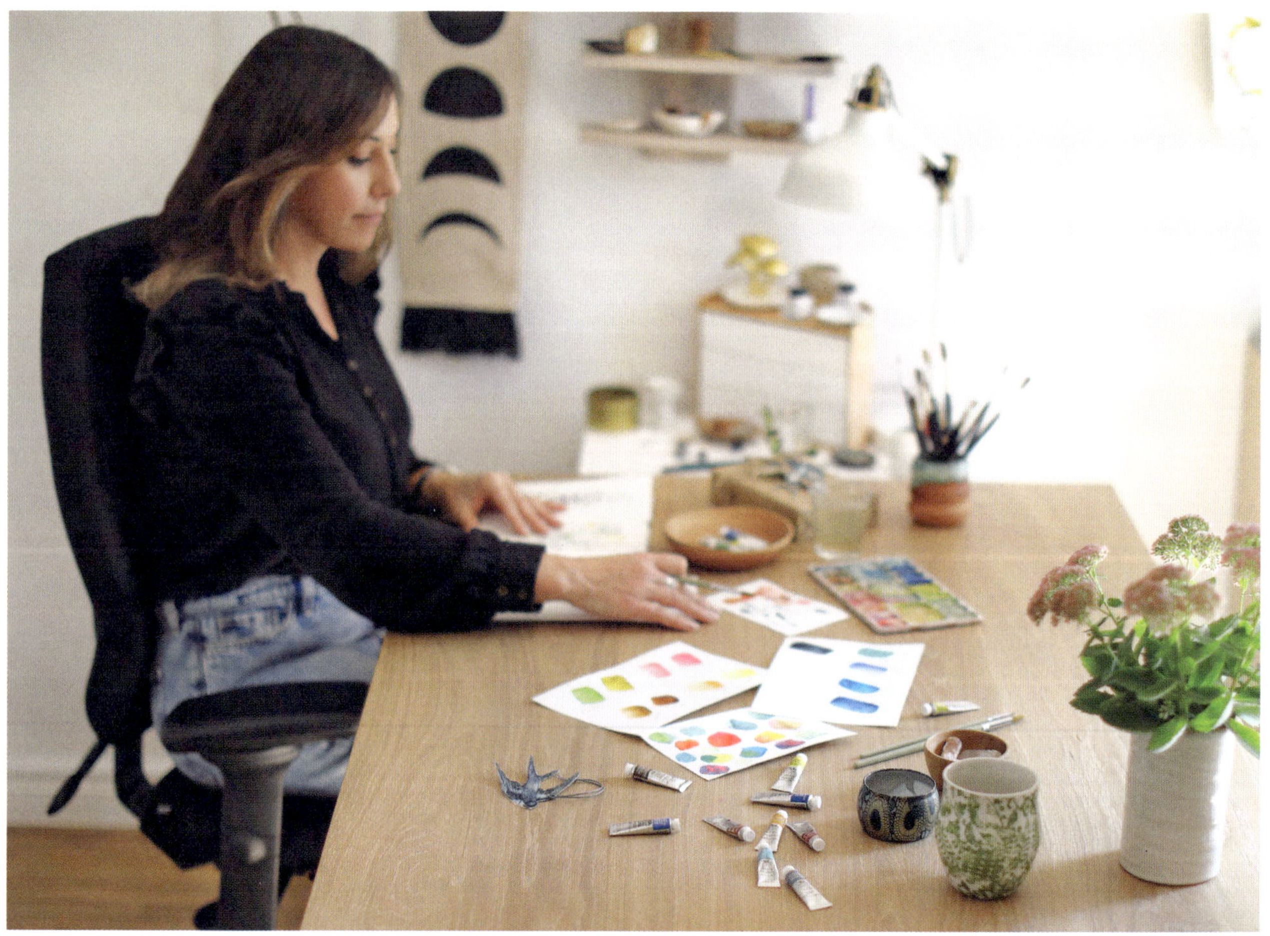

Starting each day painting in my journal is part of my daily routine.

CREATING SPACE TO PAINT

If you can, carve out a dedicated space in your house for painting. Any spot in your home will work, whether it's your living room, bedroom, or even basement. I recommend that you do your best to set up a small table near a window if possible. Painting near a natural light source is best because the glare of an overhead light on wet watercolor can be a little challenging.

It's really important that you make the space cozy, inspiring, and creatively charged with your favorite things. When you walk into a space that speaks to you, you will be even more inspired to sit down and paint, practice, and create. Guaranteed. Place a plant or fresh cut flowers close by, pour your favorite hot or cold drink, and really make your painting session inspiring and special. Hang inspiring art, or YOUR art, on the walls. Play music, put on a podcast, or enjoy the silence as you paint.

If you're unable to carve out a dedicated space in your home, then find interesting ways to store your watercolor necessities so you can pull them out quickly and easily when you're inspired to paint. Rolling storage carts are great when space is limited, but you still want to have everything in one spot and be able to move it to different parts of the house. Keeping your watercolor supplies organized and easy to access means that you will get to painting more quickly and your painting sessions can be longer, too.

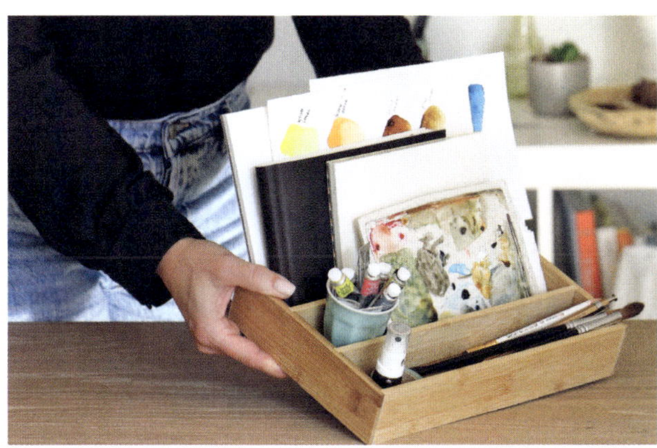

Everything you need to paint with watercolors can easily fit in a small box.

t i p ······ Remember, make it simple and easy for you to get into the groove of painting first and foremost. Give yourself permission to put your creative practice first.

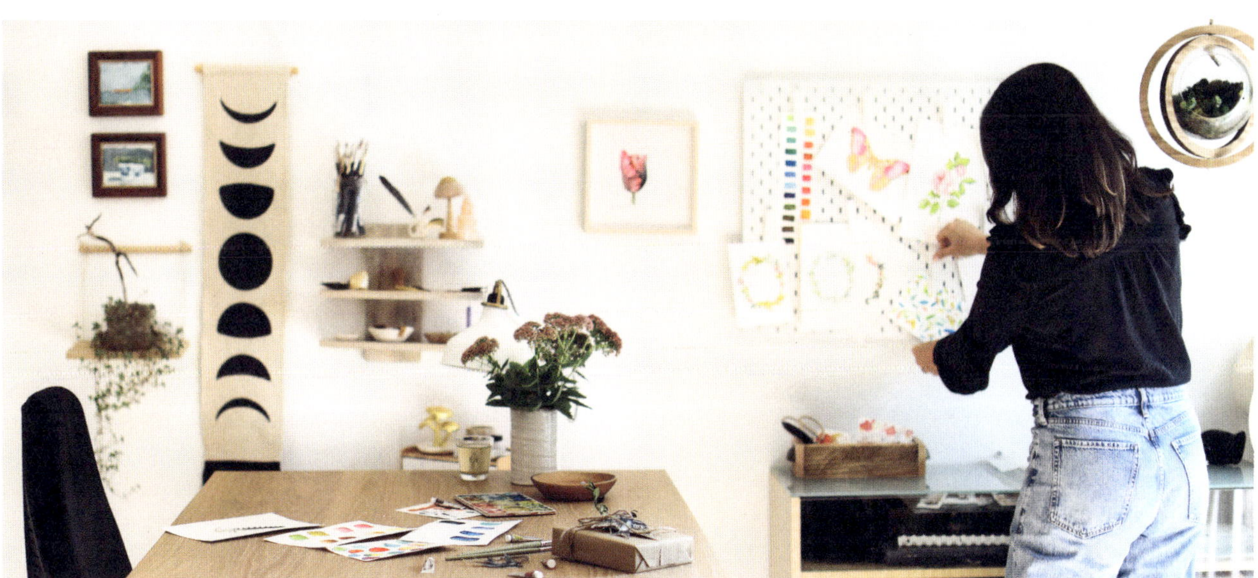

Surround yourself with inspiration to get your creative juices flowing.

ON PRACTICE

Repetition is key, especially when you're first starting anything new. The more you paint the same object, practicing strokes and techniques, the more your painting will improve. You are building muscle memory, and with practice, brushstrokes will become innate. You may not notice improvement right away, but if you keep and date your practice sheets, you will notice the gradual improvement and will be happy that you spent the time on repetition.

As the improvement happens, and the process seems easier, you will want to sit down and paint again and again. I encourage you to flip the switch and release the pressure of the outcome of your painting session—that is, the painting itself—and instead, focus your energy on the act of painting and get into the habit of practicing as often as possible. A practice routine of fifteen minutes a day is better than one hour-long session once a month.

permission to make bad art

I feel like we put a lot of pressure on ourselves when we're painting and want every piece to be one that we are proud to share or hang. I want to give you permission to be okay with painting things that you don't love or that don't turn out as expected. I want you to be okay with not being happy the first time you paint it. **You won't love everything you paint, and that's okay.**

As with anything new, it takes practice, repetition, and muscle memory—not to mention painting lots of bad paintings—to get to something great. We've all painted "bad" paintings and you'll continue to paint "bad" paintings. Trust me, I still experience painting sessions where things aren't clicking. I walk away from those sessions having learned so much more from what went wrong. Often, we learn most from painting sessions that challenge us rather than painting sessions where everything goes smoothly.

Keep in mind that the weather can affect how watercolor dries or behaves. Our mood affects our creative flow. Our stress levels can affect our painting sessions. When you are okay with painting things that aren't to your liking the first time around, you will have a much more positive painting session and moments when everything does go as planned.

Give yourself room to explore and grow, and be okay with pieces that you don't love in the end. Hold on to them, though, because I'll show you a fun idea for what to do with them in a later chapter. Allow yourself to fall in love with creating, painting, and exploring.

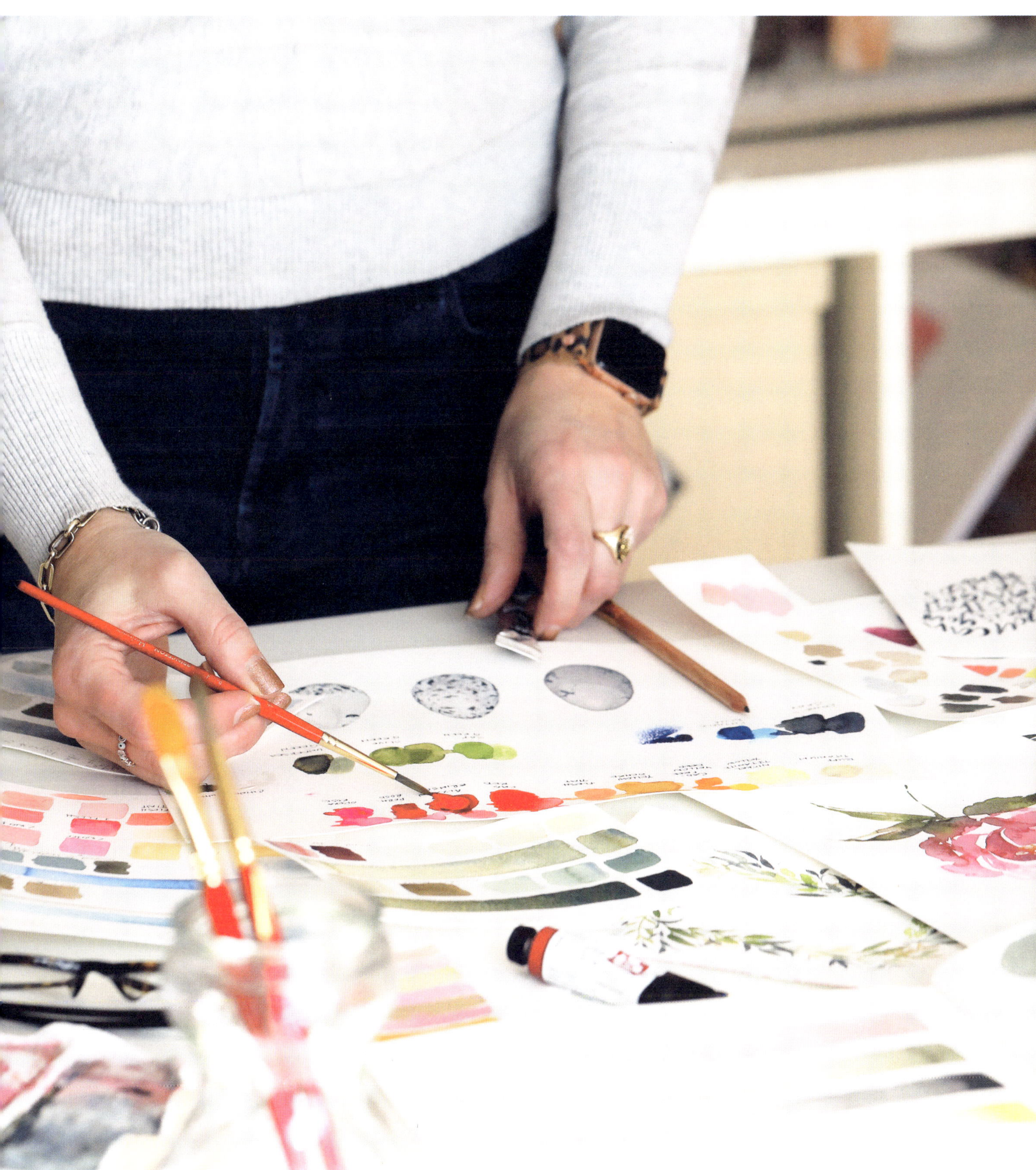

Save your practice sheets so you can see how quickly you can progress with just a little practice!

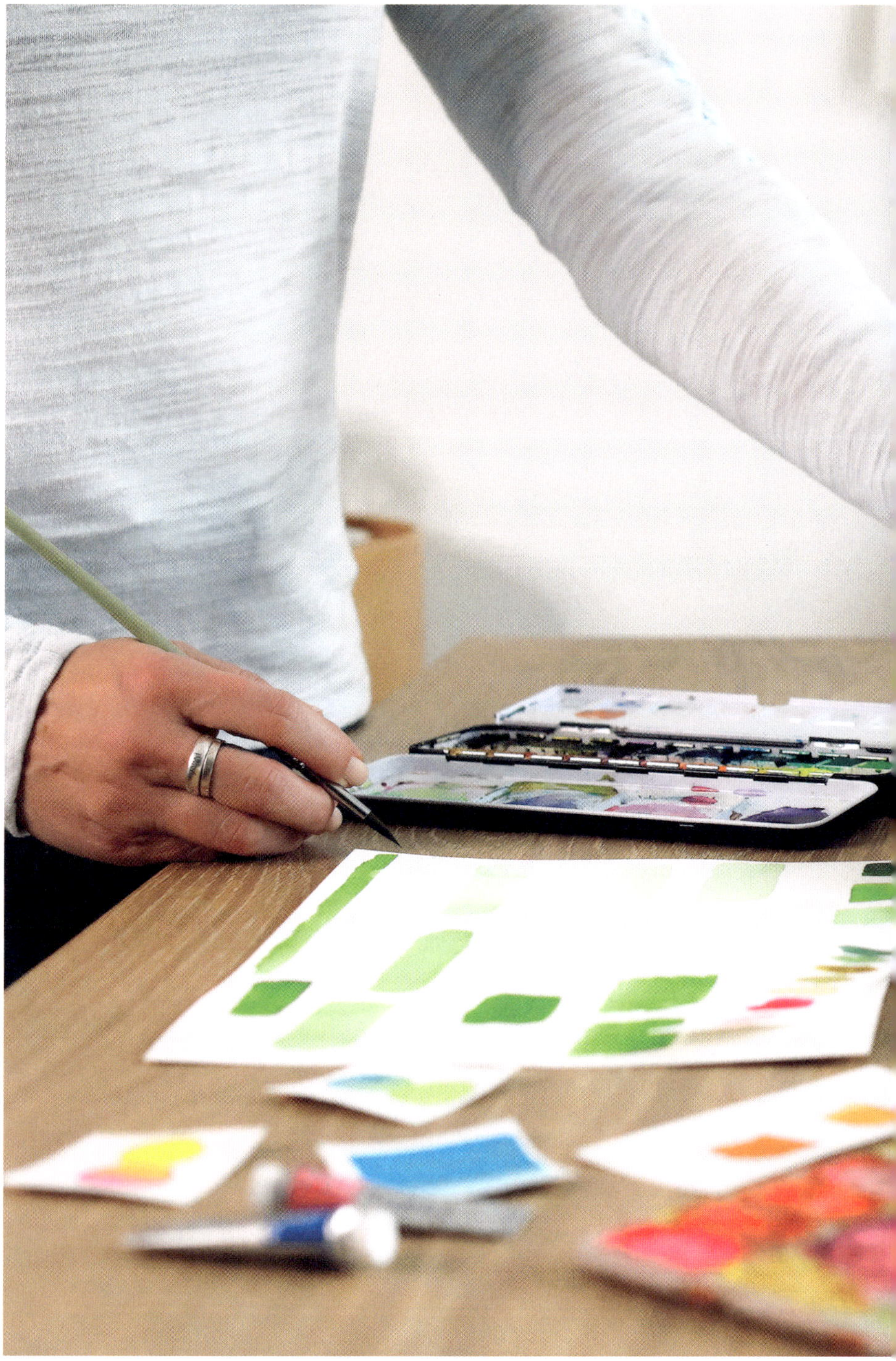

2

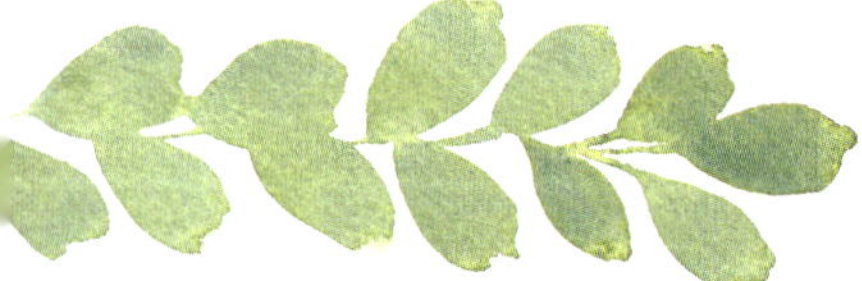

PRACTICE
AND PLAY

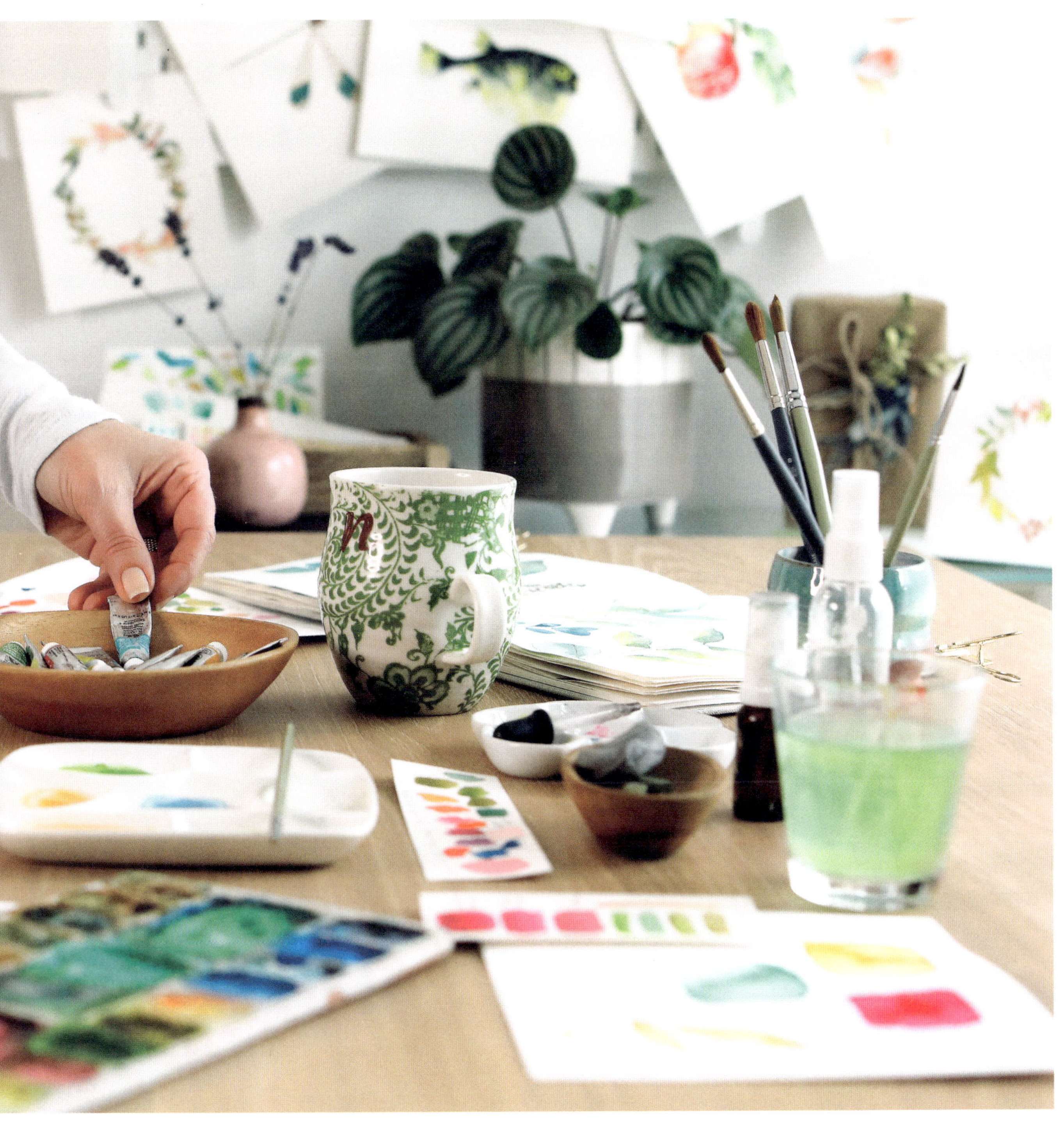

When we're learning to paint, we often want to skip boring beginning techniques and get right to the good stuff—creating beautiful paintings. I hear you on that. But I have also learned that practice is the only way to find out the "best" way to mix and apply your paint. The quality of paint, the type of paper, the temperature in your home, the humidity in the air . . . these are all factors that can affect how much water to add to a paint mix. If you follow along with the exercises in this chapter, you'll get plenty of experience mixing and moving paint around. So practice, play, explore, and make notes along the way.

WAKING UP WATERCOLOR PAINT

Because watercolor painting is a wet medium, your first goal should be getting to know how much or how little water you will be adding to your watercolor paints to get the right ratio for the task at hand. I'd love to make it really simple and say the best way to wake up watercolor paint is to add water and go paint. But there's a little more that is required to get to the painting stage. You can add a little bit of water to create a strong, opaque mix. Or you can add a lot of water for a transparent, thin wash of color.

Something to keep in mind as you start exploring watercolor paint mixing is *the more water you add, the lighter the color will be.* You do not use white watercolor paint to lighten a color, your simply add more water to your mixing puddle. If you desire a darker color, simply add less water to your mixing puddle. Doing so will result in a dark, opaque version of that color.

Don't worry, as we get practicing, this will begin to make more sense. For now, let's explore two of the most popular forms of watercolor paints: tubes and dry pans.

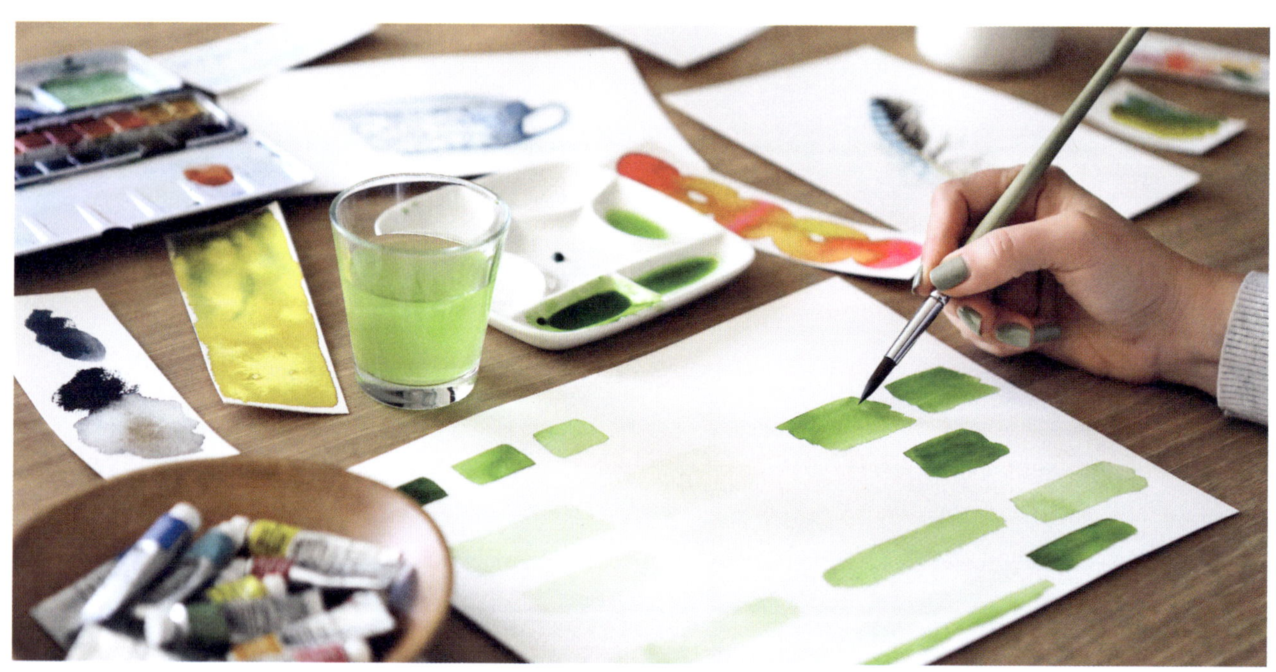

Let's use sap green as an example. The first square (above) has more paint and less water in the mix.

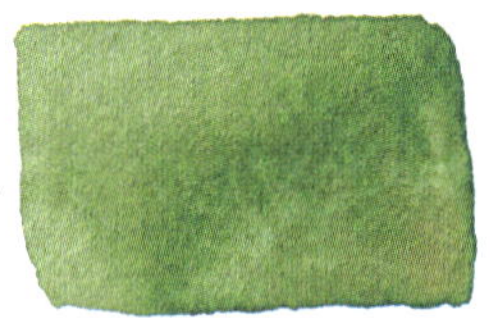

Next, use the same sap green, but add more water to the mix. See how the color is lighter and more transparent?

Try adding even more water to the mix. Here you have an even lighter and more transparent version of sap green.

t i p ······ I always use a ceramic mixing palette, whether I'm working with a dry palette or paint directly from a tube. I do not recommend plastic palettes for watercolor paints. The paint slips on the plastic, which makes it difficult to mix.

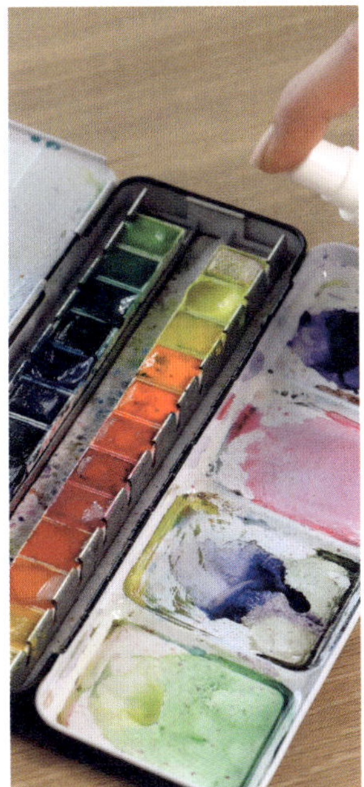

Use a spray bottle, eyedropper, or wet brush to wet your dry paints and get them ready to paint.

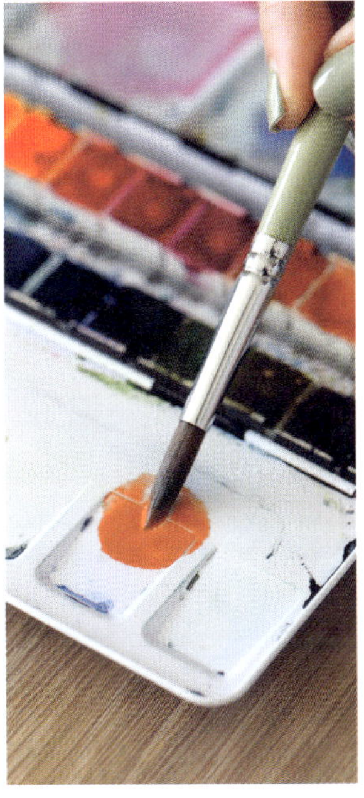

Even when working with pans of watercolor, you should mix your paints on a palette.

HOW TO "WAKE UP" A DRY PALETTE

You've probably seen beautiful sets of dry watercolor palettes and wondered how they differ from tubes of watercolor paints. Dry pans of watercolors are simply watercolor paints that have been pressed into a pan and dried. They require water to get the paint activated.

A dry pan of paint requires more water than you might think to get the top layer of dry pigment really nice and wet and moving. I like to use an eyedropper to add water to each pan, but you can also use a spray bottle or a wet brush to very gently "scrub" the surface of the paint to encourage the water and dry paint to mix and blend together.

When working with a dry palette, I recommend you use a mixing palette to mix your watercolor puddle, which allows you to adjust how much paint to water is in your painting mix. Painting directly from the pan of color will result in a very heavy, opaque, and often clumpy mixture.

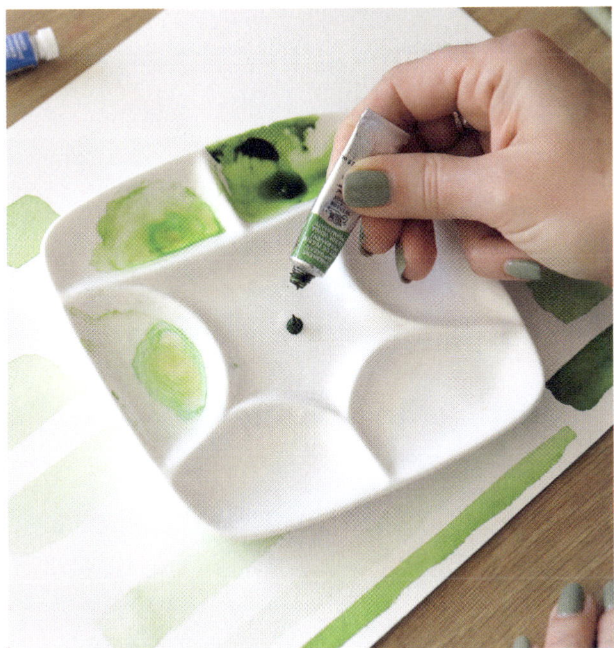

Squeeze out just a small amount of paint to start. You can always add more.

HOW TO MIX USING TUBES

Working with tubes of watercolor paint is my personal preference. Tubes of watercolor paints are highly pigmented and very convenient because you just need to squeeze out a pea-sized amount of paint to get started painting. Tubes will last you a long time.

I like that the paint is very pigmented right out of the tube, and I just need to use a bit of water directly from my brush to start mixing the consistency that I need on my mixing palette. I normally use the same colors over and over again, so working on a mixing palette means I can squeeze out more paint whenever I need to replenish that spot in my palette. Whether you choose to work with a dry pan set or directly from tubes of paint, you will achieve the same outcome. The only thing that will be different is your starting process.

WATERCOLOR PUDDLES

Understanding how to mix watercolor puddles is an essential skill. There are different ratios and even strengths of watercolor puddle mixes that will help you achieve beautiful transparency or rich opacity.

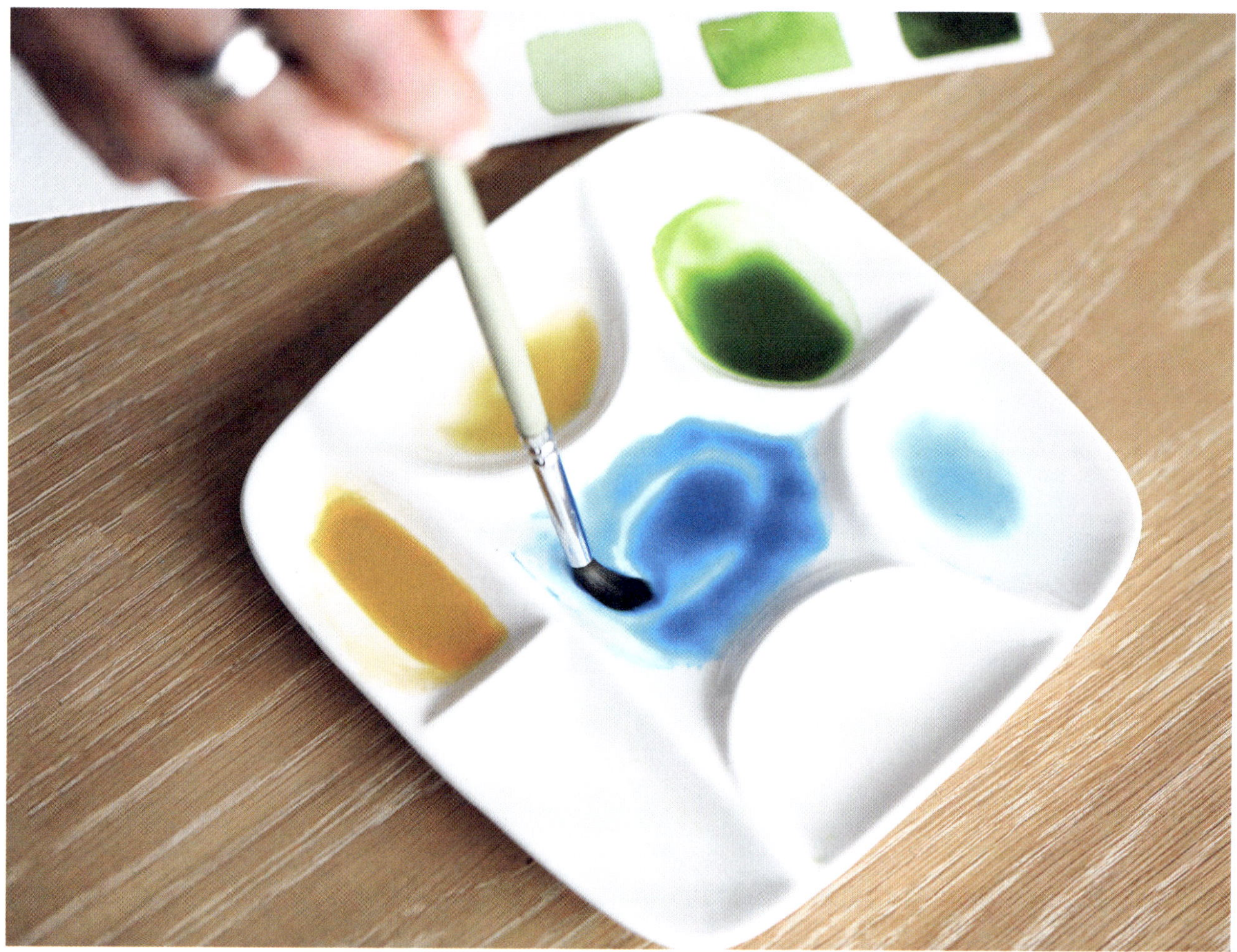

The more water you add to your paints, the lighter and more transparent they will be.

WATER-TO-PAINT RATIO

Mixing different water-to-paint ratios is where we begin exercising our observational skills. Keep in mind, the more water you add to your puddle, the lighter and more transparent your paint will be. Also, factors like the amount of water you have on your brush will affect your paint mix, and the less water you add to your paint puddle, the darker and more opaque your color mix will be.

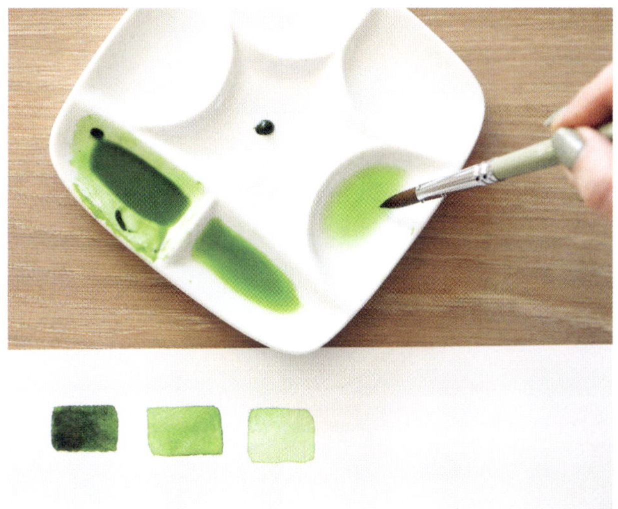

Less water in the mix to more water in the mix (left to right).

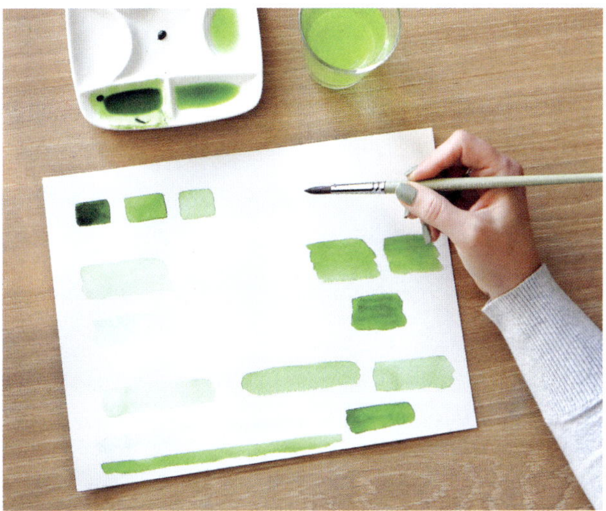

This is what your practice sheet should start to look like.

MIXING A TRANSPARENT WASH

Starting with a dab of paint on your mixing palette and a brush full of water, blend the paint and water together. Test what that mix looks like by running your brush across the paper. Is the color strong? Vibrant? Transparent? Making observations as to how much water you use in your paint mix will help down the road when you paint the subjects in this book and beyond.

Next, try adding even more water to the paint mix and run the brush across the page. Is the paint color even lighter? More transparent? Runny? There is no right or wrong here; you are simply observing the paint and the brushstroke to determine what the paint mix looks like.

In the painting section of this book, I will instruct you to mix a "transparent wash/puddle of color." This means you will add lots of water and *less paint*. When I instruct you to mix an "opaque mix/puddle of color," this means I want you to mix a puddle that has *more paint* than water so the color is strong and not as transparent.

t i p ······ To lighten a color using watercolor paints, add more water to the mix, not white paint. White watercolor paint tends to look very chalky when added to watercolor, so it's best to use water to lighten a color.

MIXING AN OPAQUE PUDDLE

Let's mix another puddle that has a higher paint-to-water ratio. Starting with a dab of paint on your mixing palette, use less water than you did when you practiced mixing a transparent wash of color. Mix it well with the brush and run the brush across the paper. What do you notice? Is the brush stroke drier? Is the color more opaque? Is the color more vibrant? Try adding a little bit more water with the brush and see if you can get the paint to flow a bit more, then paint another stroke as you make observations for how opaque and vibrant the color is. Make notes as you go directly on your practice page.

The goal is for you to start getting comfortable with your paints and building your observational skills. Noting how much water you need to add to the paint to make the color light and transparent or dark and opaque will be unique to your supplies and goals. The biggest takeaway as you work on your paint mixes is to understand that YOU are in control, and the more you can practice mixing different puddles and ultimately consistencies of paint texture, the more you will enjoy the process of using watercolors for your paintings.

At this point, you should have filled at least one page with brushstrokes from testing your different paint mixes. You should notice on this practice page a variety of lines with different degrees of transparencies and opacities. Well done.

USING YOUR BRUSHES

You might be using a brush at this point and feeling like you're really not sure how to hold it or what to do with it. Now that we've mixed our paints and put the beginning brushstrokes on paper, let's learn a little bit more about round brushes, my go-to brushes, and all that they can do.

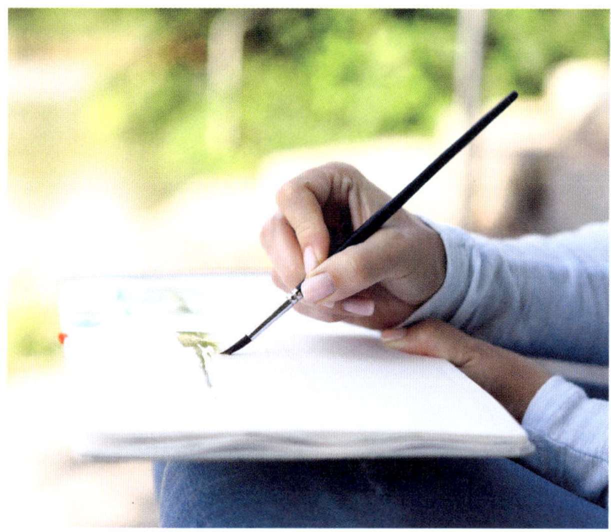

Try holding your round brush at about a 45-degree angle as you begin to play with it.

ROUND BRUSHES

A round brush is a very versatile brush to have in your watercolor kit. Just varying the angle of the brush to the paper can create a very thin line or a more expressive line, or what I like to call a "thick and juicy" line. This is where the paint can really puddle, move, and create some interesting effects when dried. Changing the pressure you place on the brush as you paint will change the amount of paint it releases. Moving the brush quickly or slowly across the page will also create different effects. As you experiment with a round brush, start to observe how your brush movement can change the way that watercolor paint behaves and even dries. Let's work on some exercises to enjoy all that a single round brush can offer.

You can create all of these different lines, and more, with a single round brush.

BRUSHSTROKE TECHNIQUES

Practicing brushstrokes before you sit down to work on your next painting is not only a great way to warm up but it's also how you build muscle memory and learn to control watercolor paint. I recommend you practice the brushstrokes I've illustrated here by following along and setting a goal for yourself to fill an entire page with these brushstrokes. As you paint lines and curves, begin to observe how much water your brush can hold and how long you can go before the lines look dry or uneven; really get to understand the unique characteristics of watercolor paint while it's wet and then as it dries.

Swirl your brush in the jar of water first to get it nice and wet. Lightly scrape excess water back into the jar or dab the tip of the brush very gently onto a kitchen towel to absorb excess water. Your brush is now ready to be loaded with paint from your mixing palette.

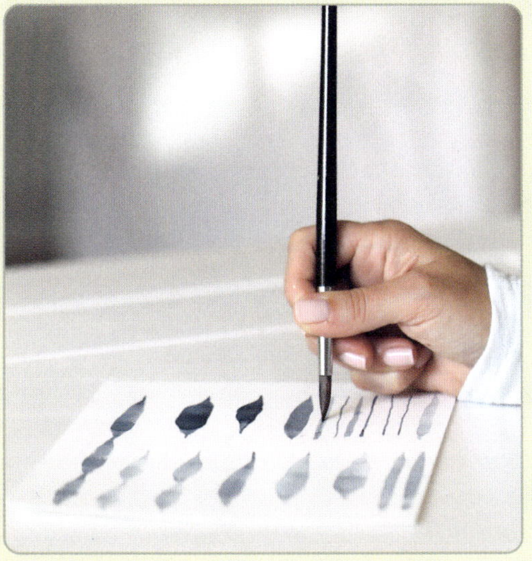

For this exercise, hold your brush straight up and down.

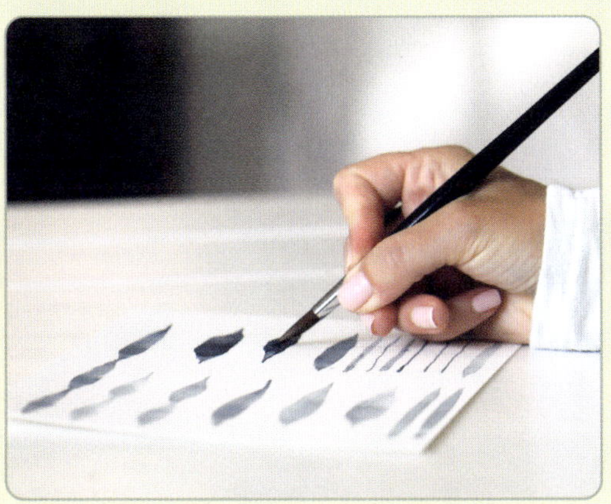

Then try holding your brush at a 45-degree angle and filling a page with brushstrokes.

The same round brush can make all of these different straight lines.

thick and thin lines

Hold the brush at a 90-degree angle to the paper. Resting your wrist lightly on the table will support your upper body and help you paint controlled lines. Press down on the brush slightly as you let the brush hairs follow behind your stroke and begin to paint thin lines with the tip of the brush. Pressing down a slight bit more will offer slightly larger brushstrokes. Using the same brush, apply a bit more pressure on the brush to paint a few lines that are a bit thicker. The more pressure you apply downward on the brush, the more the belly of the brush will open and spread the hairs outward and the larger the brushstroke will be.

Paint lines from left to right as you experiment with how much pressure you place on the brush and observe how thin or thick your lines are.

a different angle

Holding the brush at about a 45-degree angle to the paper will completely change your brushstroke and will allow you to paint with the full length of the brush hairs. You'll be able to cover more surface area with paint using a fully loaded brush. Again, I want you to paint a page of brushstrokes as you hold your brush at this angle. Doing these exercises is the best way to get to know your brush better and fully understand how much watercolor it holds, what size strokes you can paint with it, and how long you can go before you have to reload it with more paint.

t i p ······ If you run out of paint too quickly or the brushstroke looks dry, you probably need to saturate your brush with more water. Either dip your brush into your water jar and then your paint puddle, or mix more water into your paint puddle for a loose, watery paint mix. Remember, these beginning few strokes are a way to become familiar with both your brush and your paint mix.

SCAN TO WATCH
A TUTORIAL

single-stroke leaves

Now that you have a handle on painting straight lines, let's practice painting lines that have a bit more movement to them. Holding your brush at 90 degrees, allow the tip of the brush to touch the paper to start painting a thin line. As you move your brush, press down slightly on the brush as you drag it across the page, then release the pressure again to a taper. This will result in what I like to call a "single-stroke leaf" brushstroke because it resembles a leaf shape when complete. It begins with a thin line, then opens up midstroke to a full "juicy stroke," and ends with a thin line again. Work left to right but also try painting this same stroke top to bottom and see how it feels.

   Practice this stroke a few times and watch how the watercolor pools and puddles while it's wet. These puddles dry in unique ways, creating interesting effects that only watercolor paint offers. Even changing how quickly or slowly you move your brush across the page will have an effect on the characteristics of the watercolor paint when it dries. It's what I love most about this beautiful medium and what I encourage you to embrace.

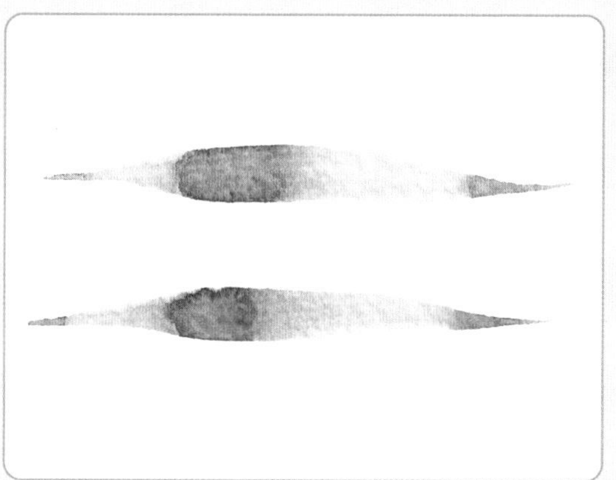

Left to right

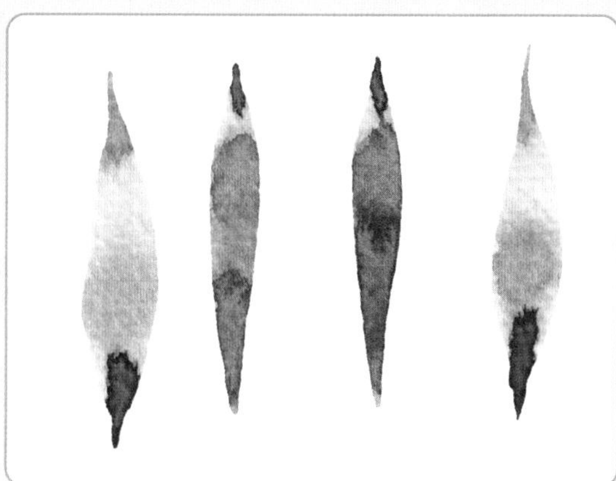

Top to bottom

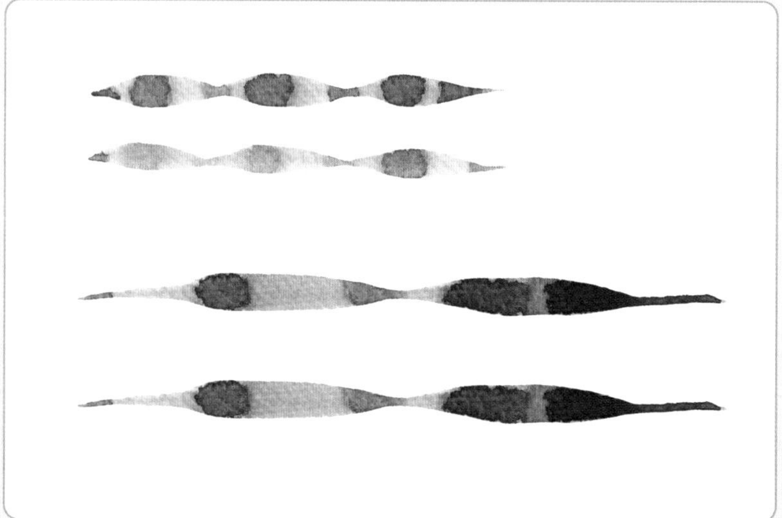

Once you practice these strokes, enjoy the flow of joining them together and painting them in a continuous line as we will do in the next exercise.

SCAN TO WATCH
A TUTORIAL

varying lines

Let's try this stroke again but expand on it. This time, painting a line from left to right, start by touching the tip of the brush to the paper, then as you move your hand, press down slightly on the brush, allowing the brush hairs to open, then release the pressure so the tip lightly drags across the page; repeat without lifting the brush from the paper. Continue this movement so you get beautiful "juicy" strokes in between thin, delicate strokes. Work left to right on this movement and really enjoy varying the thin to thick lines. Be playful with this brush practice and enjoy the fluid movement of your brush and watercolor paint. I encourage you to paint a full page of these lovely brushstrokes and choose paint colors that you love, as it will help you enjoy your brushstroke practice even more.

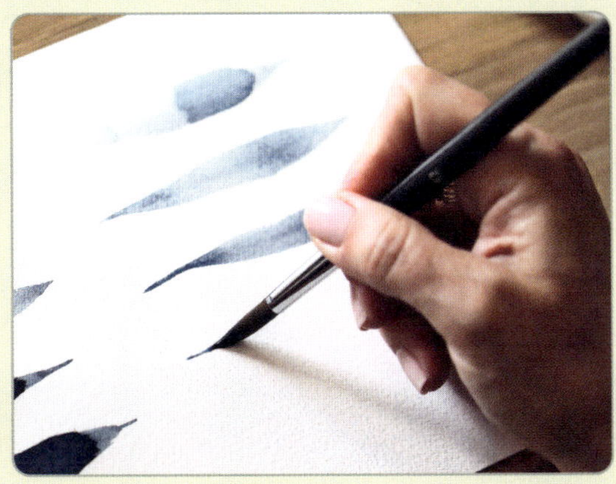

Less pressure

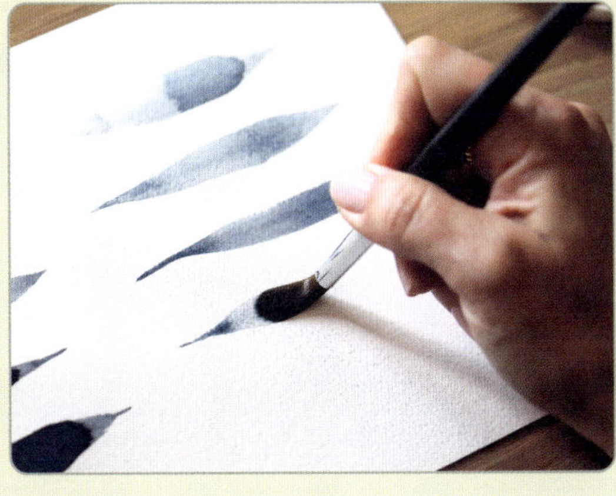

More pressure

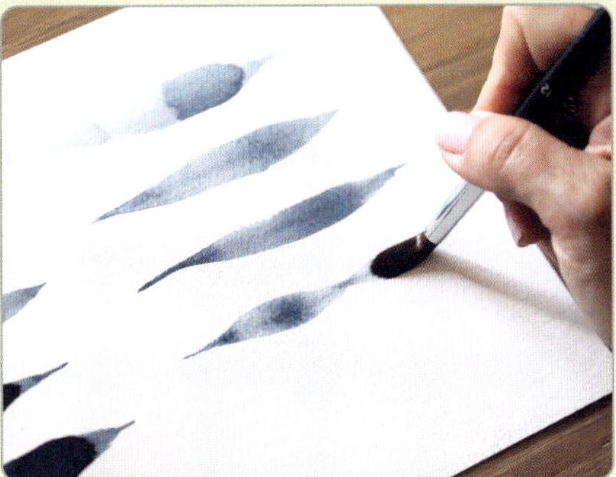

Less pressure

More pressure

SCAN TO WATCH
A TUTORIAL

c shapes

Now let's practice painting curved brushstrokes, or "c" shapes. Holding your brush at a 90-degree angle to the paper, place the brush lightly on the paper, and as you move the brush to the left, press down slightly, releasing as you finish painting the bottom of the curve. Paint a few of these and try switching the direction of the curve in the opposite direction.

   Did this feel a bit harder to do? That's very common. When you begin a new brushstroke, it takes some practice for the new movement to become automatic. With practice, these brushstroke exercises can be very meditative and a way for you to connect with your painting as you get warmed up. Do this a few times and observe how much you can vary the curves based on the pressure you apply on your brush.

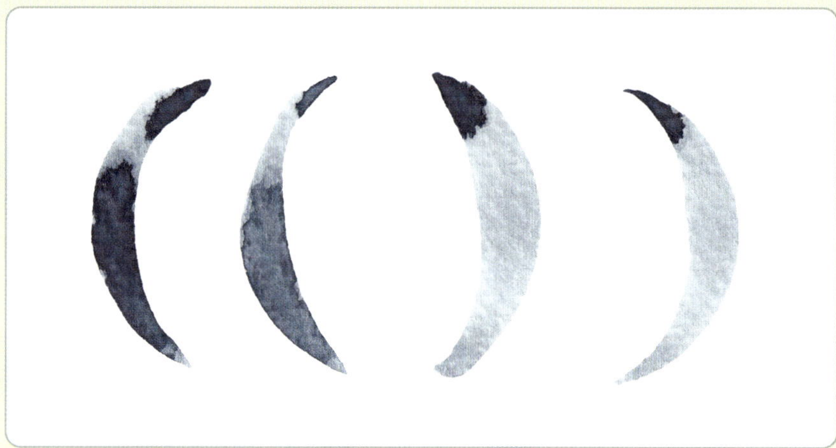

Practice painting these C shapes in different directions.

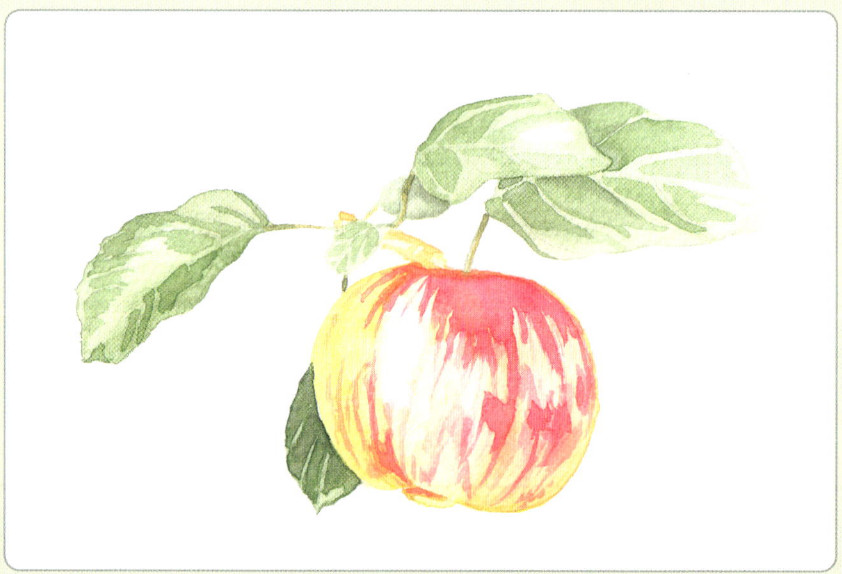

Keep in mind the shape of your subject. Your strokes should mimic the shape.

SCAN TO WATCH
A TUTORIAL

painting swatch cards
and practicing brushstrokes

There is no better way to understand what colors are in your watercolor kit than to swatch them. This exercise will leave you with a reference tool for when you are deciding which paint colors to use for your painting, and it also builds muscle memory and a deeper understanding of how to mix watercolor paint and use your brushes.

Take out a watercolor sheet and whatever paints you currently have in your watercolor kit. Using a mixing tray, begin to "wake up" the watercolor paint, and paint a generous opaque square, circle, or whatever brushstroke speaks to you. The goal is to swatch that particular color so you have a true indication of what it will look like on paper. Write down the color name below or above the swatch, and now you have a reference for what the paint color actually looks like. Do this for all the colors that you have in tubes or in a dry pan set. While you have paint puddles mixed, work on the brushstroke exercises and build that muscle memory and confidence using your round brushes.

As you put brush to paper in these exercises, not only are you building the necessary skills for watercolor painting, but you are also beginning to express your artistic style using these brushstrokes. Just like handwriting is unique to each individual, brush marks are unique too. Embrace your personal brushstrokes.

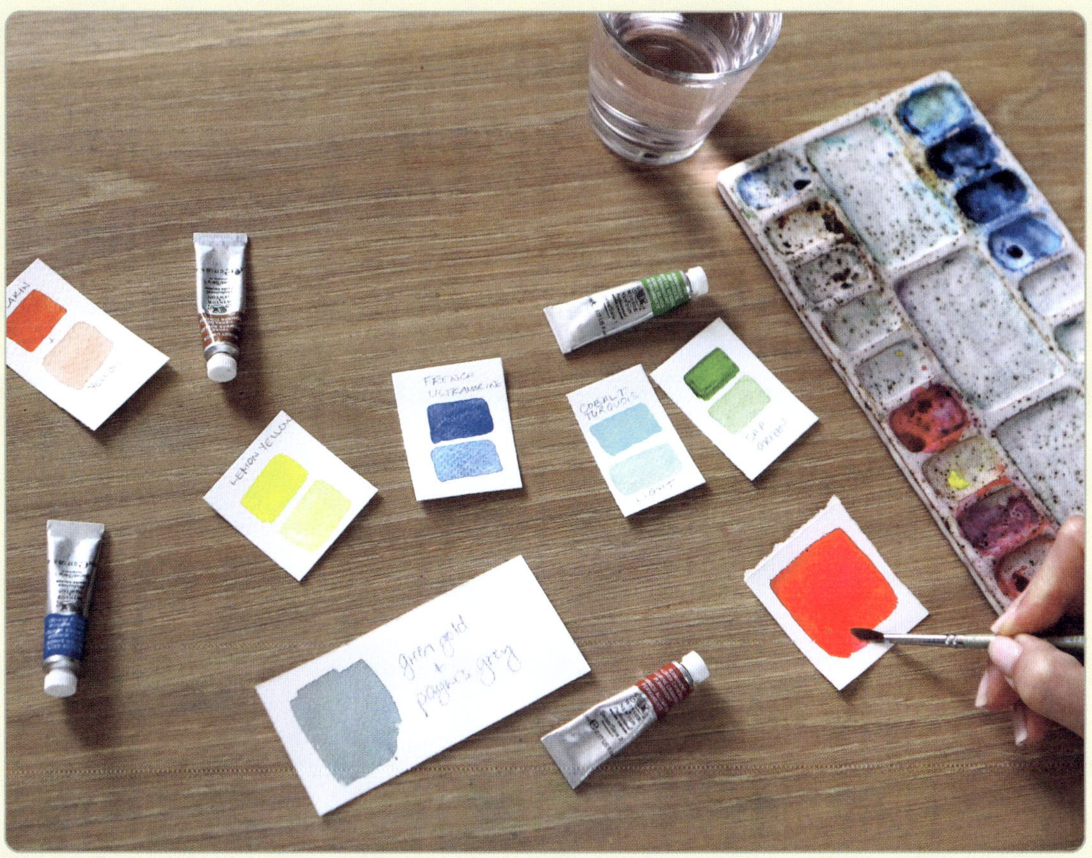

Save your swatches to use as references for mixing colors in future painting.

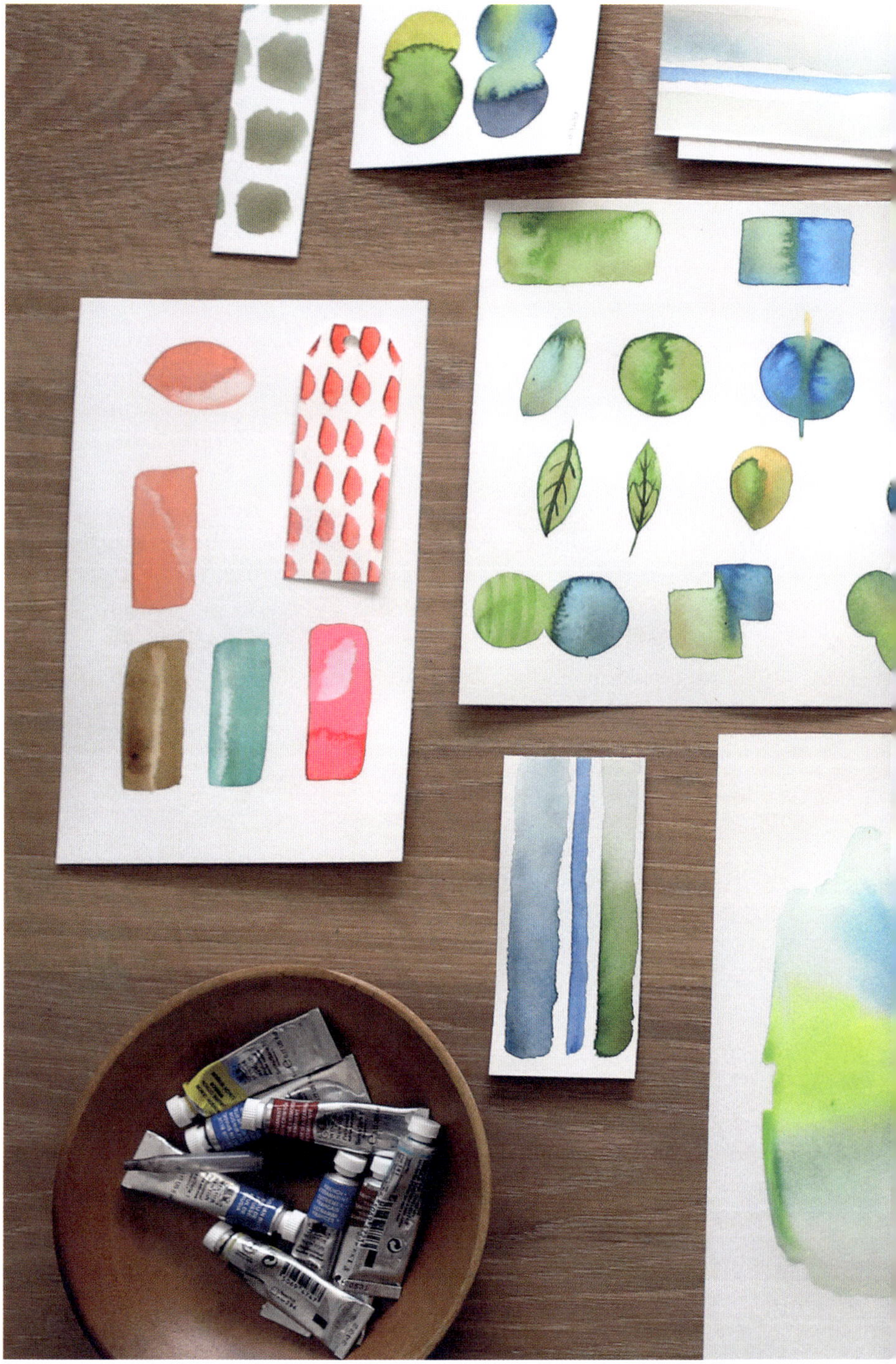

3

FUNDAMENTALS

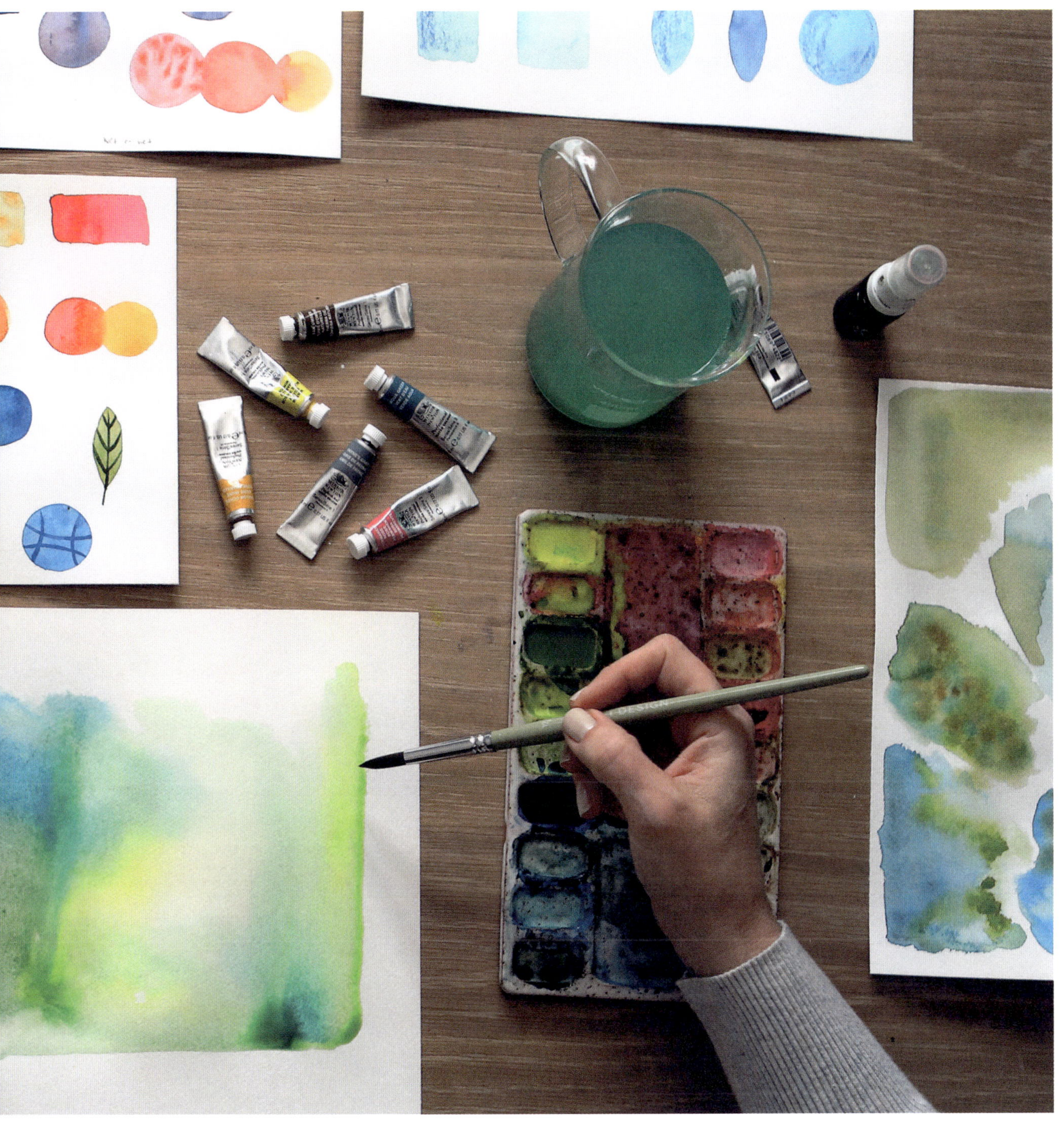

Now that you've been introduced to your watercolor supply kit, have painted some beginning brushstrokes, and have swatched your watercolors, it's time to continue to build your solid foundation of watercolor techniques. To keep it simple, in the painting projects in this book, there are three main watercolor painting techniques that we're going to use repeatedly and two additional techniques that we will use less frequently but that are really effective in creating detail and interest. These techniques will help you create watercolor paintings that have depth and beauty to them; they will also be fun to practice because you can really experience the behavior of watercolor firsthand.

WET-ON-WET

Wet-on-wet is a very common method of painting watercolors with depth and interest. I use it often to easily create darker values and shades within a brushstroke, and it's a lot of fun to practice. I use wet-on-wet for moments when I am adding depth to the center of a flower, or shadow to the outside of a shape, for example.

Keep in mind, as you practice wet-on-wet, there will be different degrees of wet strokes. The more wet the area is that you are working on, the more movement you'll observe with the freshly laid paint. This observation and experimentation process is where you truly begin to understand the characteristics of watercolor paint and how beautiful the medium is to work with.

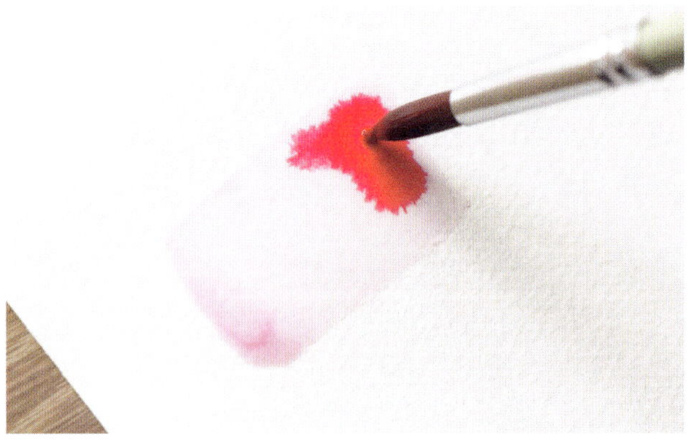

STEP 1

Using a clean but wet brush, lay down a square of just clean water onto the paper. Then using the tip of your brush, pick up a bit of watercolor paint from your mixing palette (maybe one of your favorites you swatched in the last chapter) and dab the tip of the brush onto the wet brushstroke on the paper. Watch the pigment move and mix into the wet stroke and see what happens. Use your brush to push the pigment around and watch the movement.

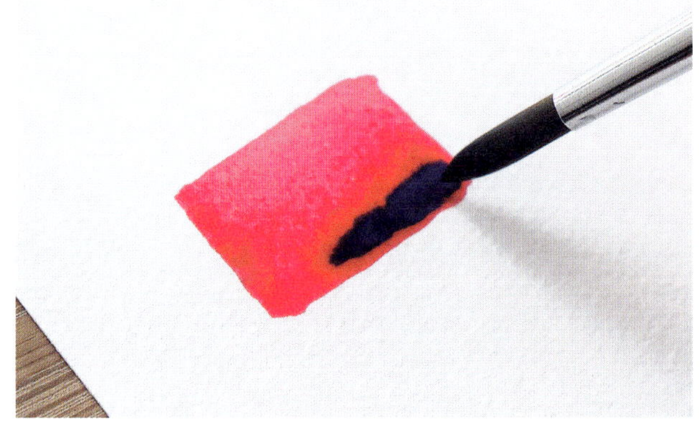

STEP 2

Now do that again. This time, load your brush with water and your paint mix, and paint another square. Then pick up even more paint (not so much water at this point) and dab more paint into the brushstroke. Feel free to use a different color like I did in this step. What do you observe now?

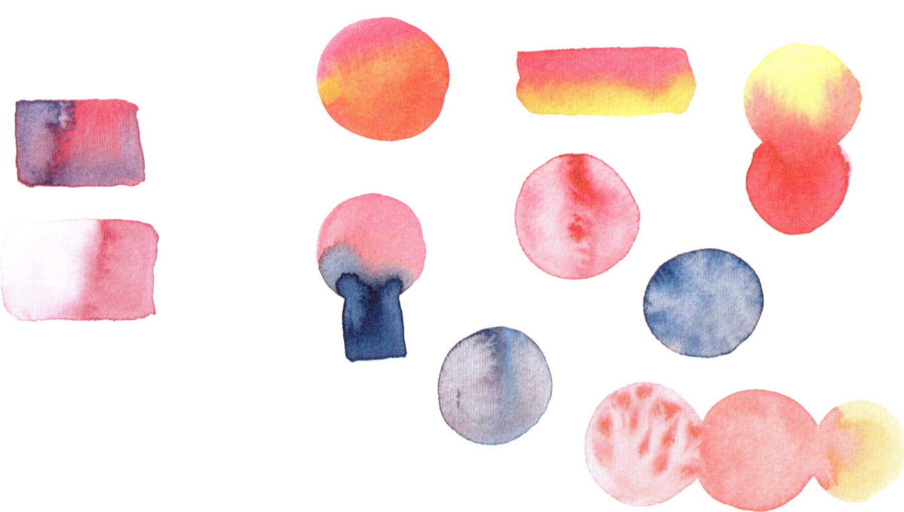

Try painting shapes that touch and see what happens. Really lean into this practice and have fun with it.

SCAN TO WATCH
A TUTORIAL

WET-ON-DRY

Another key technique that I use regularly to create depth and interest is wet-on-dry. Adding a wet brushstroke on top of dry watercolor paint adds opacity, detail, and even dimension to your painting. Essentially, you are adding another layer of watercolor paint to an existing area of dry paint.

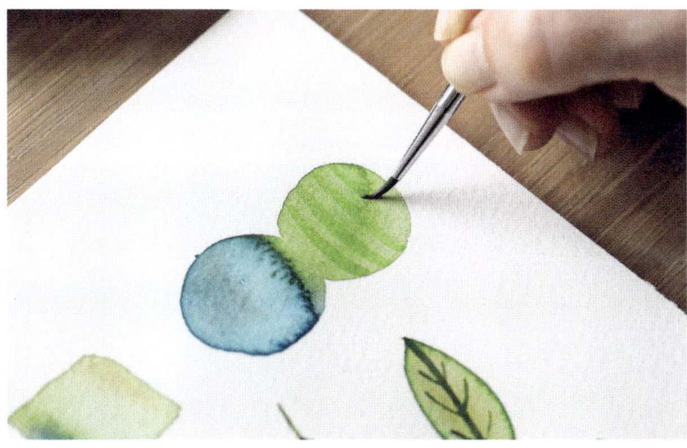

When painting wet-on-dry, you can go back over dry watercolor as much as you need to achieve the level of depth you desire.

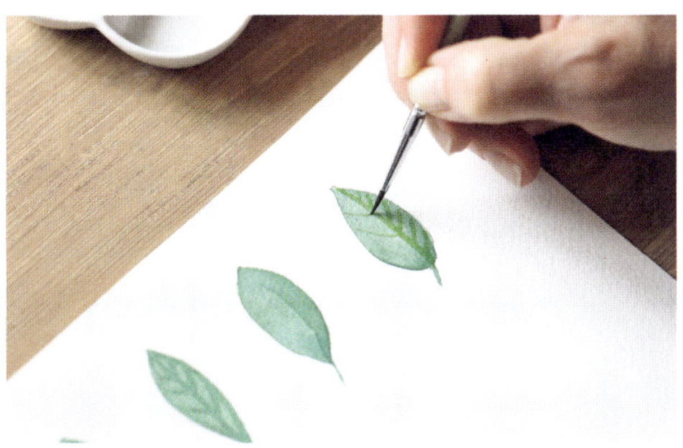

I use this technique on my botanical paintings to add veins as the last touch of detail or to darken areas that need to be recessed in a painting.

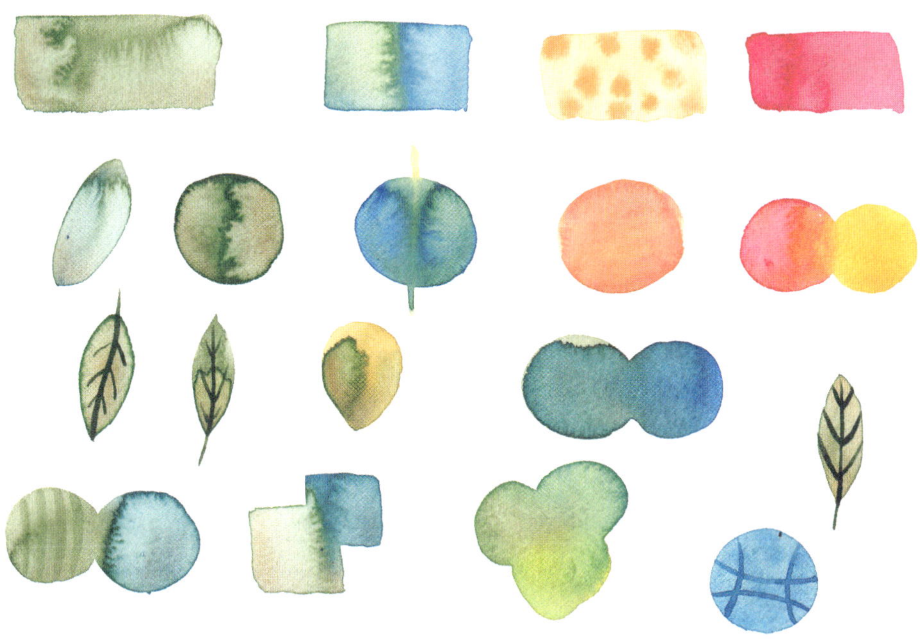

While the paint is still wet, you are in control. Use your brush to gently move the wet puddle around so that it settles where you want it to dry.

LIFTING

Lifting paint from the paper when the paint is still wet is a very common way to lighten the paint or to create a highlight. This technique is a very easy and effective way to brighten areas of the painting and add interest. Use a good-quality brush that holds a lot of water and cotton watercolor paper.

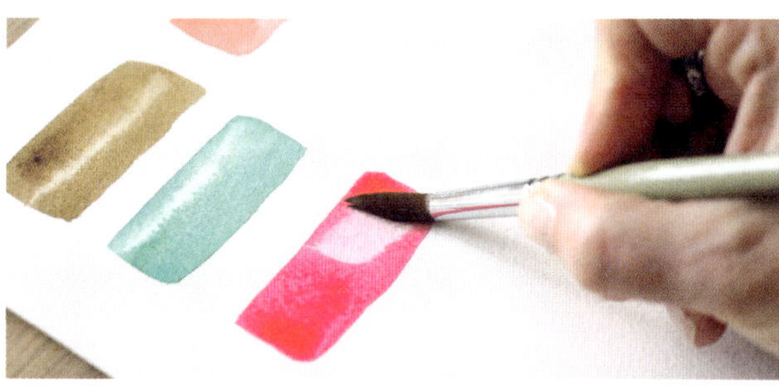

STEP 1

To practice this technique, lay down a generous amount of paint onto your paper. Give it a few moments to start to settle and be absorbed by the paper. Then swirl your brush into the clean water jar, dab the brush on a kitchen towel to remove the excess water, then swipe the brush across the wet brushstroke.

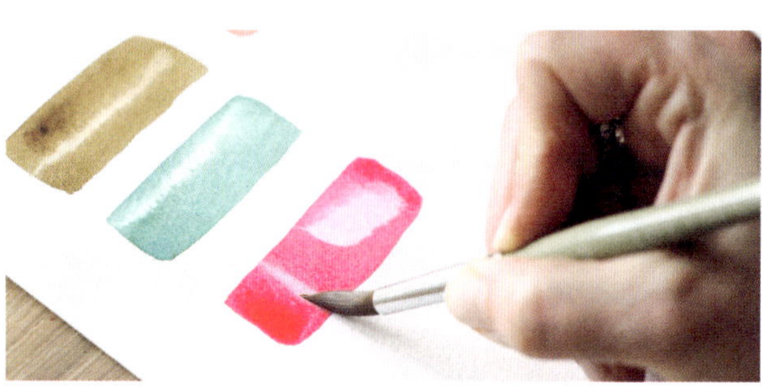

STEP 2

Watch the wet paint stroke be absorbed by the brush. Repeat. Wash the brush, dry it off using a kitchen towel, and swipe it across the lightened area. Observe what happens as the clean brush draws the paint and water from the page.

SCAN TO WATCH
A TUTORIAL

LAYERING

I use two techniques to add depth and dimension to my watercolor paintings. First, I use a wide value range in my pieces, and second, I layer those values on top of dry layers of watercolor. You will learn all about values in the next chapter.

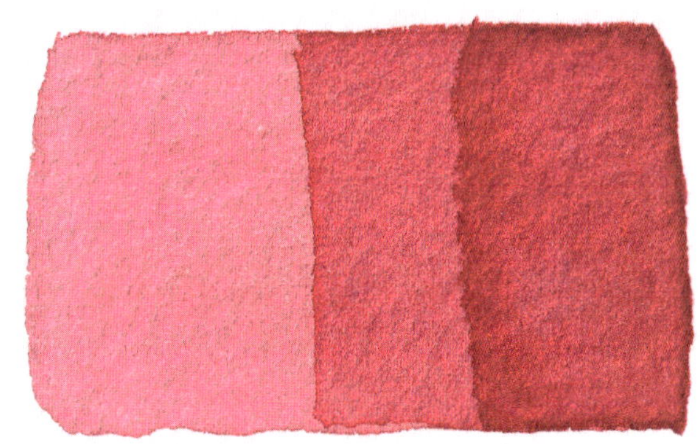

Paint a square using your favorite color. Let it dry. Then add another layer to only half of it. Let it dry. Then add another layer on top of the second layer but only by a quarter. See how much depth you're able to paint? Notice how opaque and dark the color becomes?

tip ······ Use the kitchen towel to dab off excess water from the brush if you feel you have too much water or if you are having trouble controlling the paint.

SCAN TO WATCH
A TUTORIAL

DRY BRUSHING

When I'm working on a detailed piece, I usually spend hours painting the various layers and then give myself a bit of a break before adding the finishing details. This is when I'm able to come back to it with fresh eyes and decide whether it needs more details and depth. One of my favorite ways to add fine detail is by using a dry brush technique, or what I like to call dry-on-dry.

Dry brushing with watercolor paint can be a little tricky, so don't be discouraged if it takes a few tries before you are pleased with the results. Essentially, your paint mix needs to have a higher paint-to-water ratio so that the paint is more opaque, creamy, and full of pigment. Most importantly, your brush should be dry.

Using a fine detail brush, load your brush with the paint mix only, without dipping it into your water jar first. After you've loaded it with the paint mix, dab it onto a kitchen towel and let the towel absorb all the water from the brush. At this point, I also have a scrap piece of watercolor paper handy and lightly run the side of the brush back and forth until I see that the paint is quite dry and skips across the paper.

Use this dry brush to begin adding detail to painting projects such as the feather project, the moth, and even the bird. This is also where tube paints come in handy. I will dispense just a pea-sized amount to my palette and not add any water to the mix, but dip my damp brush into the paint directly and use that for dry brushing detail.

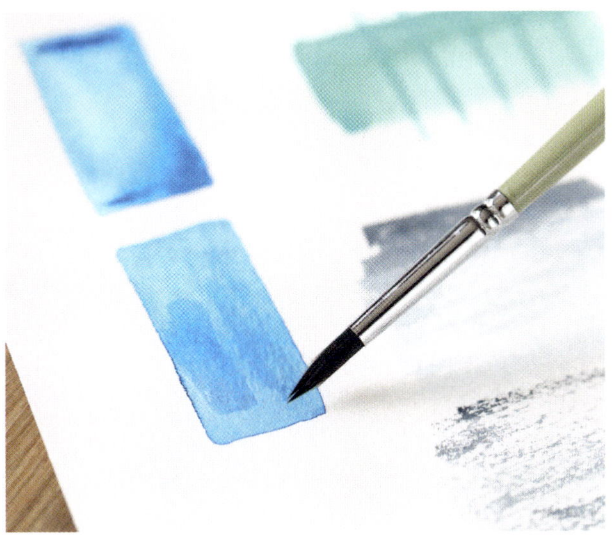

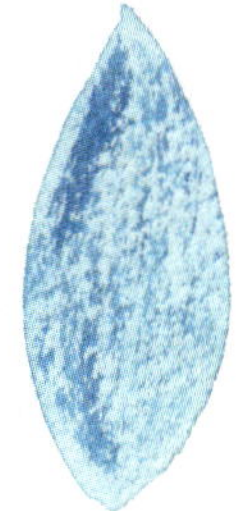
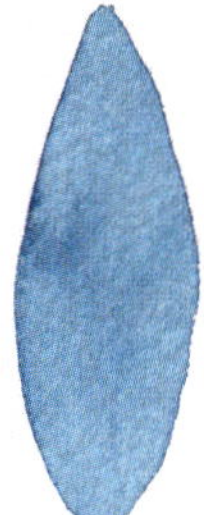
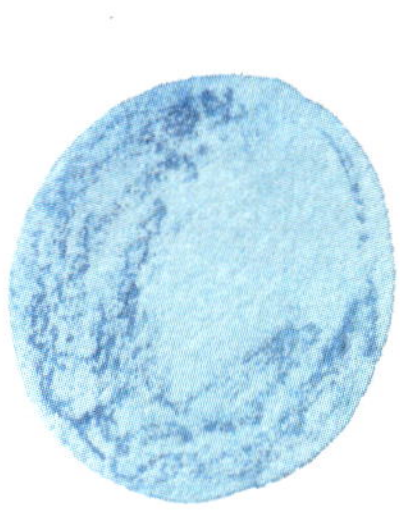

Again, this technique takes practice, but when you get it right, it's a great way to add some fine detail to your paintings without a lot of fuss.

practice fundamental techniques

It's time to practice these very important techniques. I have a challenge for you: Fill an entire sheet of watercolor paper with leaves as you practice each technique in this chapter.

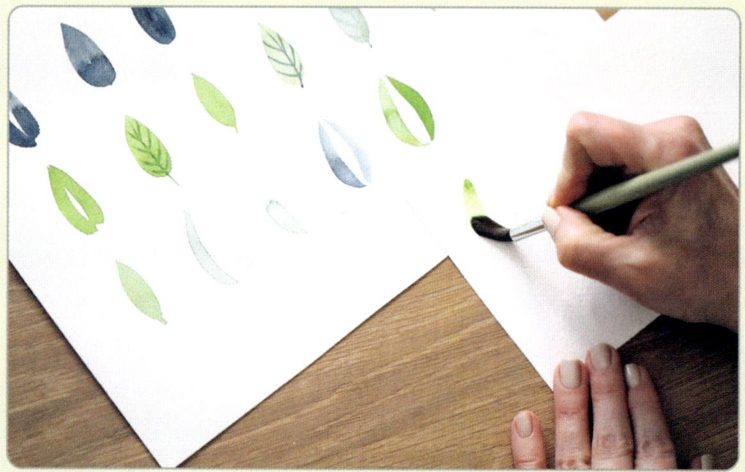

STEP 1

Start by painting leaves in two simple strokes. Place the brush on the paper and slightly push down on the brush to open the belly as you drag the brush down, and then release the pressure to create a taper at the bottom.

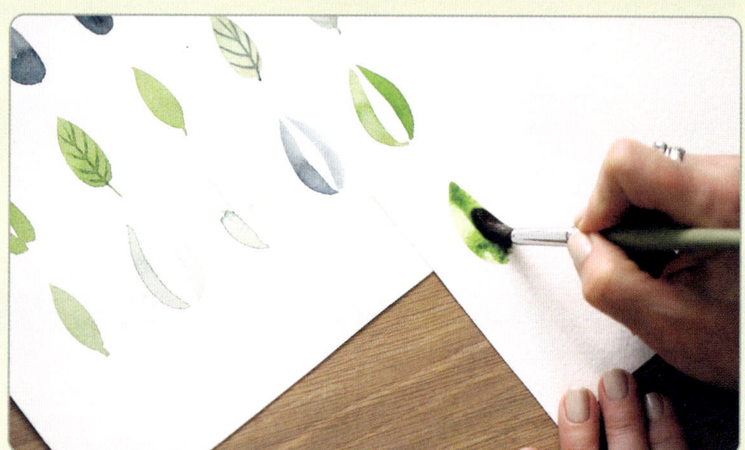

STEP 2

Repeat on the other side. You've just painted a simple leaf.

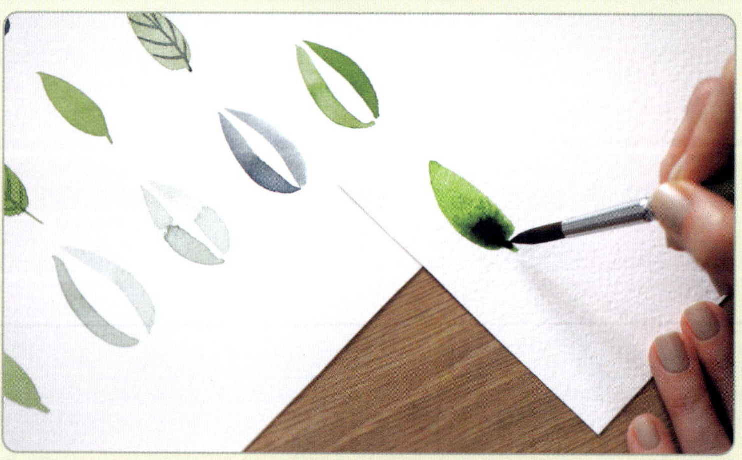

STEP 3

Now, using the **wet-on-wet technique**, drop a slightly darker color at the base of the leaf where it is still wet. I used sap green for the leaf and Payne's gray as my wet.

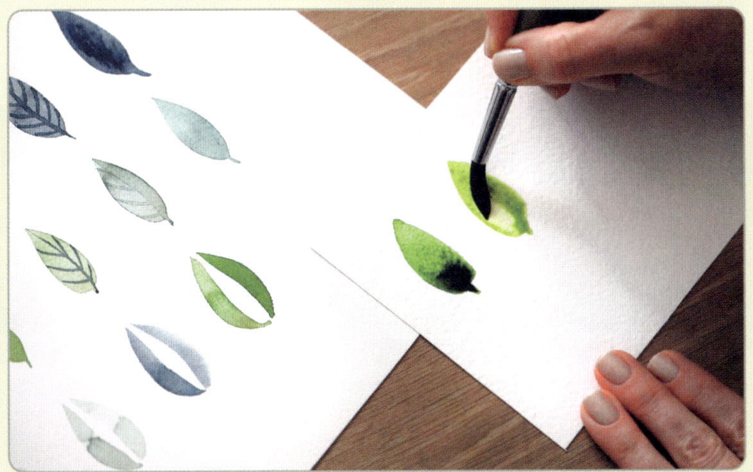

STEP 4

As you work on wet leaves, try **lifting** color and creating highlights in the leaves.

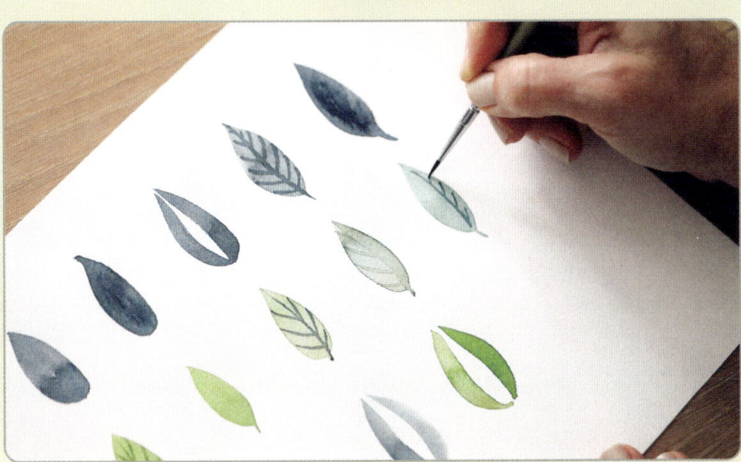

STEP 5

Next, when your leaves are all dry, paint a few stems and veins by using the **wet-on-dry technique** or even **dry brushing.**

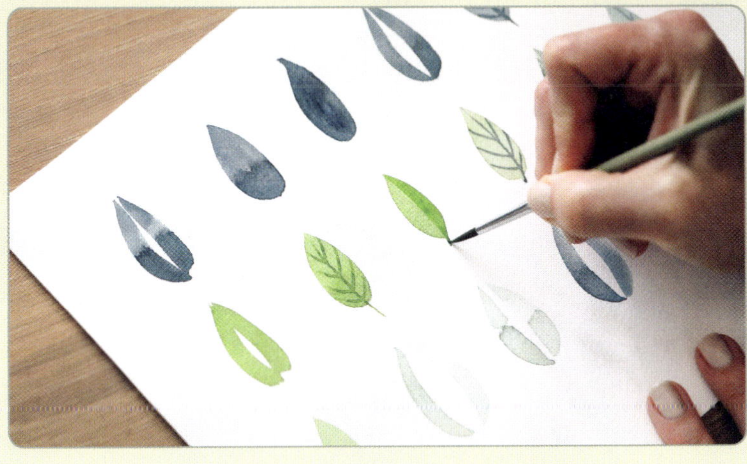

STEP 6

Lastly, paint a second layer of color on top of a few of the leaves to practice **layering** and adding depth.

t i p ······ Save those practice sheets because we will do something fun with them in chapter 8.

SCAN TO WATCH
A TUTORIAL

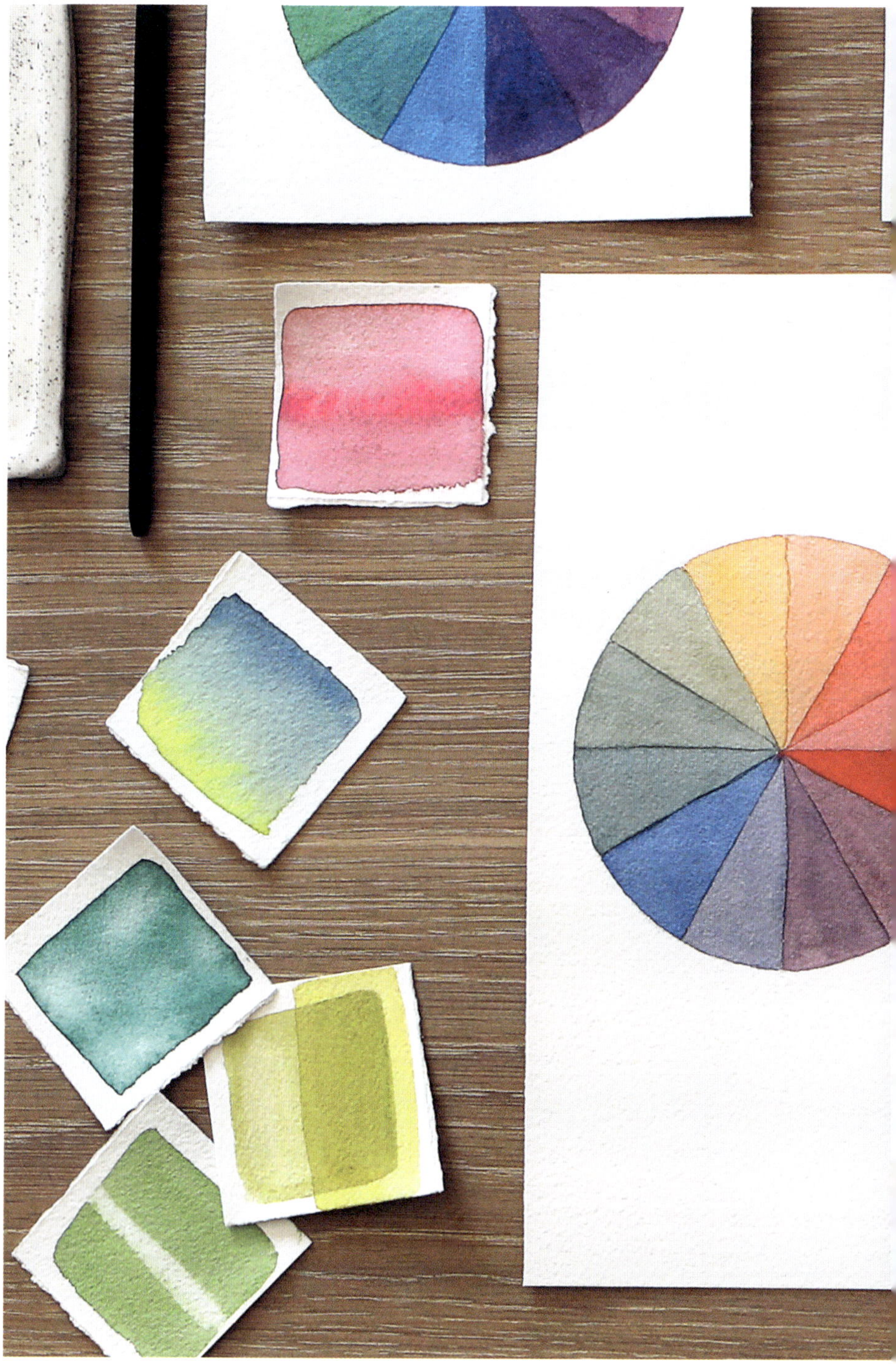

4

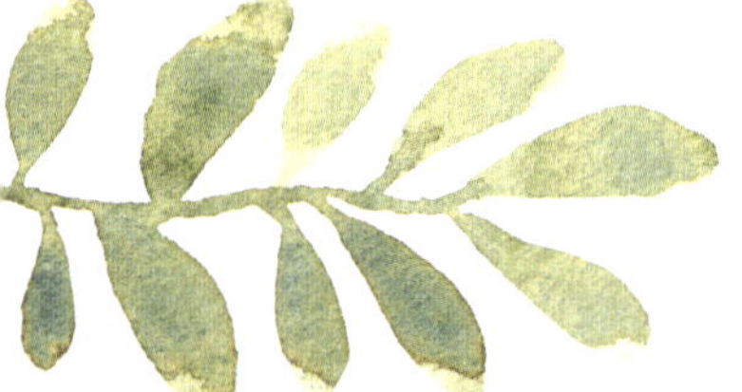

COLOR MIXING

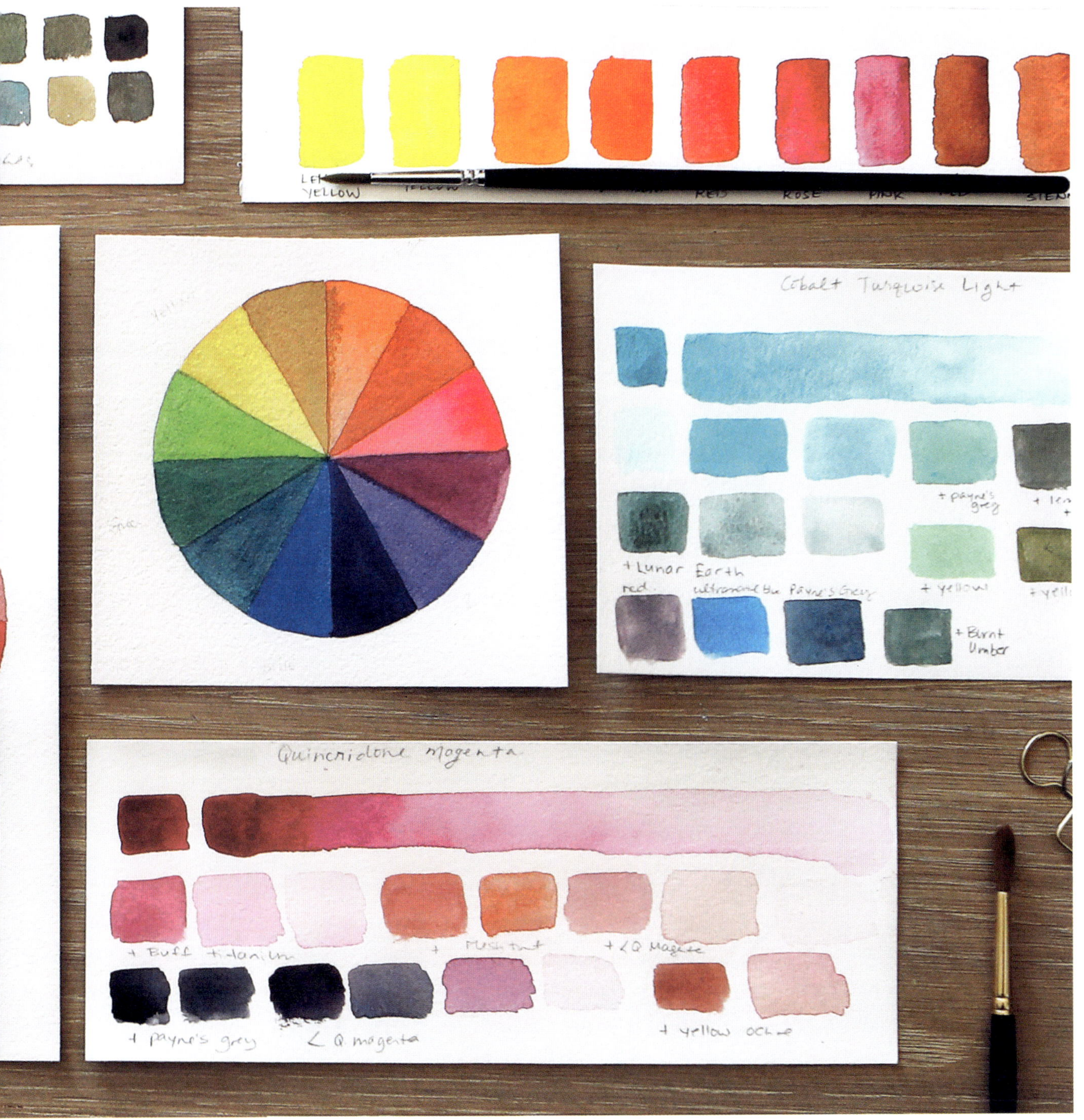

Color plays a big role in our lives and affects many choices we make, from the clothes we wear to how we decorate our homes. Color also plays an important role in our paintings. It creates a mood, makes a subject familiar, and can offer a unique point of view. Color is very personal, and using colors that make your heart sing will lead you to pick up your paintbrush and explore that color more. In this chapter, you'll learn a few simple but important aspects of color mixing and color theory. But if you want to nail color mixing and be confident when deciding which colors to use in your paintings, a bit of courage and a lot of practice are the keys.

THE COLOR WHEEL

Before we dive in, I want to offer you some definitions that I suggest you become familiar with. **Hue** is the name of the pure color, for example, yellow or green.

All colors are derived from by combining two or more **primary** hues, which are yellow, red, and blue.

Mixing these primary colors will create three new **secondary** colors of orange, green, and violet (purple).

Mixing one of the three original primary colors with one of the secondary colors will result in a **tertiary** color. The tertiary colors are yellow-orange, red-orange, red-violet, blue-violet, blue-green, and yellow-green.

A color wheel is a way to organize these twelve colors and show the relationships between them. This color wheel is something that I have handy when I'm painting and use as a reference when I need a reminder of what to use for my color mixing.

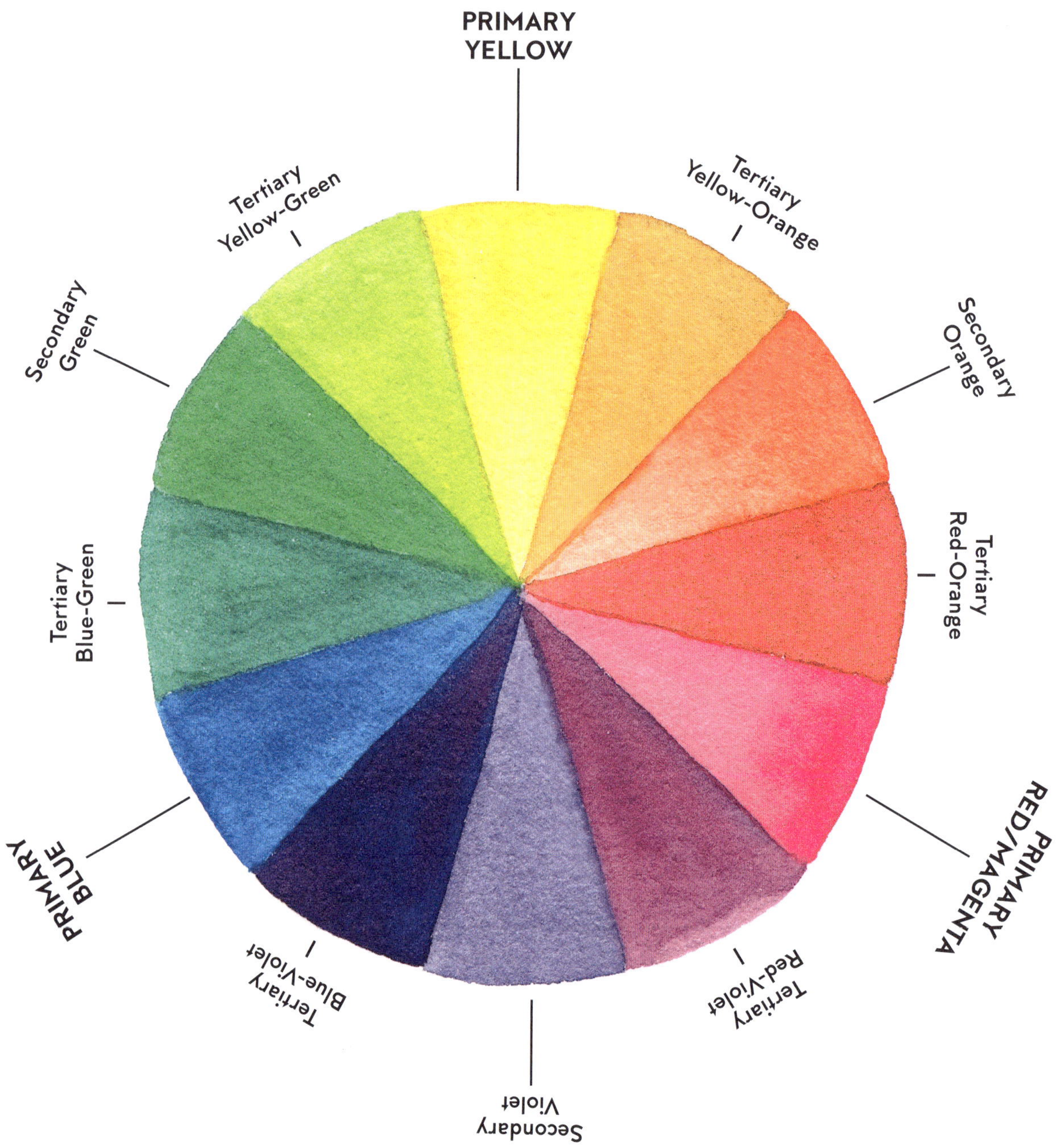

painting a color wheel

Having a color wheel near you when you're painting is a great reminder of how to mix colors that may be missing in your watercolor kit. For this exercise, you will paint a color wheel using the primary colors of yellow, red, and blue. Looking at your paint swatches that you created in chapter 2, decide which yellow, red, and blue look the brightest and most pure, and start with them. For reference, I'm using permanent rose, Winsor yellow, and Winsor blue (green shade). Alternate primary colors that can be used are magenta, cyan or phthalo blue, and yellow.

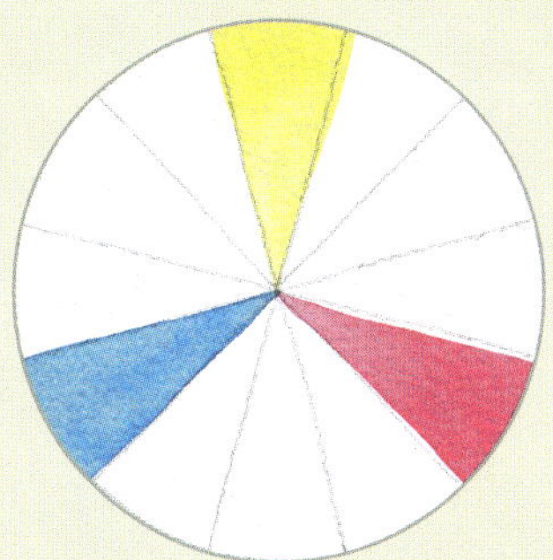 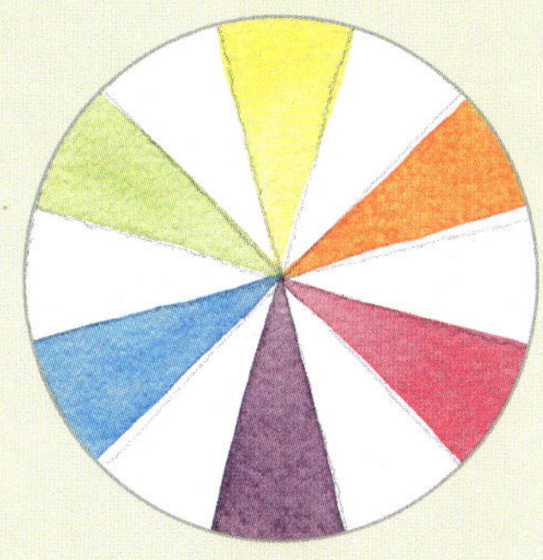 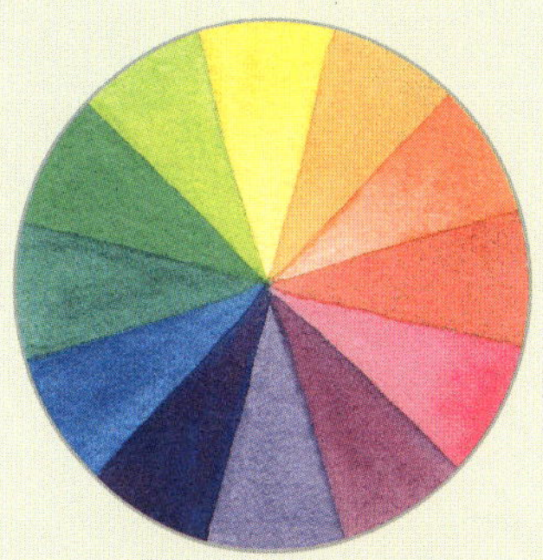

STEP 1. Trace the color wheel from page 42 onto watercolor paper. Paint primary yellow in one section, primary red in the fourth section to the right of yellow, and primary blue in the fourth section to the right of red. These are your primary colors in your color wheel. Let dry.

STEP 2. Mix equal parts yellow and red in your palette. Paint the orange color in the second section to the right of yellow, between your red and yellow sections. Mix equal parts red and blue in your palette to get violet. Paint it in the second section to the right of red. Mix equal parts yellow and blue in your mixing palette to get green. Paint it in the second section between yellow and blue on your color wheel. You've just mixed all three secondary colors.

STEP 3. Mix equal parts of the secondary orange and primary yellow together to make yellow-orange and paint it to the right of yellow. Mix equal parts secondary orange and primary red to make red-orange and paint it to the left of red. Mix equal parts of violet and red together to make red-violet. Paint it in the section to the right of red. Mix equal parts of violet and blue together to make blue-violet. Paint it in the section to the right of blue. Mix equal parts of green and yellow to mix yellow-green and paint it in the section to the left of yellow. Mix equal parts of green and blue to make blue-green and paint the section to the left of green. You have just mixed nine new colors using just yellow, red, and blue.

COLOR MIXING FOR BRIGHT OR MUTED COLORS

As you begin to explore color mixing and even painting your own color wheel, you will continue to build your observational skills as an artist and understand your watercolor palette even more. For color mixes that are brighter and crisper, begin with primary colors as close to the purest form of that color as possible. For example, look for the brightest red rather than a red that has an orange tinge to it. Don't worry if you can't tell the difference between a bright red and an orange-red yet; you will learn these distinctions using some of my techniques along with practice.

I have come to realize that I really love using colors that are muted. As you continue to grow your watercolor painting experience, you too will be drawn to certain colors more than others.

Mixing muted colors can be a little tricky because you want beautifully muted tones and not mud. I mix using two different methods. First, you can mix a secondary color wheel by using colors that are not pure colors (see page 44).

Secondly, you can mix small amounts of warm colors with cool colors to "tone" the mix. By doing this, you'll be able to mix gorgeous deep greens, smoky blues, and even rusty orange tones—colors that can create a moody vibe.

Color wheel using brighter colors (left) and color wheel using more muted colors (right).

tip ······ Knowing the basics of color theory is important, but I don't want you to stress out about it. Some beginning artists dwell on the semantics of having the exact paint color, or brush, or even time to paint, and it stops them from just playing and allowing themselves to experience being creative. While it's important to use the primary colors for color mixing or good quality cotton paper, I don't want it to stop you from trying, exploring, and enjoying watercolors!

alternate color wheels

Try the color wheel exercise you just completed again, but paint an alternate version using nontraditional primary colors. For example, try using yellow ochre, alizarin crimson, and Prussian blue. Observe the unique mixes that you create using these colors. Remember to make note of what colors you use to paint your color wheel so you can recreate that color mix again and again.

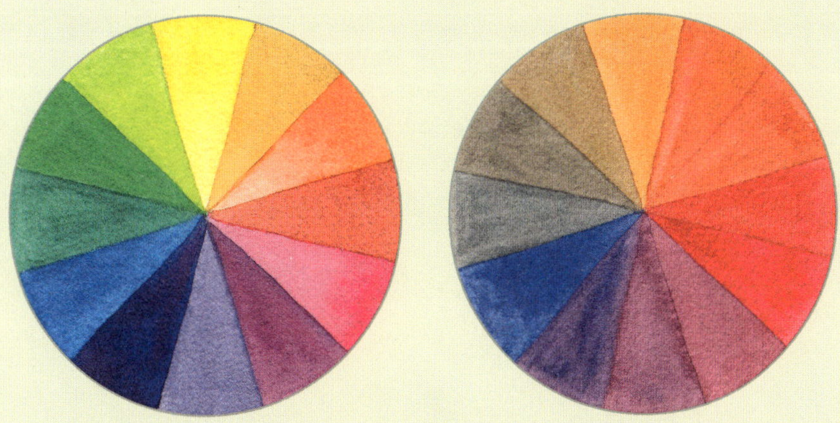

Color wheel using primary colors (left) and nonprimary colors (right).

mixing colors

Pick a bright green from your palette and swatch a small square onto your watercolor paper. Choose a red from your palette, and swatch a square next to the green. Then mix in a very slight amount of red to the green and swatch it again. What do you observe? Adding a bit of warmth to the green will really change the color and give you freedom to mix colors that are opposite on the color wheel. Remember, if you add too much, you can end up with a muddy brown, so add slowly until you get the color you're imagining. Make notes about your color mixes and continue to observe what happens when you mix colors.

When you mix sap green and alizarin crimson, you get a muted deep green.

THE VALUE SCALE AND HOW TO USE IT

Value relates to how light or dark a color is. Highlights or bright areas (light value) in a painting appear to reflect light, while darker areas (dark value) draw the eye in and create depth. A well-composed painting usually has a variety of values within the same color.

When using watercolor paints, the way we achieve lighter and darker value is by the amount of water we mix into our paint puddle. Remember, more water means the watercolor puddle will be more transparent and lighter in value. Less water in the watercolor puddle will result in more pigment and a darker value of that color.

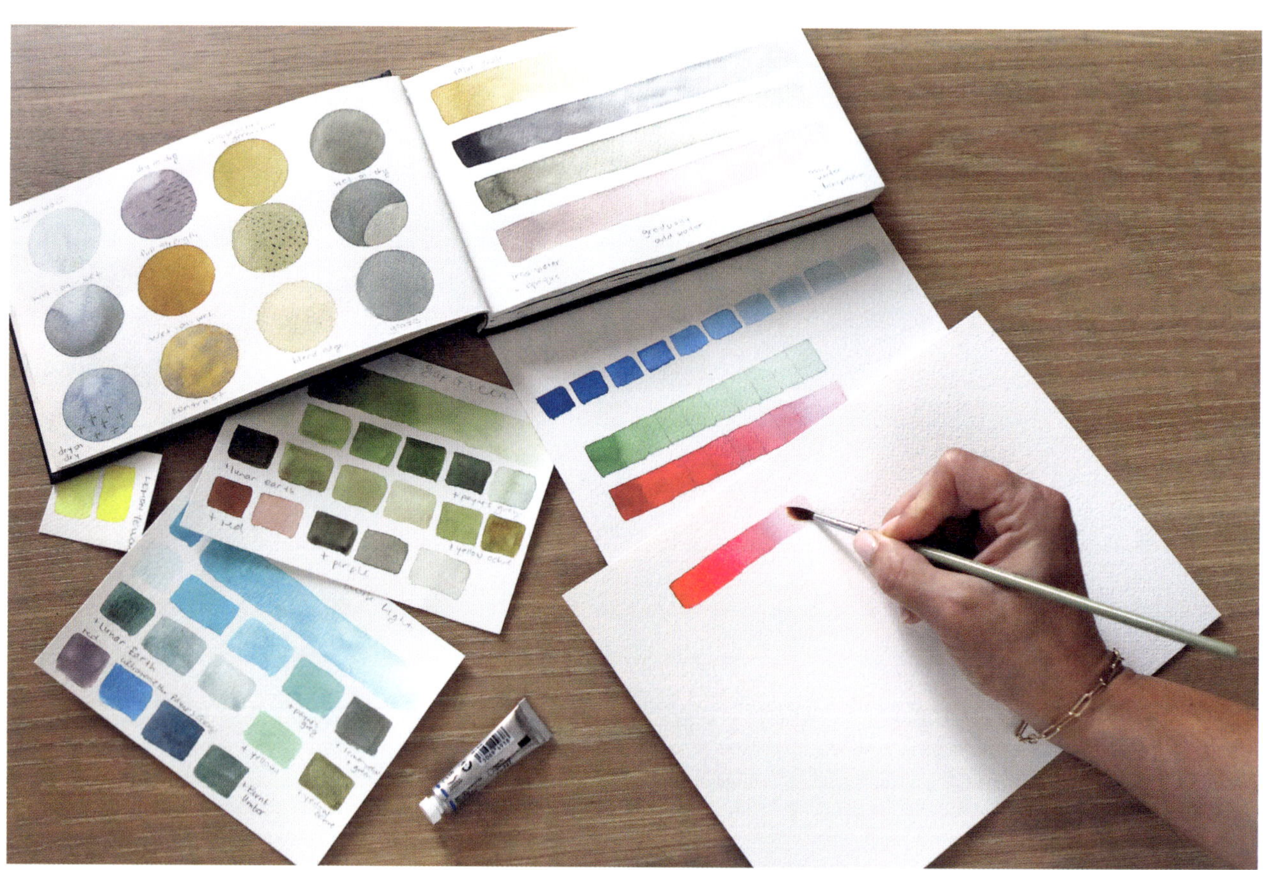

It's a helpful practice to create value scales of different colors. You will learn to control the values of colors and also have a wonderful record of colors you can use in your paintings.

t i p ······ I suggest you explore color theory beyond the basics to grow your color-mixing confidence. Start a journal dedicated to color-mixing practice and note colors and mixes that make you excited to paint.

paint a value scale

Choose a color and create a puddle using a high paint-to-water ratio so it will be very pigmented. Swatch it on your paper. Then add more water to your brush and add it to the swatch on your paper as you pull a slightly lighter shade, diluting the color as you lighten the value of the pigment. Repeat this step and continue to do this until you have about ten different values of the color across your page. How light can you get that color?

In our painting projects, we will use a variety of values to paint depth and dimension. If everything was painted in the same value, it would be flat and lack interest. Each time you put brush to paper, you are growing your watercolor skills, understanding, and confidence. Please put this new information to practice. Go ahead, make yourself a yummy hot or cold drink, grab your watercolor kit, and really enjoy practicing color and values.

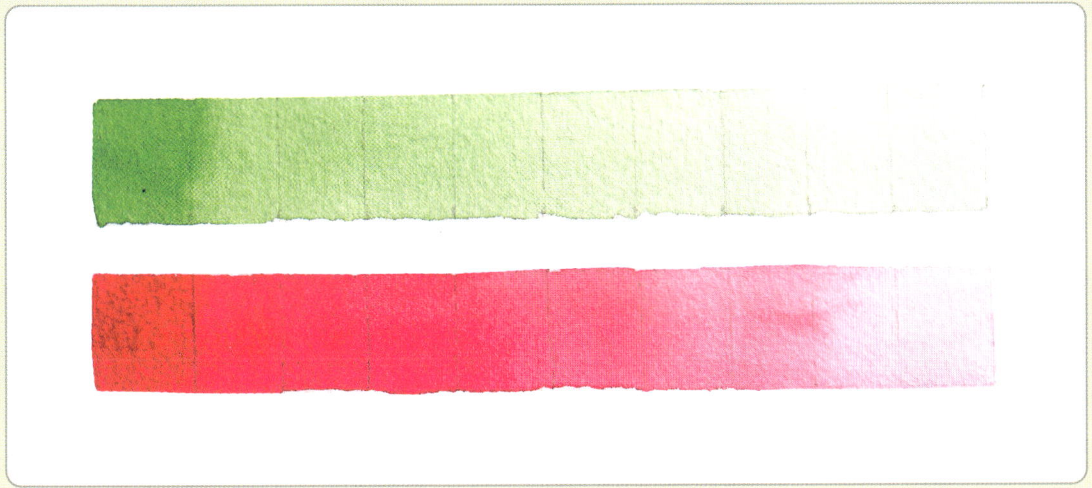

Value scales using green and red. See how much variety you can get with one color!

t i p ⸱⸱⸱⸱⸱ Follow the watercolor puddle. When painting, move the puddle that forms on the paper from your brush and pull it across the area you want to fill. This will allow you to paint seamless transitions, especially when adding a new brushstroke to your painting.

SCAN TO WATCH
A TUTORIAL

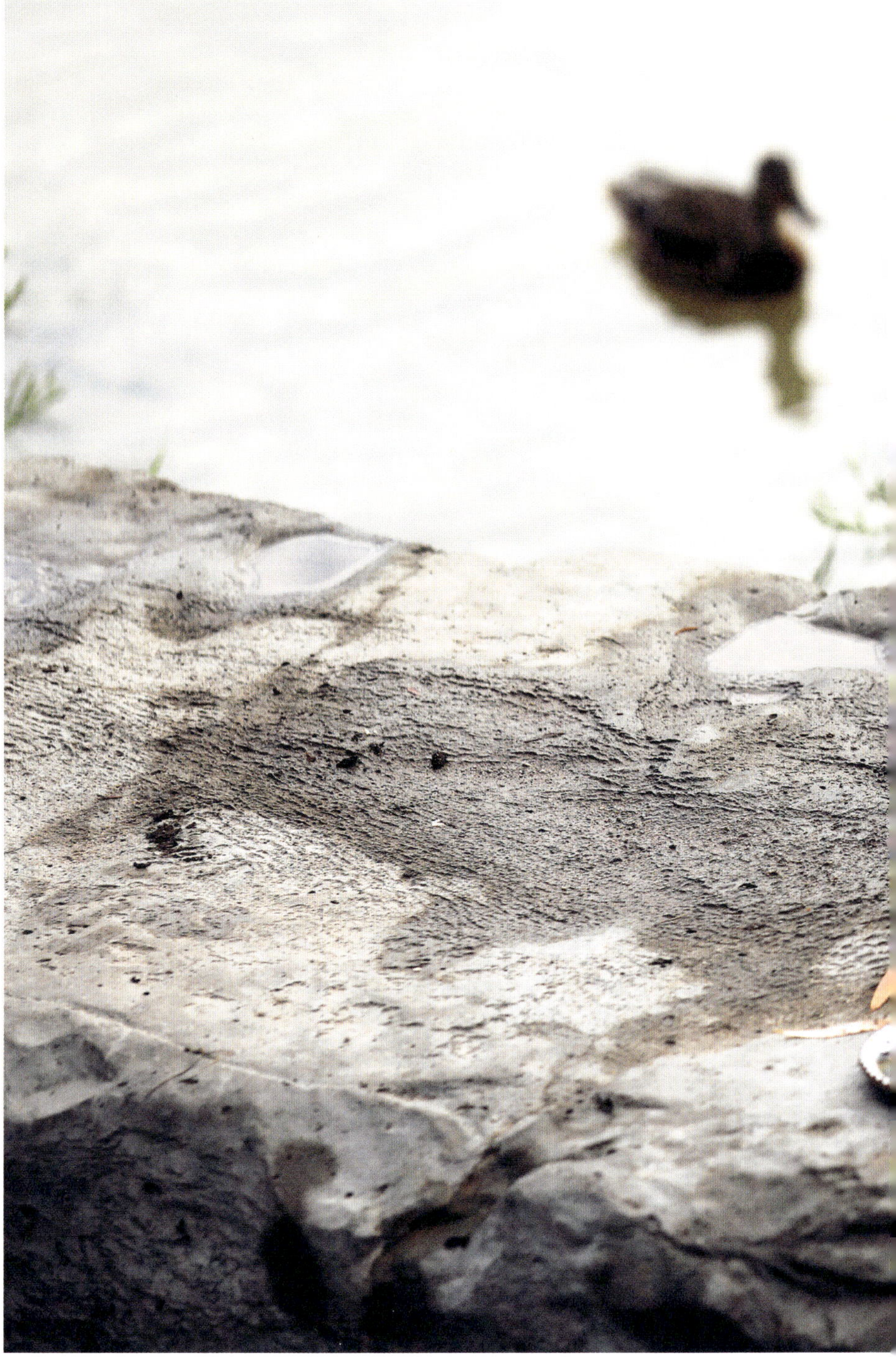

5

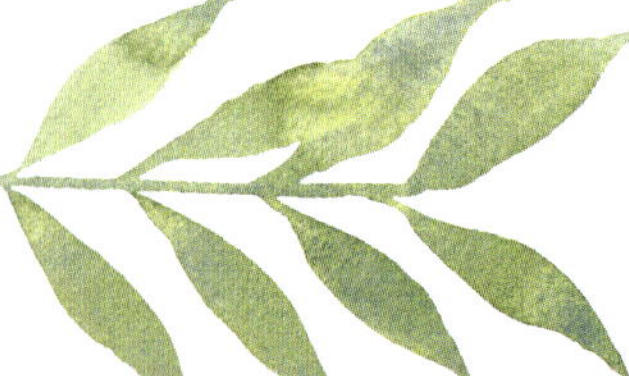

BE CURIOUS

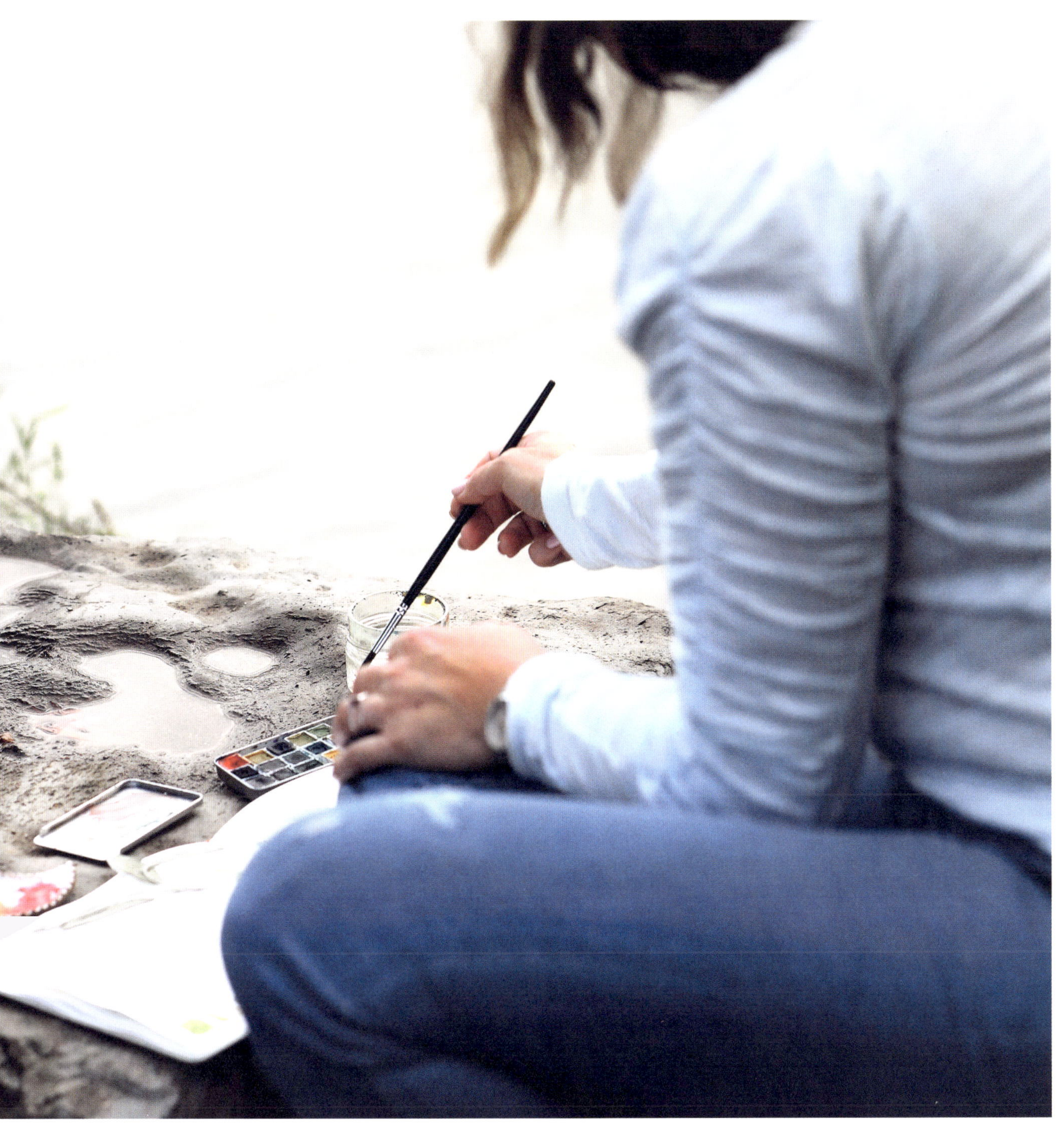

I hope you're already working on your observational skills and making notes as you practice the techniques we've explored so far in this book. I'm a firm believer that we artists need to continuously learn, explore, and experiment as we paint and practice our art. When I'm preparing for my next painting project, I love to look for color palette inspiration, paint swatches, and sketch ideas. This preparation helps get the creative juices flowing, and it's a very important step that many people skip. I want you to get into the habit of filling yourself up with ideas that make you want to pick up your watercolor supplies again and again.

LOOK AT YOUR DAILY LIFE FOR CUES

What do you naturally surround yourself with? Is it plants? Fabrics with patterns? Rich textures? What colors do you like to wear because they make you feel good? Is your closet filled with color, or is the color palette muted like mine, with black, white, gray, and a bit of green or blue? Look around you, what do you observe?

I encourage you to learn to take cues from your daily life and really lean into painting imagery that you love while using colors you're naturally drawn to. Pick up your sketchbook, grab a pencil, look around your home and wardrobe, and make notes of color, patterns, and motifs, then start brainstorming.

Next to your notes, use your watercolor paints to swatch a few of your favorite colors and make notes of how the colors make you feel, what season they remind you of, and what subjects the colors can be found in.

For example, I love the colors green and blue and often take photos of nature and landscapes as we travel or even as I go on my morning walks. I often think about ways to mix the unique blues and greens I observe and how to use them in my paintings. My morning walks make me happy and excited to start my day and are often where I find inspiration.

What do you want to paint? What colors make you excited or happy? What are some of the things that you surround yourself with?

I always say, paint what you love, using colors that you love, and you'll love what you paint!

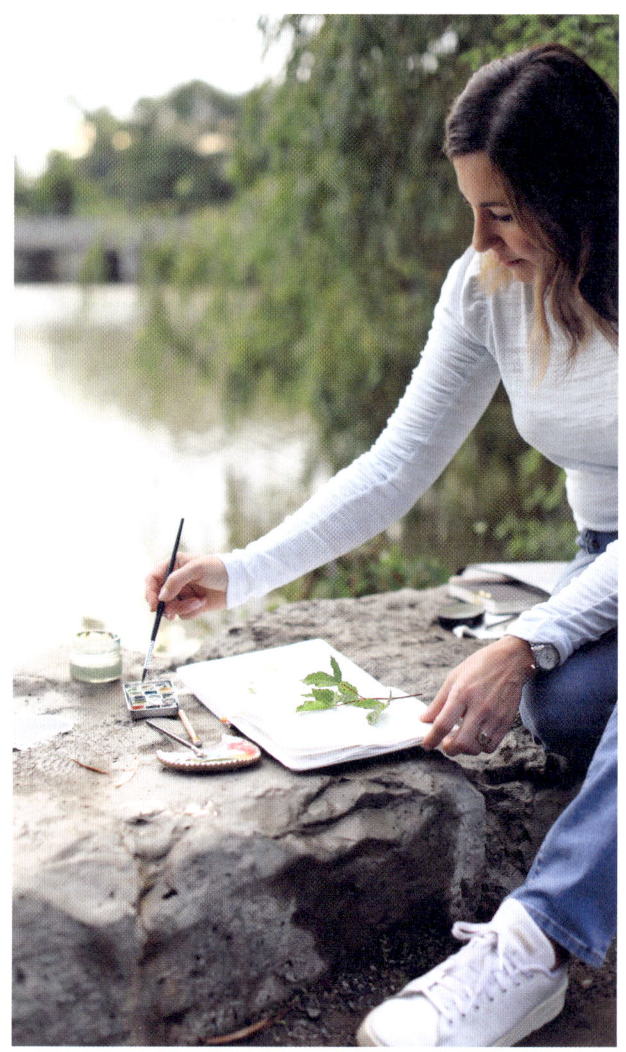

I encourage you to take a sketchbook outside to record your favorite motifs and colors.

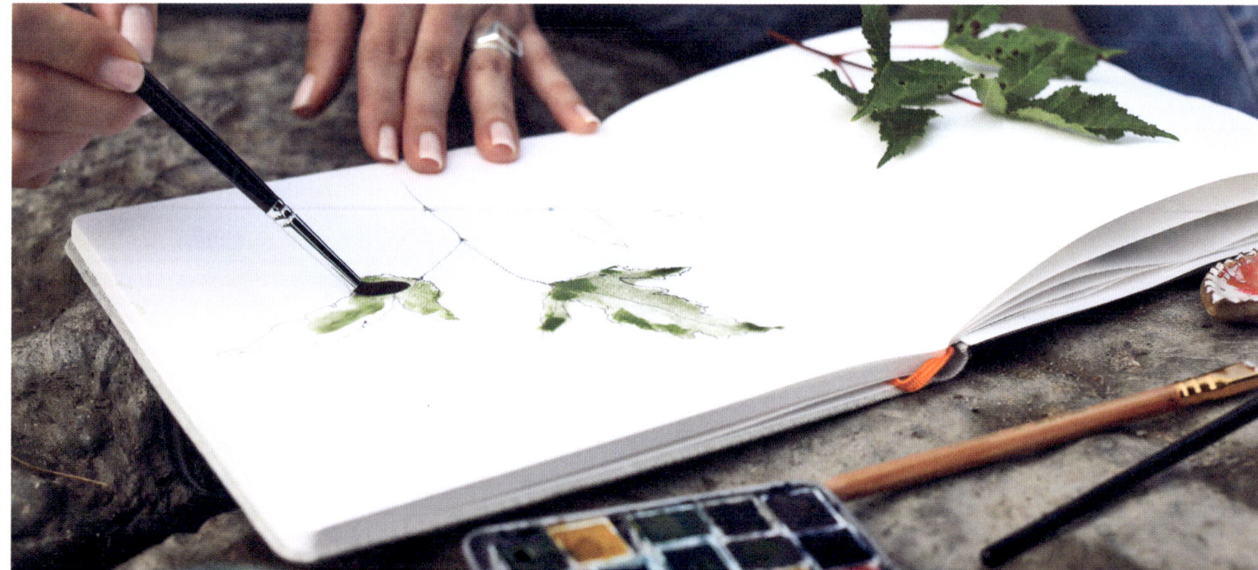

HOW TO PICK A SUBJECT AND EXPLORE IT

For the next chapter of this book, I've purposely chosen a variety of subjects that are found in nature, have interesting shapes, offer different color combinations, and open you up to painting something that perhaps you wouldn't have thought to paint before.

This is where your sketchbook comes in handy. Whether you're using a watercolor journal, a mixed-media sketchbook, or a simple sketchbook and pencil, it doesn't matter. You just need to record your ideas and take notes, looking for cues that can be found around you. Like I said earlier, your job as an artist is to be curious and examine subjects that speak to you and that you want to express using your brush and watercolor paint.

As you probably know by now, I am a nature lover and specifically love the color green. I love to examine plants and greenery and explore their shapes, curves, and movement. When I look around my home, my studio, my closet, and my bookshelf, I notice similar colors that I am drawn to and imagery that repeats around me. I recognize what I like and what I want to explore more. These areas are where I get my personal cues. Yours might be more noticeable when you look through magazines or explore online searches. Think about where you get your inspiration.

Visit your favorite sites online for things that you love and create a virtual mood board if you like to work electronically rather than in a sketchbook. Once you start looking for inspiration, you will notice it everywhere and will start to see repetition in imagery that you enjoy and that you will want to explore more. I will take you through one of my favorite personal exercises that helped me lean into imagery that made me excited to paint.

If you can't explore an item in person, use a variety of photos as reference. I love using Pinterest for research when I don't have books to look at. Pinterest is a photo-driven reference site where you can look up everything from home decor inspiration to recipes to art and photography. You are able to create multiple albums, save these photo references, and organize them to refer to later when researching things that you want to explore painting.

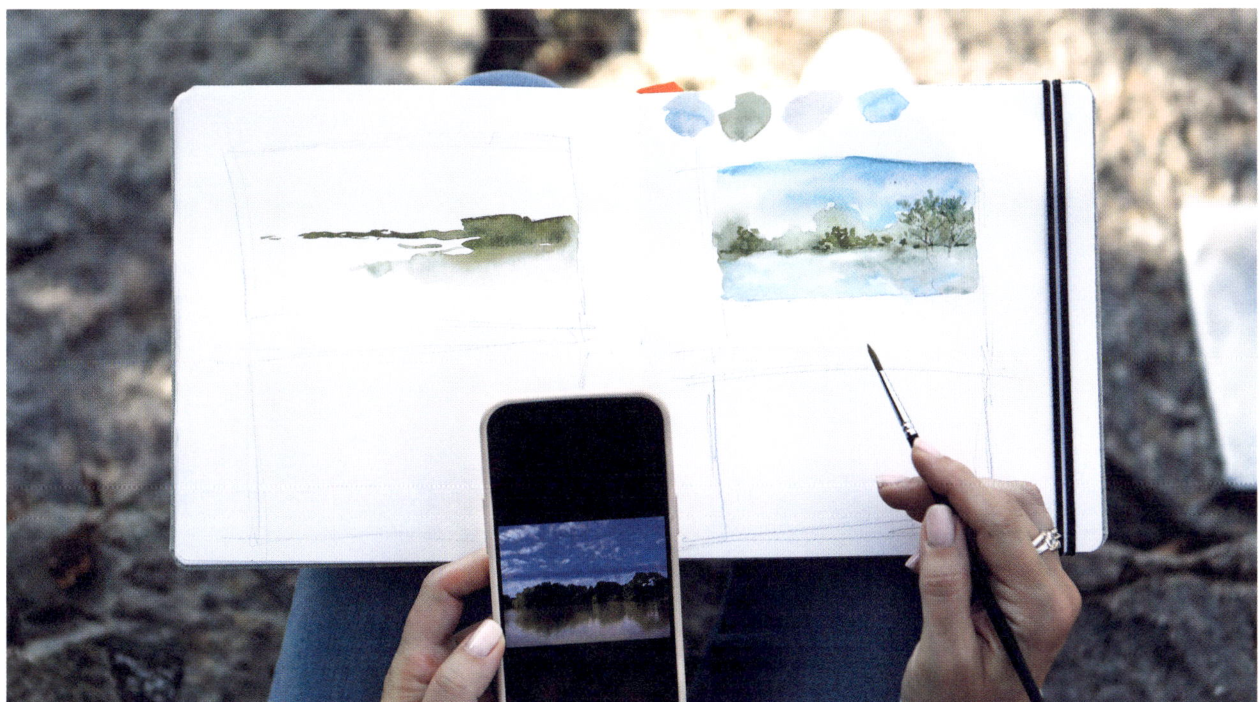

When you're sketching and collecting inspiration, take photos so you can refer to them later.

sage plant sketchbook

Let's work on a brainstorming session together. I love plants and flowers and even have a small veggie and herb garden in my yard. I love fragrant herbs and, as you now know, one of my favorite colors is green. So let's explore sketching, color mixing, and painting a sage plant.

Sage is an herb and has an aroma that reminds me of Thanksgiving, turkey, and gathering the family together for one of my favorite occasions. It's a time when the cooler weather brings us indoors more and makes the house feel warm and cozy. This is how simple things to paint become a bit of a story and create a mood even before we get started. Through this process, I can easily recognize what I love, and that directs me to ideas for what to paint.

I like to work from life when possible. I bought a small sage herb plant, which allowed me to observe details and sketch it using pencil. Now I can mix colors based on what I see and what I want to explore. I'm using artistic liberties to explore my version of the sage plant. I mix colors that I'm called to mix to interpret the grayish-green tones in my own unique way by using blues and whatever greens I have handy in my watercolor kit. My goal is not to create a literal version of the sage stem, but to explore it and interpret it as I choose while I have fun filling a few pages of my sketchbook and getting warmed up.

Using my sketchbook pages as examples, how would you explore painting the bumpy leaves of the sage plant or the colors of the stems? Are you able to observe the plant from life yourself? If so, what do you notice?

Next, what can you do with your painting? How can you expand on this exercise? Can you explore more herbs or foods that you have a fond memory of enjoying? Allow this exercise to inspire you and record your exploration regardless of how formally or informally you paint it.

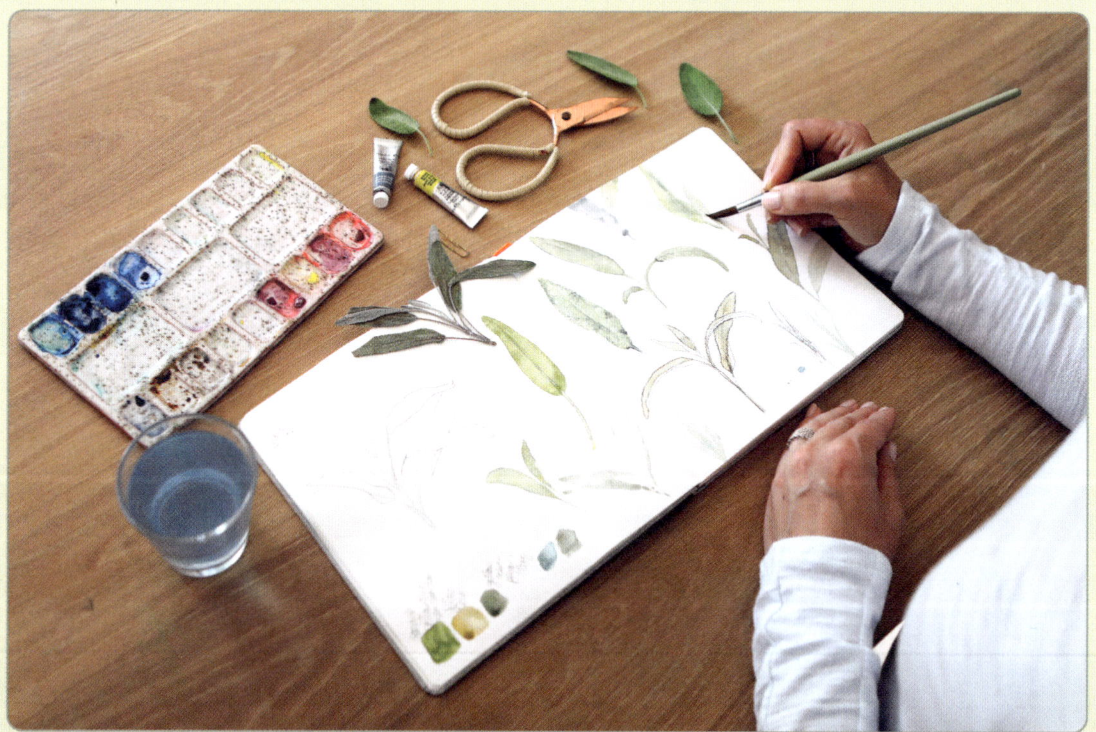

Use a sketchbook with watercolor paper so you can use your paints to add color to the pages.

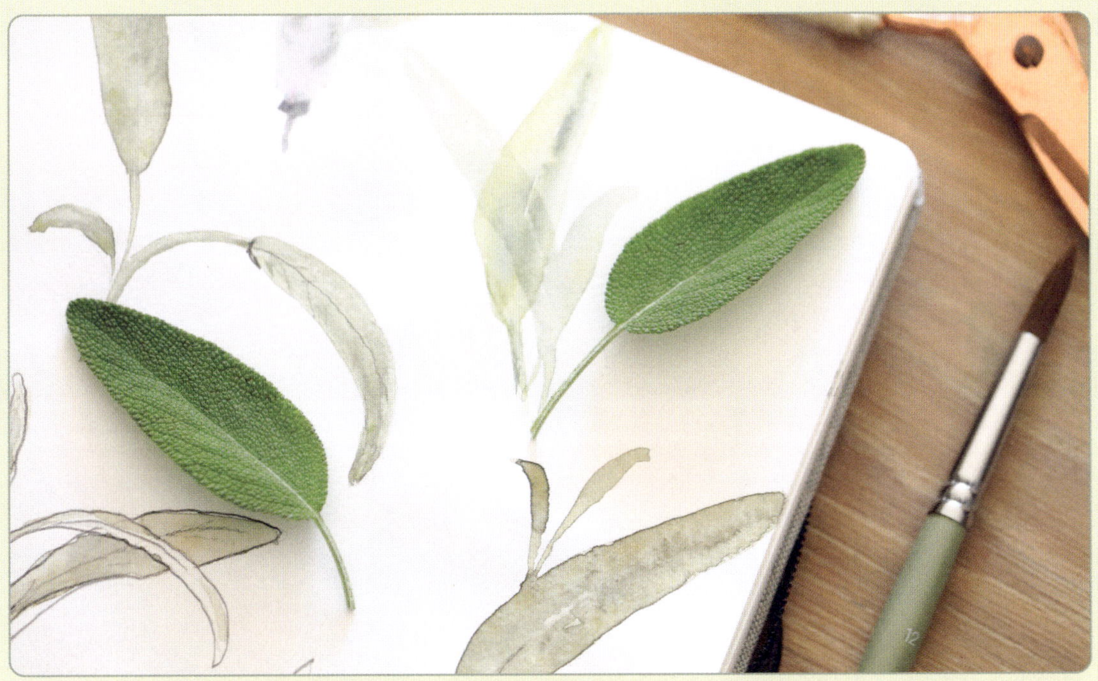

Working from life, such as these sage leaves, allows you to touch, see, and smell a subject. Look closely at the details and try to recreate them in your sketchbook.

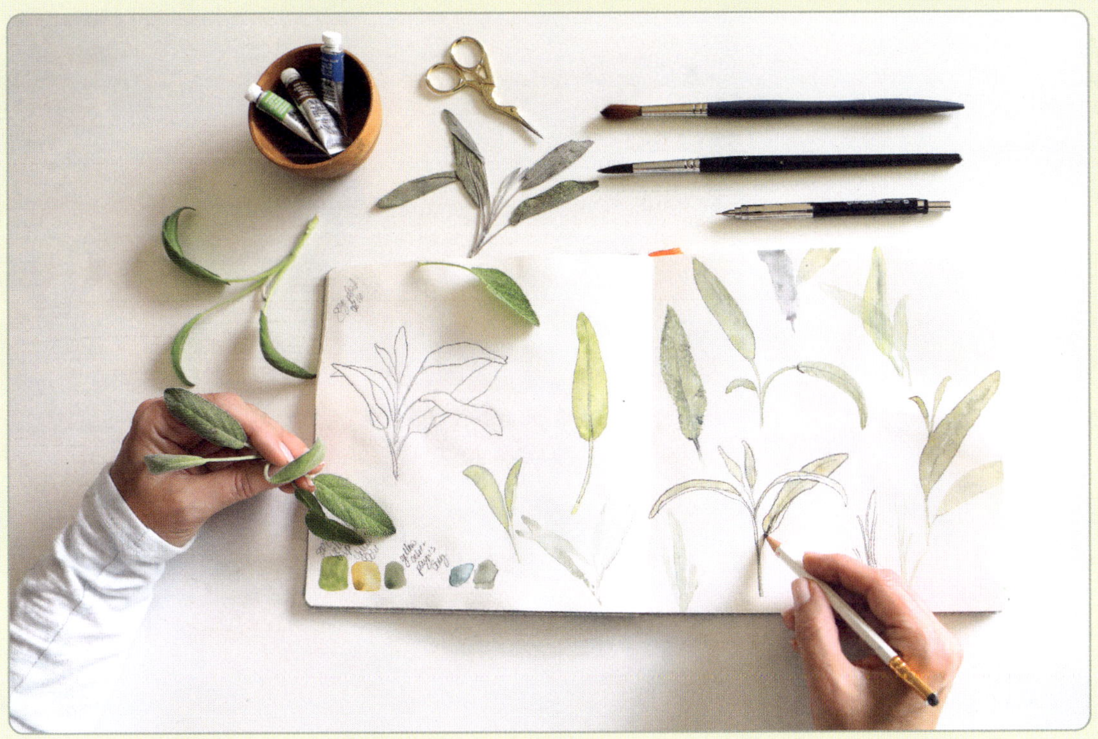

Fill the page with sketches and notes you can use in future paintings.

t i p ······ When you take time to observe and explore the subject you're studying, it's easier for you to draw from memory its unique characteristics to the point where you no longer need a visual reference to paint from.

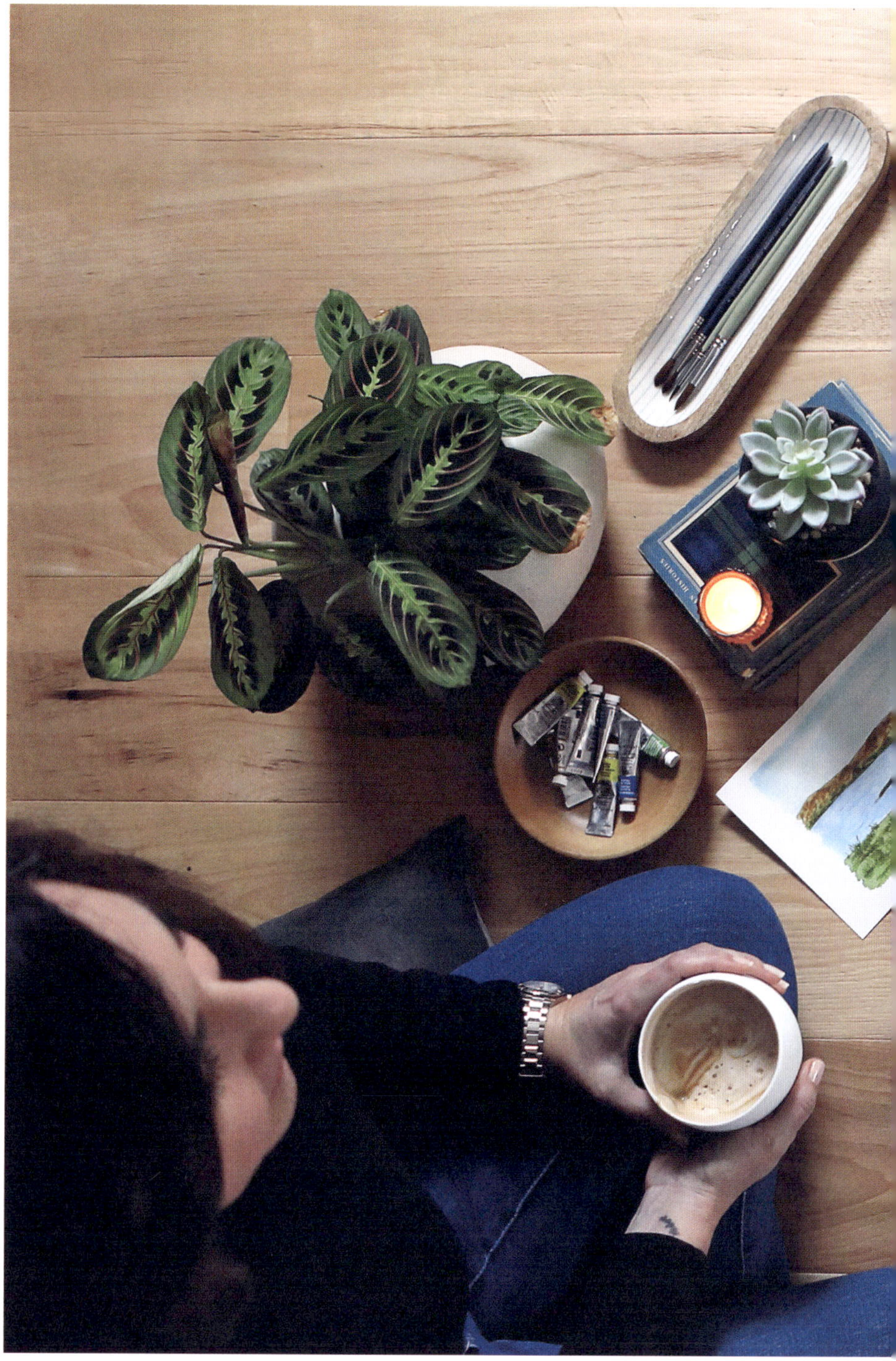

6

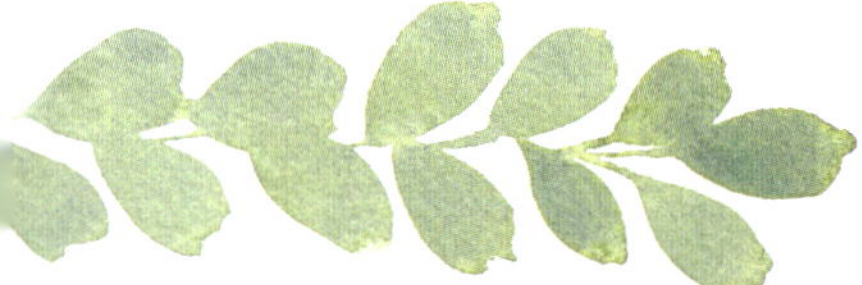

LET'S PAINT!

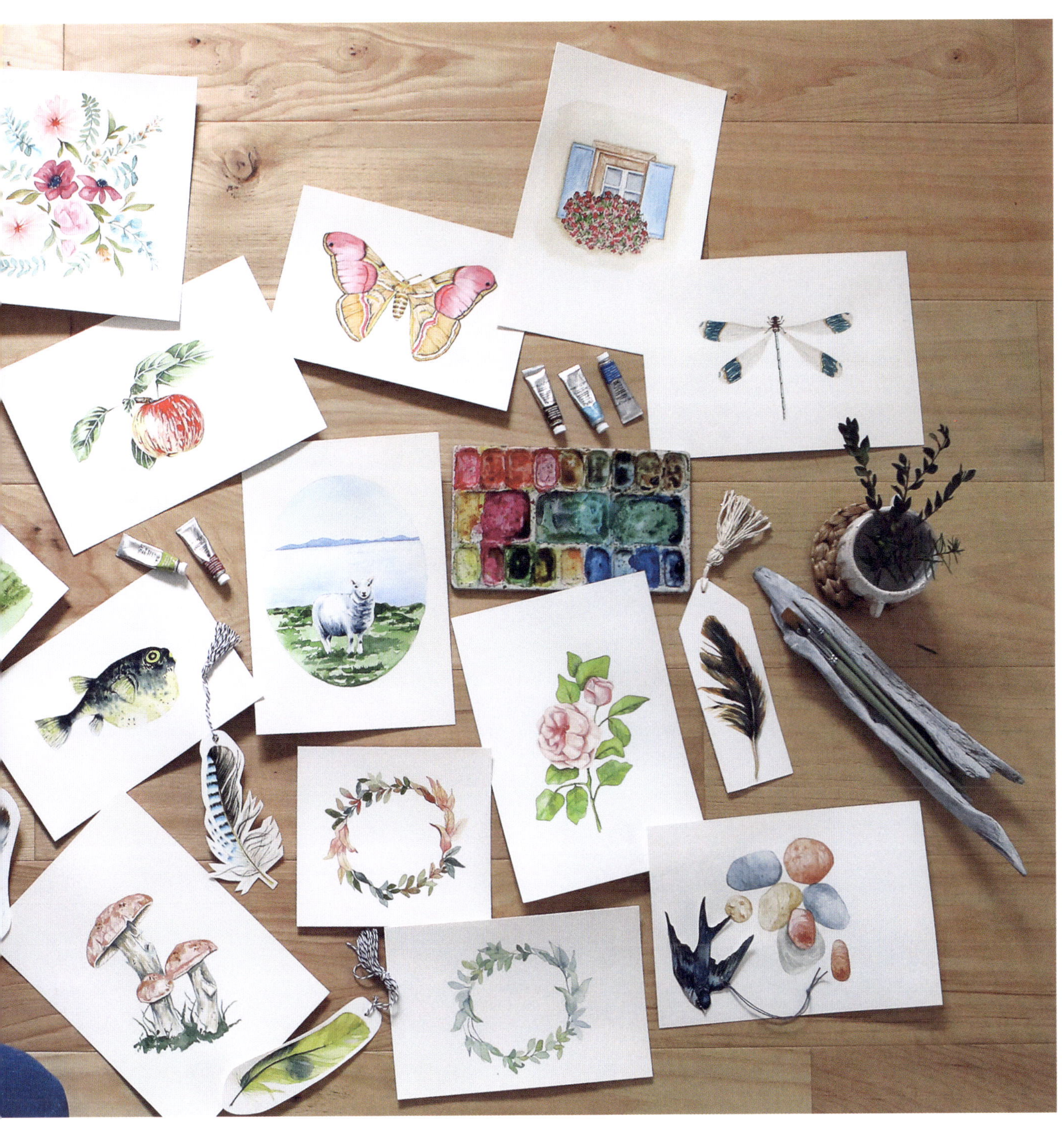

Now that you have learned some watercolor fundamentals and the process for approaching a watercolor practice, it's time to get started painting! I chose imagery that will stretch you and get you excited to paint. I encourage you to try every motif, even if it doesn't interest you at first. I have had students share that they were surprised at how fun something was to paint once they tried it. As you go through these projects, take your time and be okay with painting pieces that you may not love the first time around. Think of these first attempts as warm-ups. You can paint each project multiple times. In fact, I encourage you to do just that.

SOME THINGS TO KEEP IN MIND

Before you get to the fun painting projects that I have in store for you, I just want to give you a few more bits of advice on getting started.

PAINT LIGHT TO DARK

Because watercolors are a transparent medium, I recommend that you paint using the lightest colors first, then build the depth of color by adding layers of darker colors. For example, yellow is lighter than blue, so start with yellow as the first layer, then add blue once the yellow layer is dry. You can also use the white of the paper by leaving areas unpainted. This creates nice highlights and will really make your paintings pop.

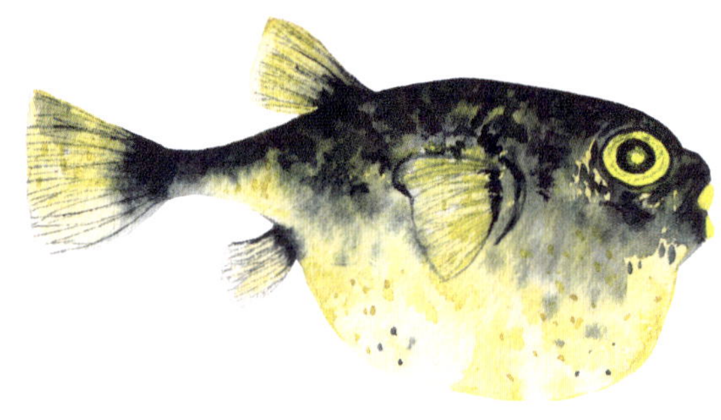

This fish painting (page 68) is a good example of painting from light to dark.

EMBRACE THE PENCIL LINES

I love pencil lines and how they offer a slight shadow in my watercolor paintings. Embrace the pencil lines and the wobbles that you will inevitably have with watercolor painting. We often over-edit ourselves, which doesn't leave enough room for play and joy. I have left all the pencil lines and wobbles in my painted examples to help you embrace yours too. If you want to soften the pencil lines, wait until your painting is completely dry before erasing any pencil marks. Keep in mind that if the watercolor paint goes on top of the pencil marks, you will not be able to erase them fully. You can use an eraser to lighten the pencil marks before you get started painted to help fade them slightly.

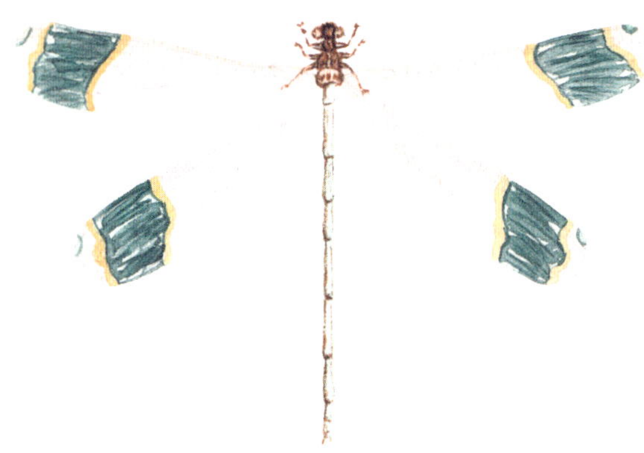

If you like, you can erase pencil marks or leave them in as I did in this dragonfly painting (page 88).

tip ······ To make it even easier to start painting, on pages 126 to 139 I have included templates of all the painting projects and instructions on how to trace them onto watercolor paper.

COLORS DRY LIGHTER

As watercolor paint dries and gets absorbed by the cottony paper, your colors will dry lighter. Don't be afraid to add bolder, pigmented washes of color, and always use a variety of value in your paintings to create depth and interest. If you use the same value of color throughout your painting, it will result in a painting that is flat. Work light to dark and keep in mind that everything will seem lighter when it is dry. At this point, once everything is dry, you can always go back with darker tones to continue to add depth to your painting. Feel free to come back to your painting days later, even weeks later, when everything is dry, and decide whether it needs another layer of a darker value.

TEST YOUR PAINT MIX FIRST

Have scrap pieces of watercolor paper nearby so you can test color mixes before you paint directly on your painting. By using a test sheet, you can swatch your paint mix and get an idea of how transparent or opaque your mixes will be on paper. This gives you an opportunity to adjust the paint mix if you need to. Testing on a spare piece of paper will save you from making frustrating mistakes as you paint your piece.

BLOOMS HAPPEN

When you add a very wet stroke to part of your painting that is almost dry, you get what is called a "bloom." The wet stroke reactivates the paint layer that is still drying and the water pushes the pigment. These blooms can be lovely accidents and are what I consider to be a beautiful characteristic of the watercolor paint medium. So go with it and know that blooms happen and when dry can offer a beautiful element to your painting.

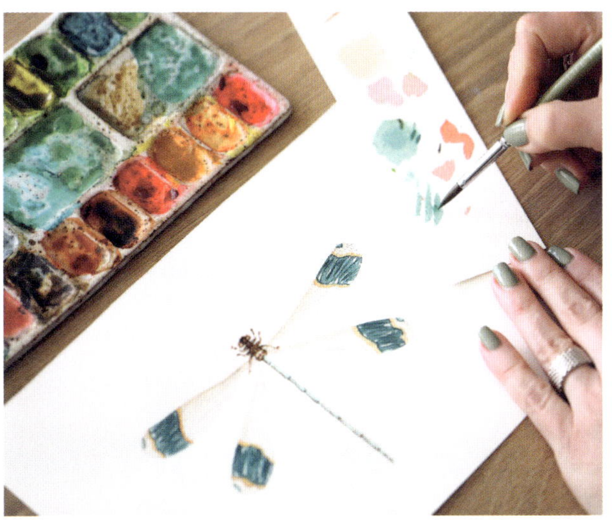

Always test your paint colors on a scrap paper before adding them to your painting in progress.

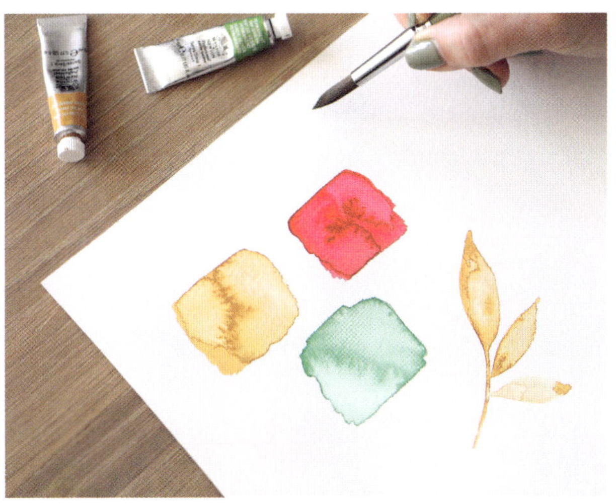

Some people look at blooms as mistakes, but they add a beautiful spontaneous element that is unique to watercolor painting.

t i p ······ Repetition is key. The more you paint the same subject, the more comfortable you will become with it. Don't limit yourself to painting each motif only once. This is worth repeating: Attempt to paint each project a few times and see how much your painting changes each time.

 permanent rose

 raw umber

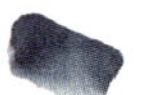 Payne's gray

river rocks

This painting project is a really great way to warm up, practice the watercolor techniques you learned in chapter 3, and enjoy using color and value to paint smooth, subtly colorful river rocks. You will begin to build layers and use value to create depth and shadows. This is a great painting project to use as practice whenever you want to review essential watercolor painting techniques. Let's get started.

STEP 1

If desired, trace the template on page 127. Mix a transparent wash (more water than paint) of permanent rose and raw umber. Use a small brush to paint the first layers of a few of the rocks. Use your brush to lift away some of the paint, revealing highlights on parts of the rocks to start creating roundness. Don't worry if the pencil lines show through; they will add to the character of your painting.

STEP 2

Mix a transparent wash of Payne's gray using more water than paint and add in a few other rocks. Try adding in some of the raw umber to tone the Payne's gray and warm it up slightly. Paint the remainder of the rocks, allowing the paint to move and dry where it wants. Let the paint bleed and create interest and character in your rocks.

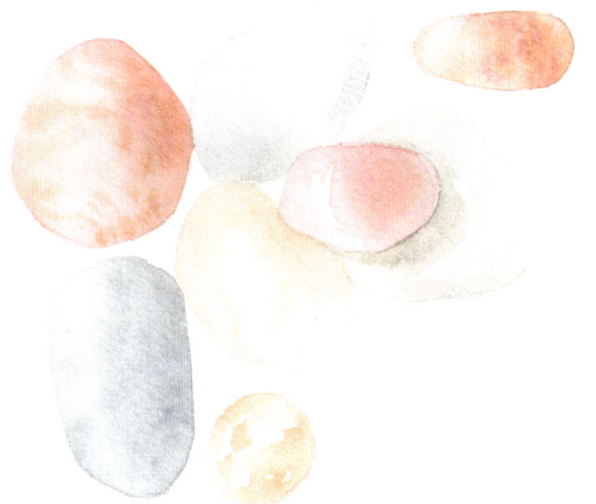

Go back to your color mixes for each stone and add
a second layer of paint, focusing on the outer edges
to create depth. Use wet-on-wet and a detail brush
to paint dots, lines, and fine texture in each rock. Lift
away paint while it's still wet using a dry brush for
lighter values and highlights. Use a darker value on
the areas of the rocks where the rocks touch, and
even overlap slightly. The more variation in value and
interest, the more interesting the finished piece will be.

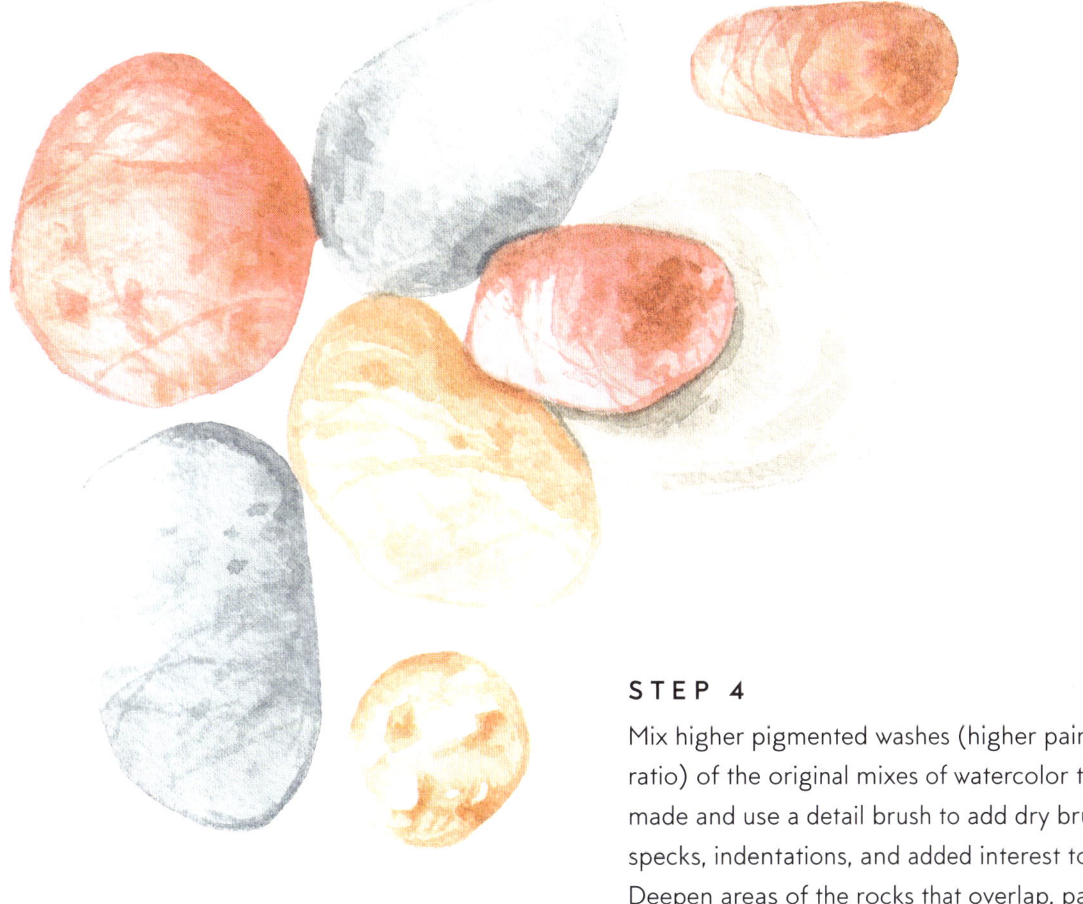

STEP 4

Mix higher pigmented washes (higher paint-to-water
ratio) of the original mixes of watercolor that you
made and use a detail brush to add dry brush lines,
specks, indentations, and added interest to the rocks.
Deepen areas of the rocks that overlap, painting more
value for a three-dimensional effect.

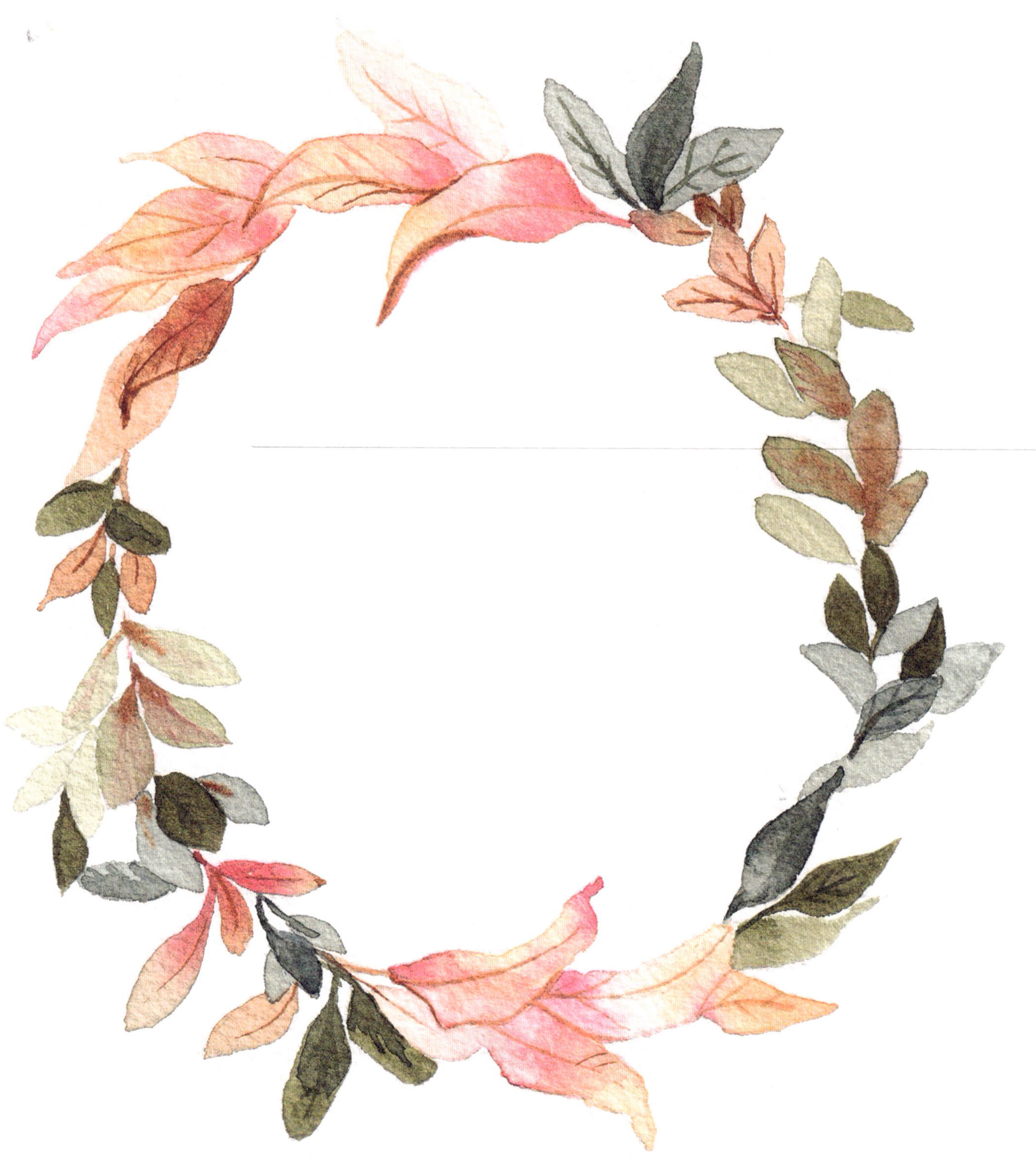

 yellow ochre

 alizarin crimson

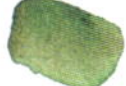 sap green

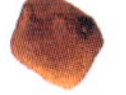 burnt umber

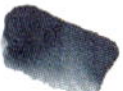 Payne's gray

leafy wreath

Painting a leafy wreath is my go-to project when I'm looking for a simple, relaxing painting session to ease into. This project is one that I hope you paint often and explore different variations, changing up the colors you use depending on what time of year you paint it. I suggest you use a variety of colors to mimic the seasons, paint it using nonrealistic colors, or add more details with a fine brush.

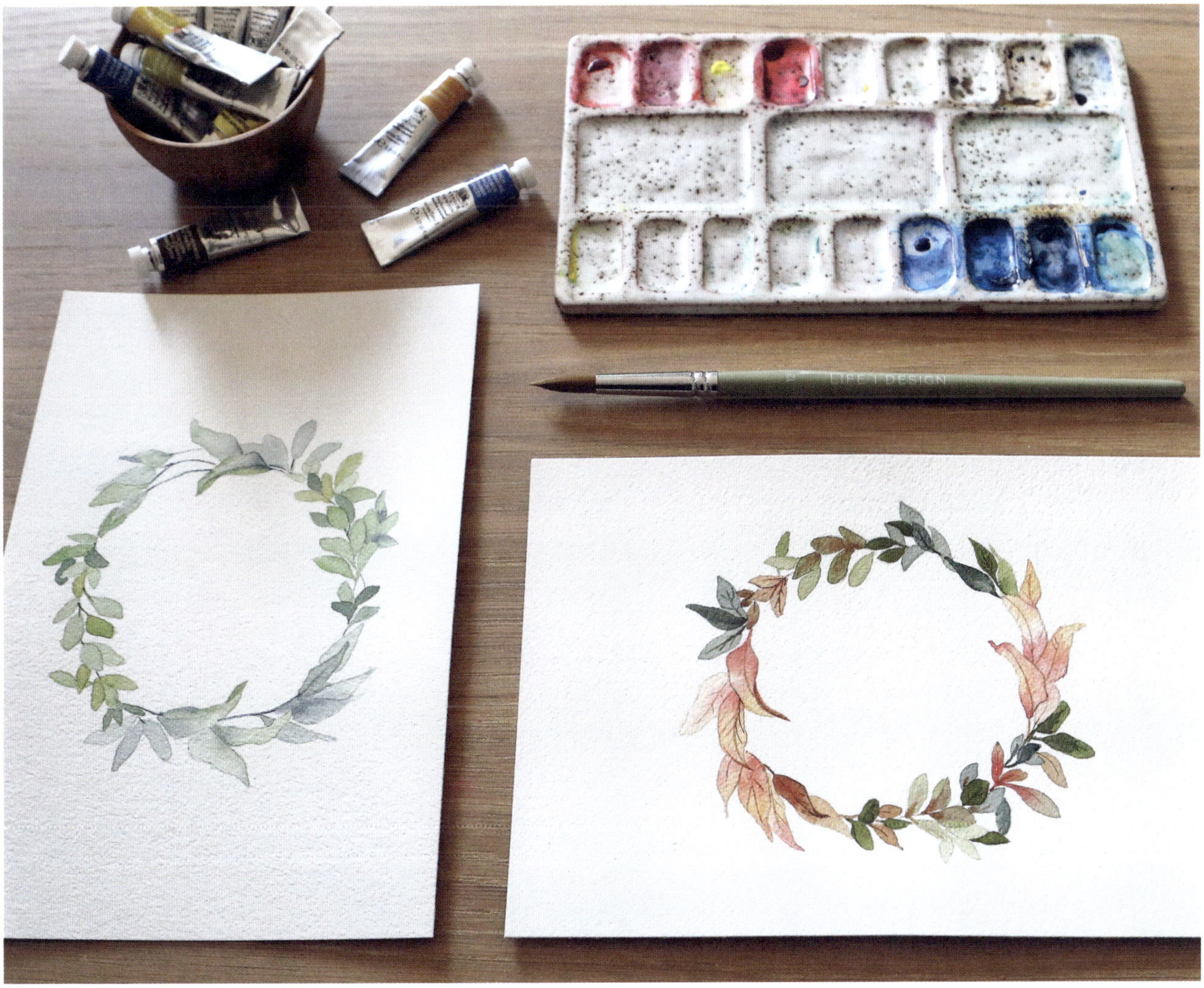

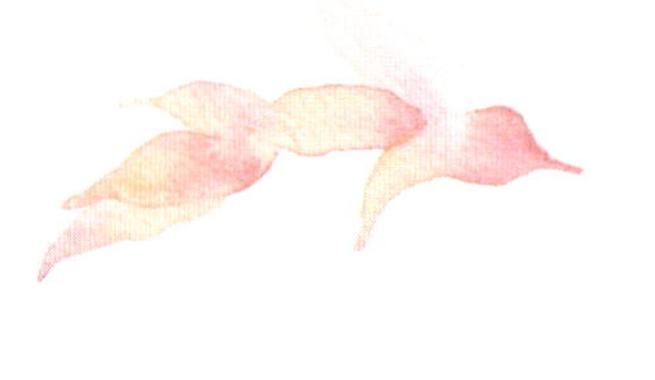

STEP 1

If desired, trace the template on page 127. Working wet-on-wet, paint larger leaves with a wash of yellow ochre. While the paint is still wet, add a bit of alizarin crimson with the tip of your brush and let the colors bleed together. Because the leaves touch and overlap in parts of this wreath, I suggest you work on painting leaves that do not touch, allowing them to dry fully before you paint the one next to it. Also vary the transparency of the leaves to create lovely variation.

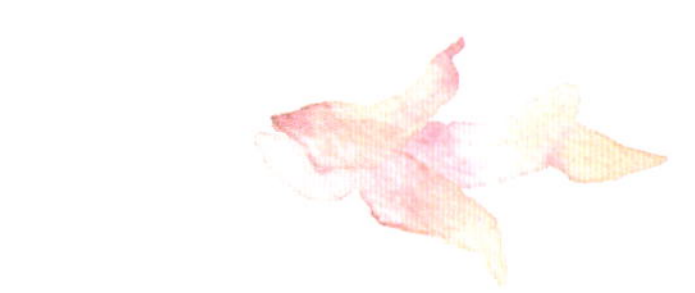

STEP 2

Mix equal parts sap green and burnt umber to achieve a deep forest green color. Start with a very watery, transparent mix and work wet-on-wet again to achieve some nice variations. Use the tip of a fine brush and a concentrated amount of burnt umber (dry-on-wet) to paint some dark values into the wet areas of a few of the leaves.

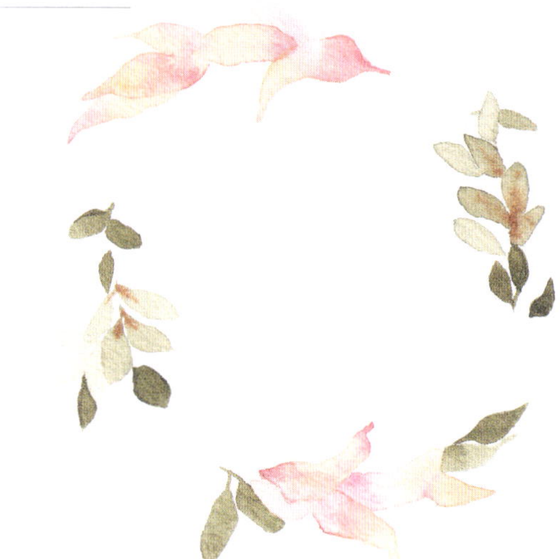

t i p ⸱⸱⸱⸱⸱⸱ Remember, you can always use your brush to absorb some of the water from the leaves if there is too much; this will lift away some paint, creating a bit of highlight on parts of the leaves.

STEP 3

Mix a bit of Payne's gray with sap green to achieve a blue-green for the next leaves. There is no "exact mix" other than swatching your color mix until you're happy with the new color that you've created. Use a higher water-to-paint ratio for a range of light, transparent leaves to contrast with the darker leaves. Use a light wash of burnt umber on the remaining leaves. Play around with mixing a bit of the alizarin crimson into the wet burnt umber, too.

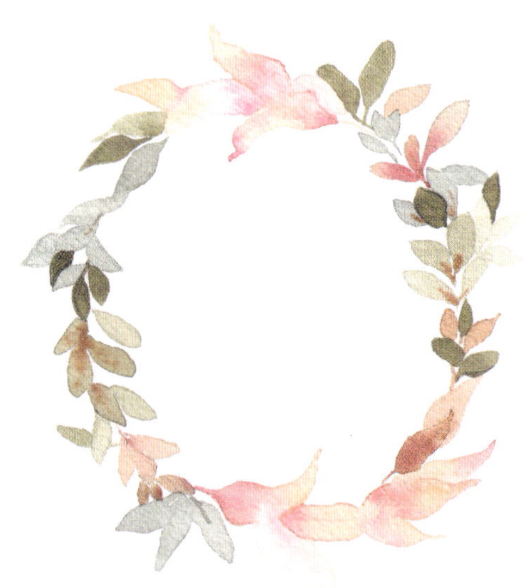

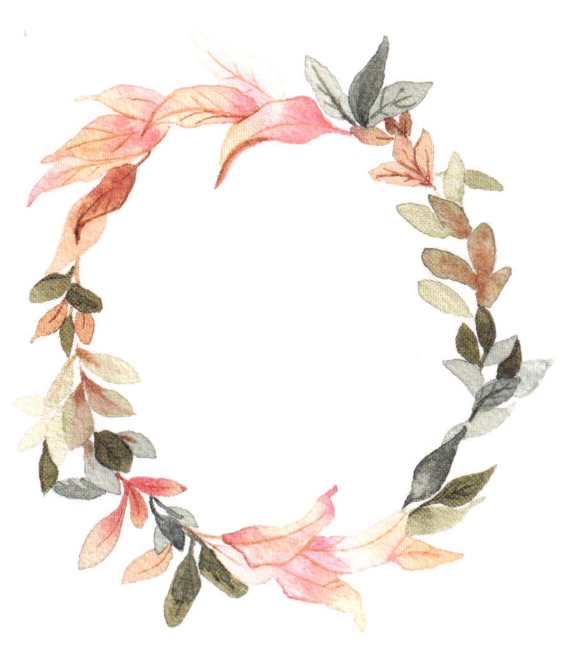

STEP 4

At this point you can choose to add as little or as much detail as you like. Here are some ideas. With a fine brush and the dry-on-dry technique, paint stems in the same color you used to paint the leaves, or use one color to paint all the stems. Exercise your artistic style and decide what you'd prefer to use. You can also choose to use a wet brushstroke to add an extra layer to some of the leaves, creating deeper values and more variety. Play around with darker values to add some depth and dimension. Outline lighter leaves if the edges are a little lost where they overlap.

t i p ⋯⋯ Keep your wreath paintings handy—I have a fun paper project coming up in chapter 7.

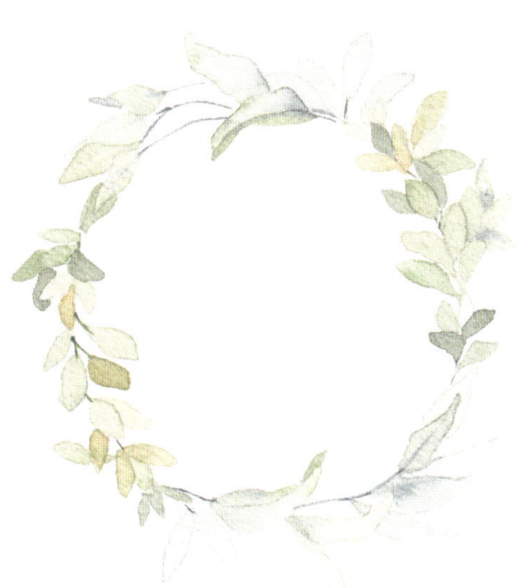

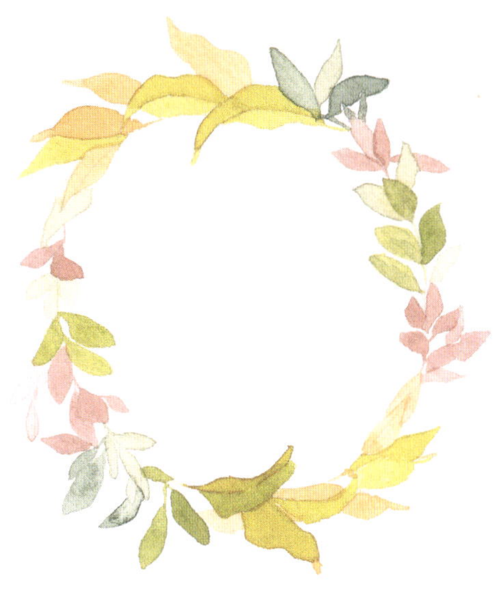

Prussian blue

sap green

green gold

Here are two variations on the Leafy Wreath painting. Have fun creating your own color palettes, as you experiment and become more comfortable with mixing unique colors.

alizarin crimson

yellow ochre

Payne's gray

green gold

sap green

 Winsor yellow

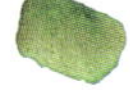 sap green

 alizarin crimson

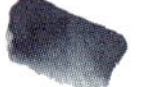 Payne's gray

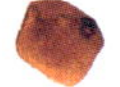 burnt umber

white gouache

apple on a stem

My love for vintage illustrations inspired this painting. This is how I chose to paint and interpret this lovely apple. Painting in layers will help define the veining in the leaves as well as create interesting lines and marks on the surface of the apple.

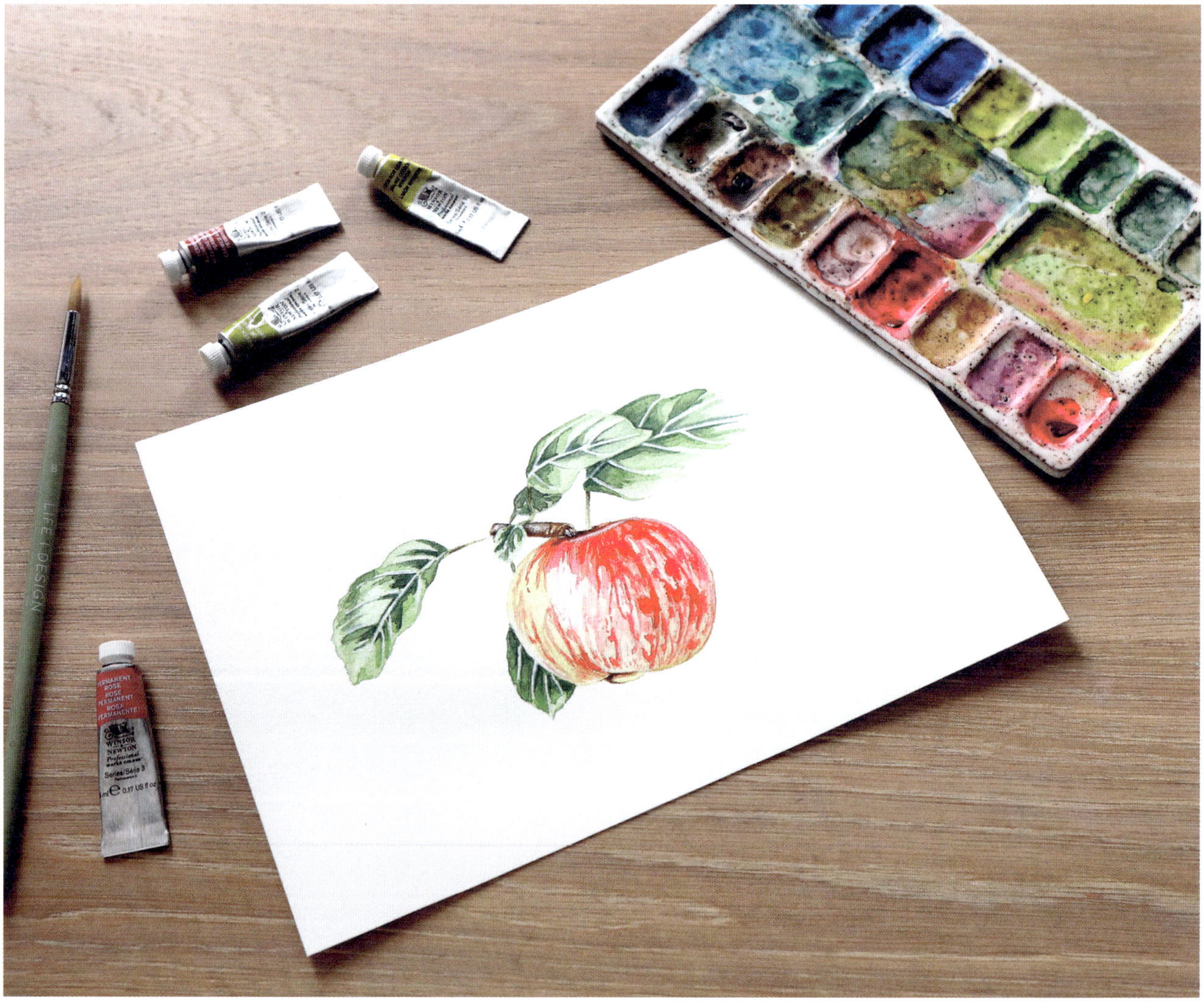

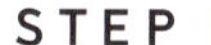

STEP 1

If desired, trace the template on page 129. Paint the entire apple using a transparent mix of yellow with a touch of sap green. Pull a highlight using a dry brush on the left side of the apple, making sure to keep it nice and bright. Use the same paint mix to paint the first layer of the stem.

STEP 2

Mix a transparent wash of sap green and paint the first layer of all the leaves. Keep in mind that the underside of the leaves as well as the parts where they overlap will be darker.

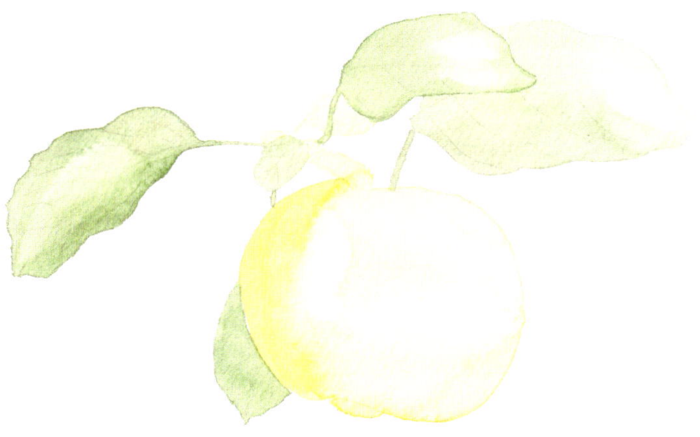

STEP 3

Add a dab of alizarin crimson to the first color mix of yellow and sap green to achieve a warm reddish-brown, ensuring your mix is really watered down. Paint in the outer right side of the apple, the bottom of the apple, and where the stem meets the apple at the top. You can also add a touch on the stems of the leaves, too. You are slowly building value.

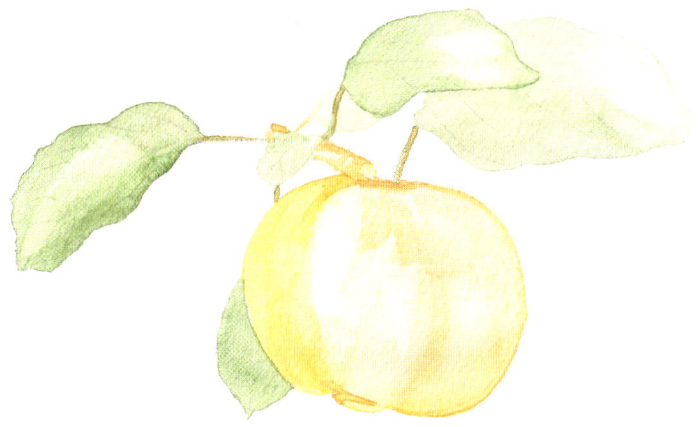

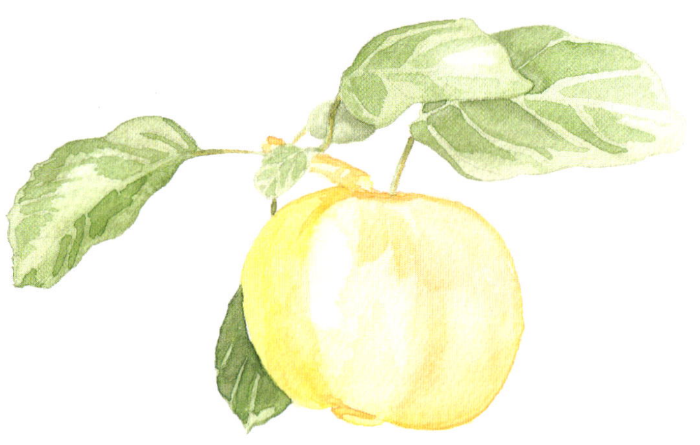

STEP 4

Mix a transparent wash of Payne's gray with sap green and paint in the second layer on the leaves, keeping in mind that the veins of the leaves will be lighter in this painting, so leave white space for the veins. I painted in between the pencil lines in the leaves to achieve this color-block effect on the leaves.

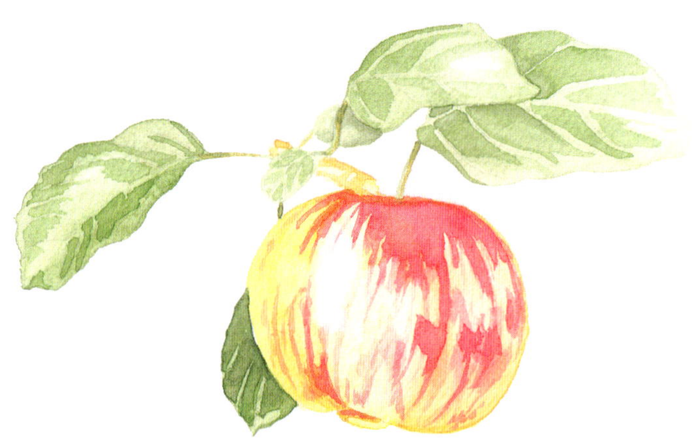

STEP 5

Mix a transparent wash of alizarin crimson and paint in the red of the apple using individual brushstrokes rather than painting it in solidly. Keep in mind the shape of the apple is rounded, so your strokes should mimic this shape. Think about the curved brushstrokes we practiced in chapter 2. Vary your lines by painting some thick and others thin as we build this first layer of alizarin crimson on the apple.

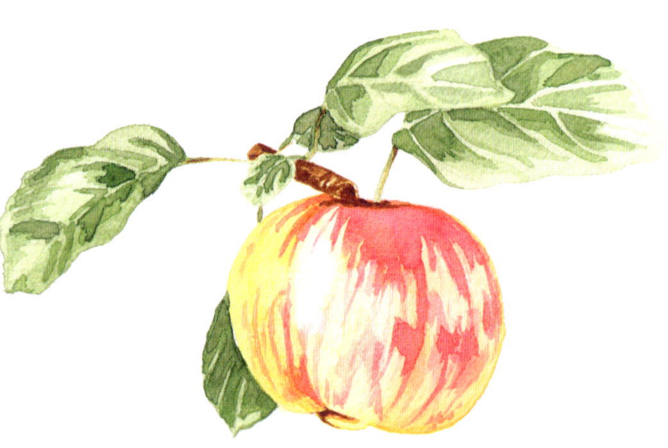

STEP 6

Mix a semi-opaque mix of burnt umber (half water–half paint ratio) and paint in the outer edges of the branch as well as the shadow of the apple where the stem meets the apple. Using a detail brush, paint the shadow on the underside of the apple as well as the shadows where the stems meet the leaves. Paint another layer of the sap green and Payne's gray mix to add another layer of value on all the leaves as you did in step 4.

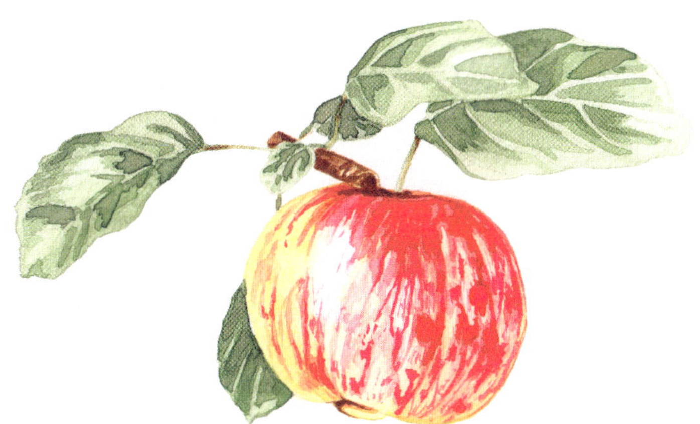

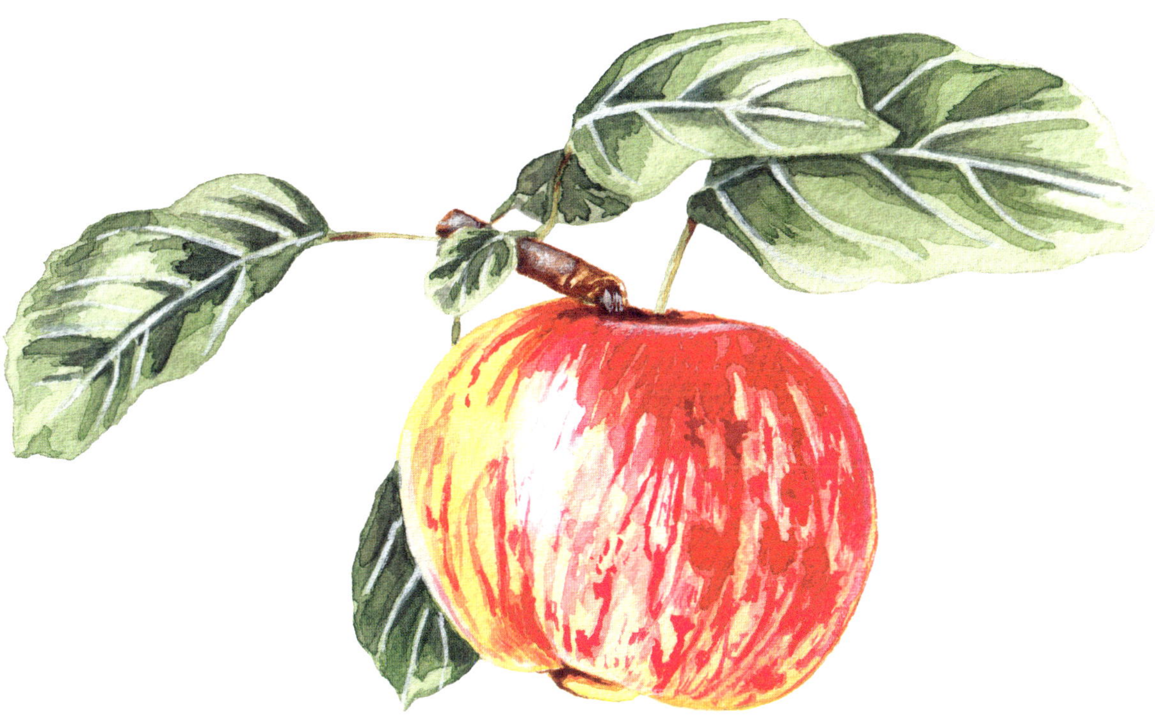

STEP 8

Time to add some finishing touches. Use white gouache and a detail brush to paint in thin veins in the leaves. Paint
a thin highlight in the center of the stem coming out from the apple as well as the outer edges of the apple for
added brightness. Using the detail brush with the Payne's gray and sap green mix, deepen the edges of the veins
on the leaves for a final layer of value, really making the leaves come to life.

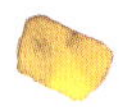
green gold

Payne's gray

Winsor yellow

vintage-inspired fish

This fish requires a lot of wet-on-wet technique to allow the contrasting colors to bleed and mix into one another. Here is where the unique characteristics of watercolor paint really shine. Have fun with this fish painting and play around with different color combinations to interpret various versions of this fish. I worked in my sketchbook first before deciding on how I wanted to express this vintage fish, which allows room to practice as well as trial and error.

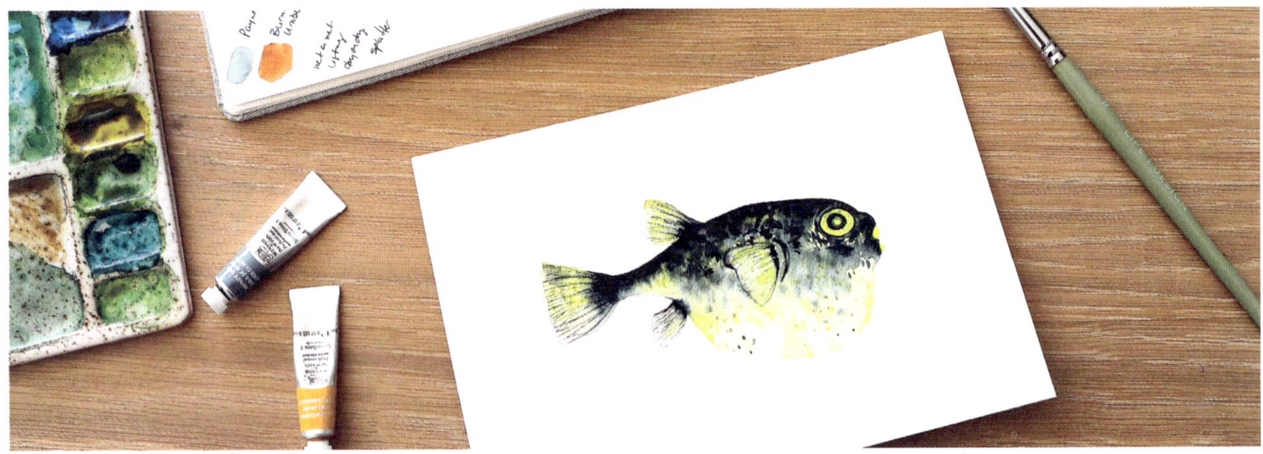

STEP 1

If desired, trace the template on page 129. Mix green gold with water for a transparent mix. Wet the entire fish, using your brush and clean water and avoiding the eye area. Starting from the top of the fish, using the wet-on-wet technique, start to dab the green gold, allowing the paint to move and bleed into the wet surface of the fish. Allow the white of the paper to show through in spots. Let dry.

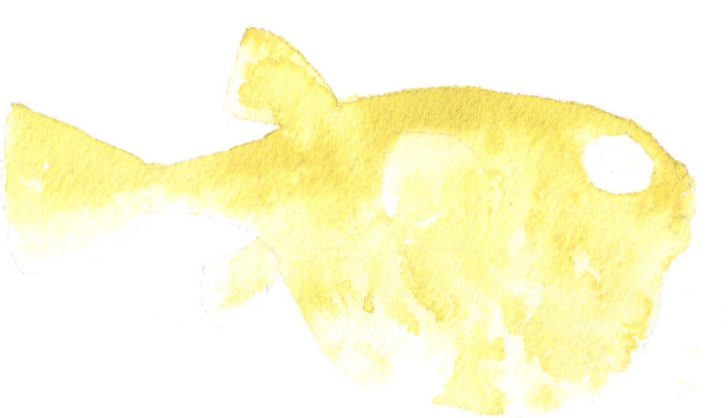

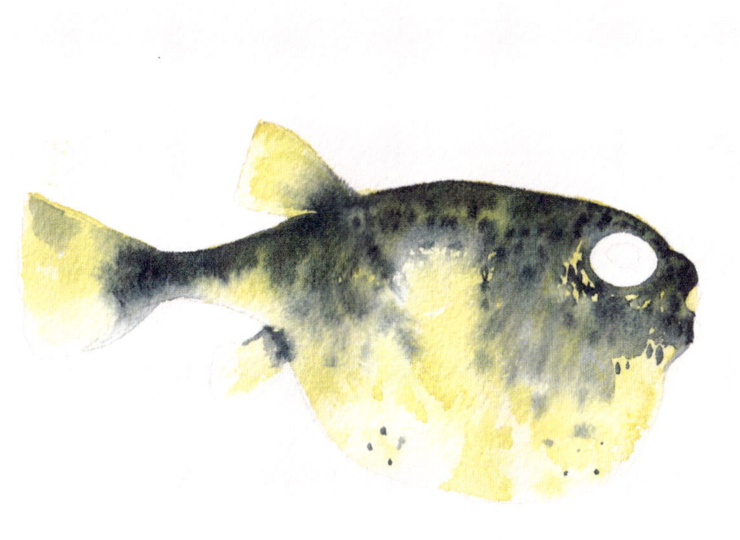

Mix Payne's gray with water, creating a loose but opaque mix. Using a wet brush, wet the entire area of the fish once again, being careful not to disturb the first layer of paint. Starting from the top of the fish, dab Payne's gray and let the paint flow toward the bottom of the fish, keeping the fins and belly area lighter. Work wet-on-wet, dabbing the brush and watching the texture and blooms happen. The more you let the paint flow here, the more interesting the piece will appear when dry. Allow to dry fully.

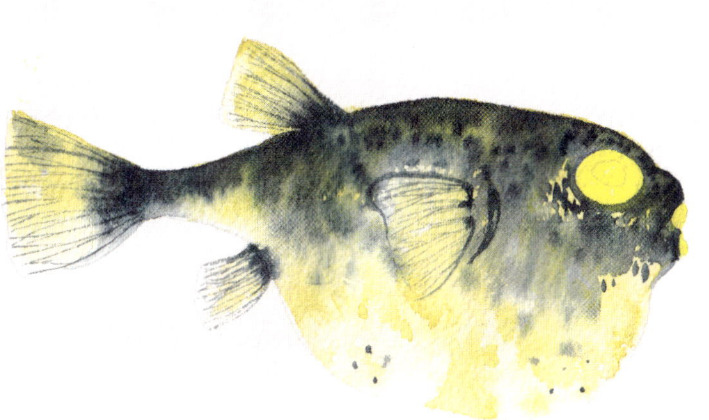

STEP 3

Use an opaque mix of yellow to paint in the entire eye area as well as the lips of the fish. With a detail brush, go back to your opaque mix of Payne's gray and start to paint in the lines on the fins. Use Payne's gray to paint a darker value in areas like the base of the fins and the very top of the fish. Doing this will create varieties of value and depth.

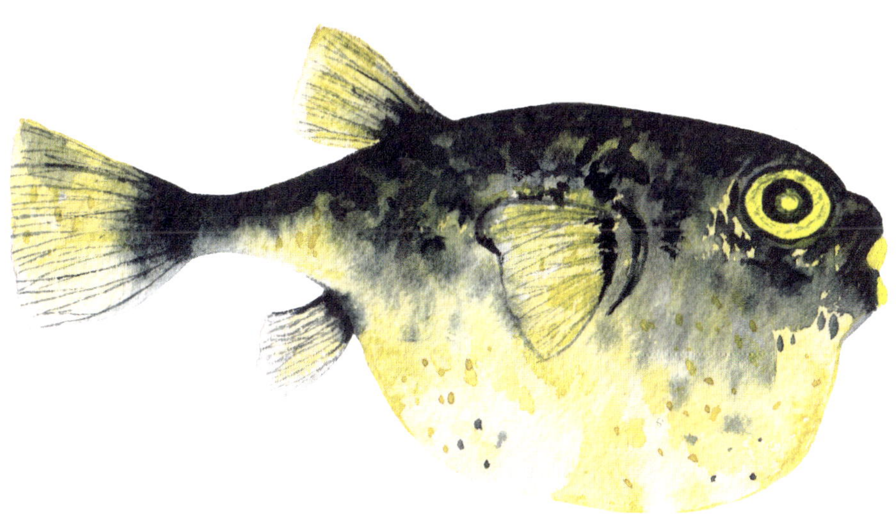

STEP 4

Paint the center of the eye of the fish using Payne's gray and a detail brush. Start around the outer edge, going inward and making sure to maintain a light spot toward the center of the eye. Use concentrated amounts of Payne's gray as well as green gold to add smaller spots and dots to the body of the fish for added interest and character.

PAINT COLORS

a feather

Once you try your hand at painting feathers, I'm sure you'll be amazed at how easily they come together and how beautiful they look finished. Painting in several layers creates depth and fine lines that emulate the soft hairs of the feather. Feel free to go beyond the four steps I illustrate here to add as much detail as you choose, layering and letting it dry, then layering some more.

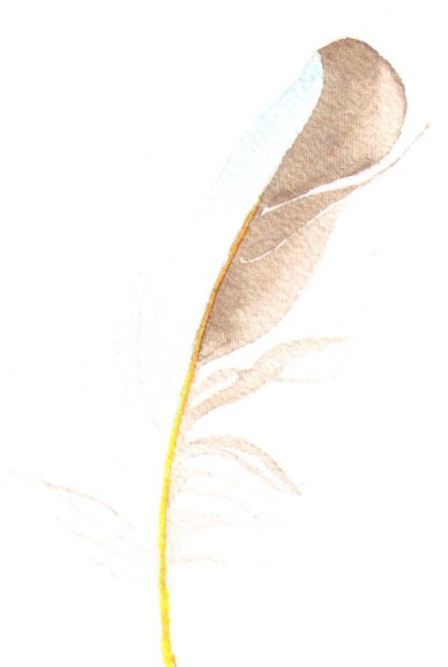

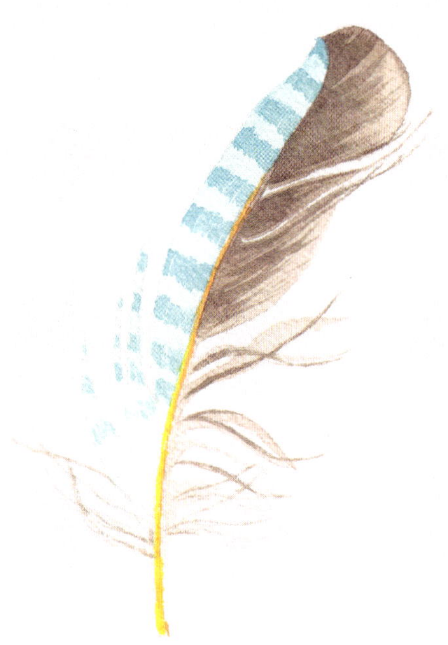

STEP 1

If desired, trace the template on page 131. Mix a transparent wash of turquoise and paint the left side of the feather. Mix a transparent wash of burnt umber with a touch of Payne's gray and paint a light layer on the right side of the feather. While still wet, lift a highlight at the edge of the feather. Use a wash of yellow and yellow ochre to paint the bone of the feather with a detail brush.

STEP 2

Using a detail brush and an opaque mix of Winsor blue, paint the stripes of the feather with short, fine strokes. Using the burnt umber and Payne's gray mix, paint a darker layer on the right side of the leaf, starting from the bone outward; use longer strokes and leave space to show the fine hairs of the feather. Build up the fine, wispy hairs, using steady strokes.

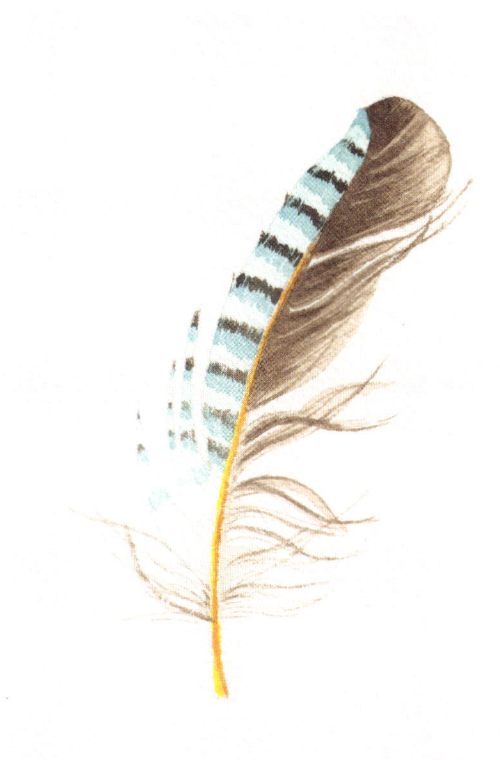
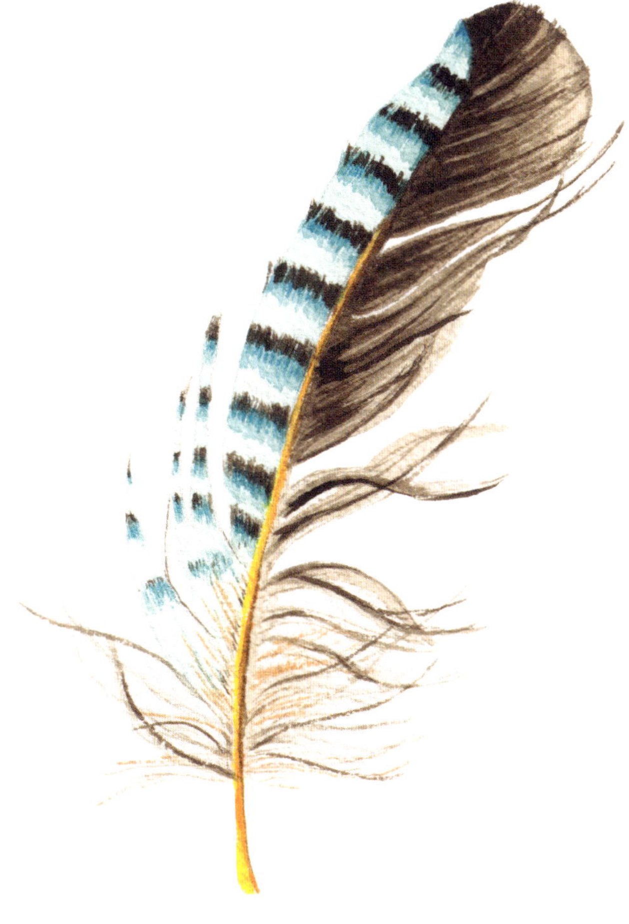

STEP 3

Using the burnt umber and Payne's gray mix and a detail brush, paint darker stripes above the blue stripes, making sure to leave space randomly between strokes to show the fine detail between the strands of feathers. Paint another layer of the same mix on the right side of the feather to create even more depth, making sure to use long, thin strokes that follow the shape of the feather.

STEP 4

Using a fine detail brush that is dry, paint in final details. Make darker areas even darker using the burnt umber and Payne's gray mix. Add more yellow ochre to the right side of the bone for depth. Paint another layer of blue underneath the darker stripes. The more detail and layering you paint in, the more this feather will come to life.

t i p ······ Try finding a variety of feathers to use for inspiration.

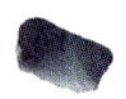 Payne's gray

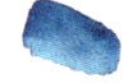 Prussian blue

fun with a teacup

I used a monochromatic color scheme and shadows to paint this teacup, but you can really have fun using colors and painting this a few different ways, based on your color and style preferences. My hope is that you enjoy the simplicity of this project and paint it again and again as you find new ways to express it.

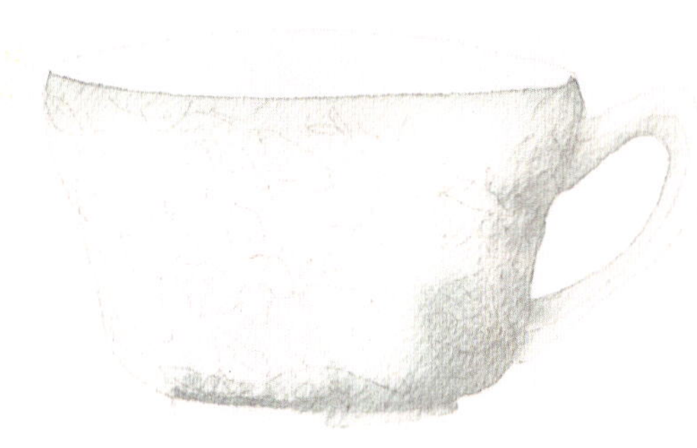

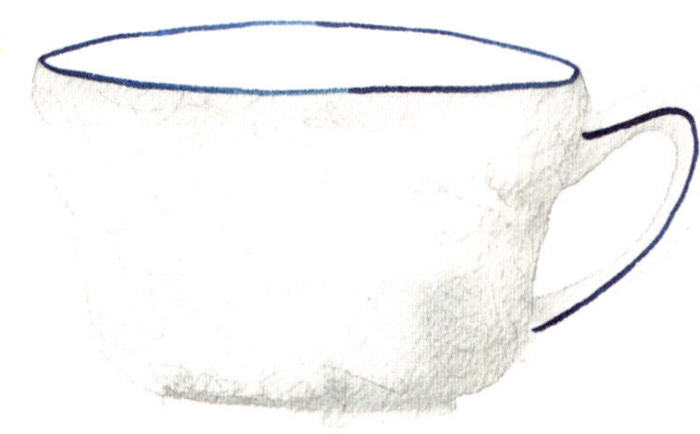

STEP 1

If desired, trace the template on page 131. Using clean water and a large brush, paint the outside of the teacup. Mix an opaque puddle of Payne's gray and, using a small brush, paint the top edge of the cup, allowing the paint to spread as it wants. Paint the outer edge closest to the handle and bottom edge of the cup working wet-on-wet. Paint the underside of the handle as well. You are slowly building shadow while keeping the rest of the cup light and using the white of the paper to articulate a white cup.

STEP 2

Mix an opaque puddle of Prussian blue. Using a small or detail brush, paint in the rim of the cup and decorative line on the handle.

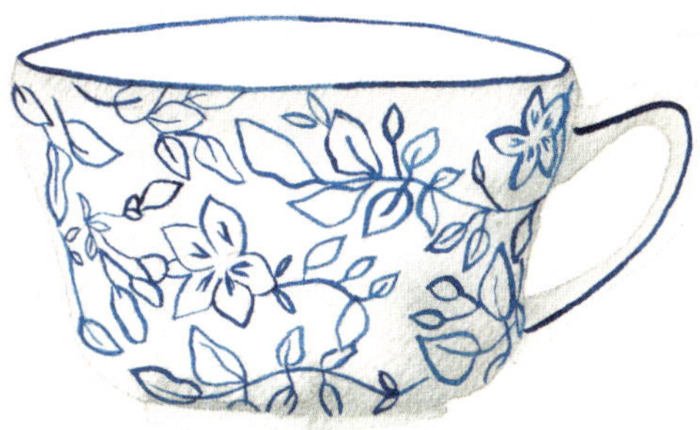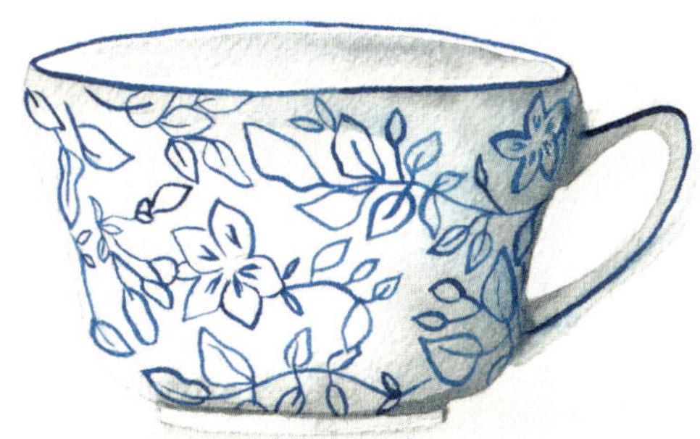

STEP 3

Using the same mix of Prussian blue, paint in the fine decorative details using a detail brush. Feel free to add more florals and leaves if you like. I personally like the rustic, handmade feel, so I embraced lines that are wobbly and interesting. Let fully dry.

STEP 4

Use a transparent wash of Payne's gray to add shadow to the inside of the cup. Add another layer of shadow toward the right side of the cup near the handle, creating depth. With a very wet brush, dab into your Payne's gray wash and add a shadow below the cup. The detail you painted in the cup may run slightly as you paint in the shadow, but it will create a unique effect to your teacup.

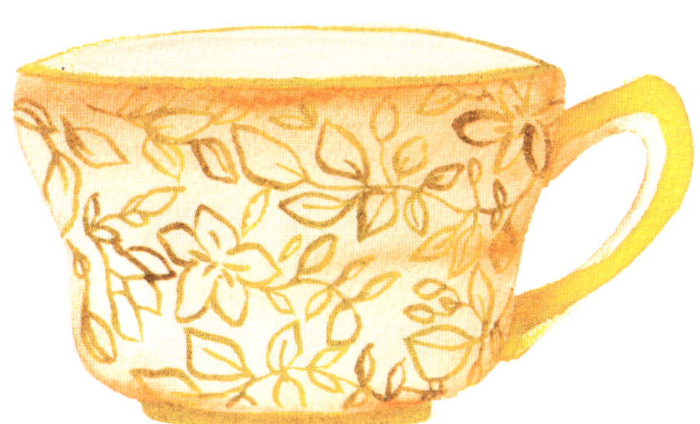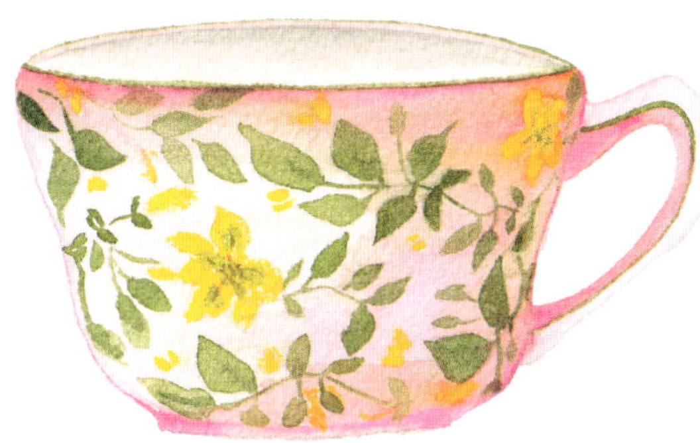

Paint this cup a few different ways using a variety of colors.

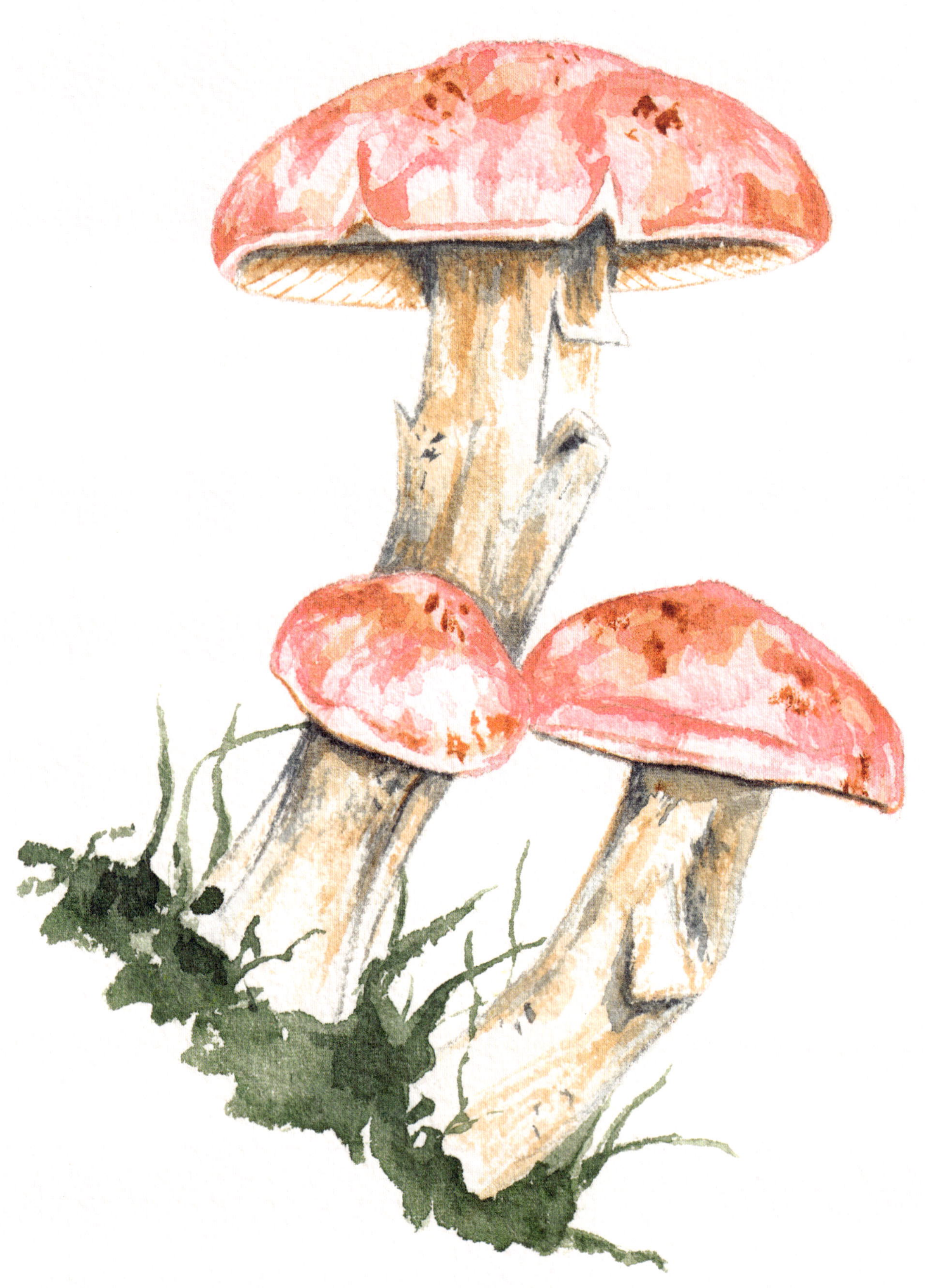

 permanent rose

 raw umber

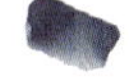 Payne's gray

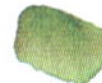 sap green

woodland mushrooms

I didn't realize how fun painting mushrooms could be until I started exploring all the different types of mushrooms. Their interesting shapes and color combinations allow room for artistic expression and a bit of whimsy. As you paint these colorful fungi, work in light layers to begin with, but then add dark marks and dry brushing to really bring these mushrooms to life.

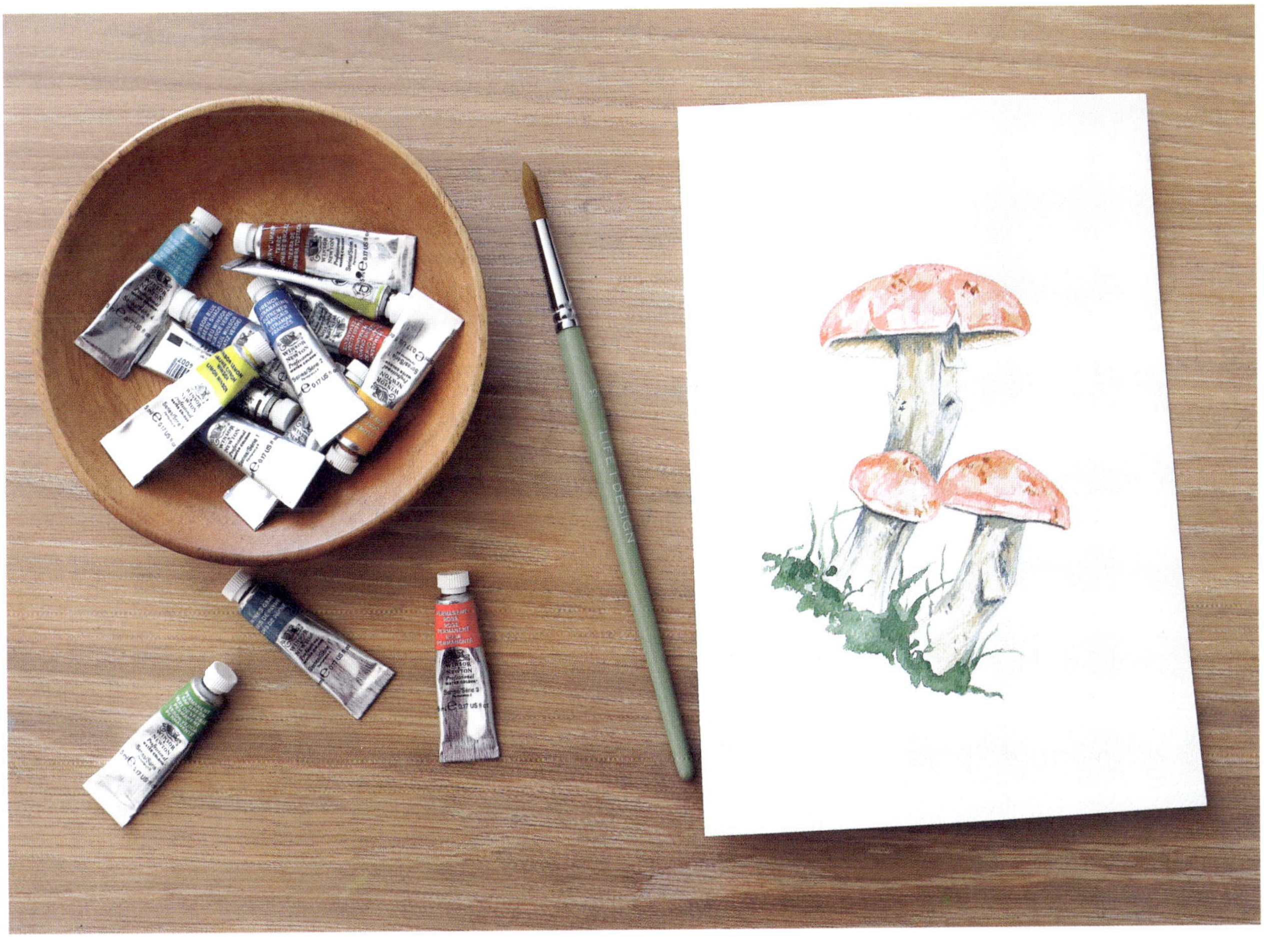

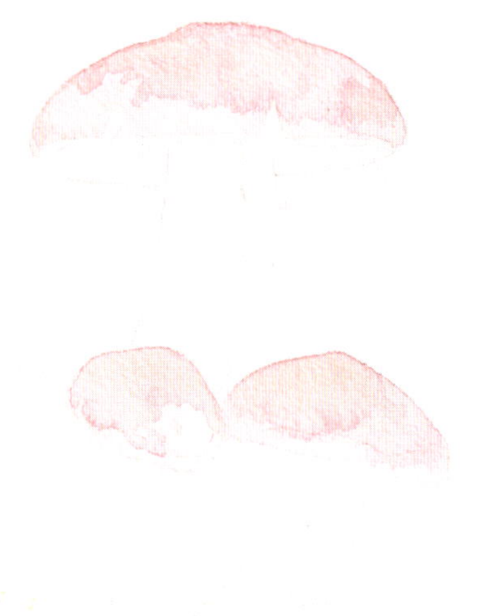

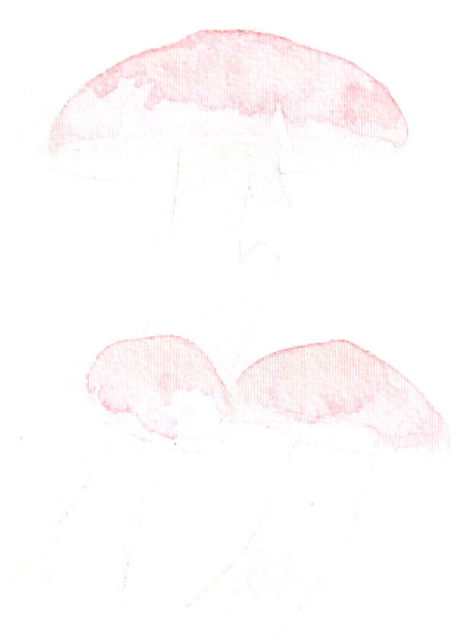

STEP 1

If desired, trace the template on page 133. Mix permanent rose with a slight bit of raw umber to create a dull pink mix. Remember to use your scrap sheet to test your paint mix and adjust it until you're happy with the color. Add lots of water to create a transparent wash and paint the first layer of the mushroom caps. Paint wet-on-wet and allow interesting variations to happen.

STEP 2

Mix a very transparent wash of Payne's gray to paint the stems. Keep areas very light where the stem is peeling back slightly. Work wet-on-wet to darken areas that are shadowed by the caps and where the mushroom caps meet.

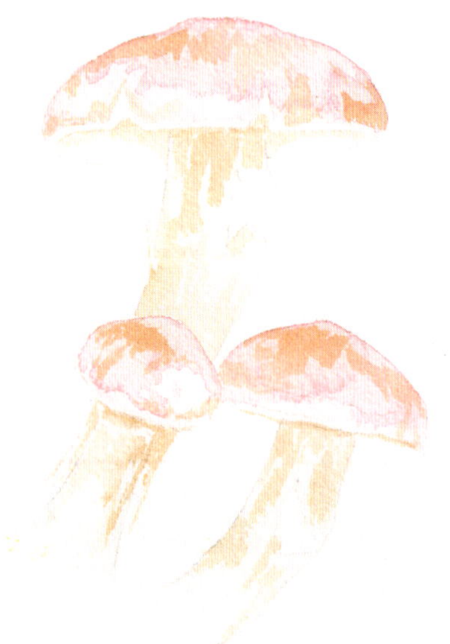

STEP 3

Using a transparent wash of raw umber, paint in shadows and marks on the mushroom caps. Use the same mix to paint the shadows below the caps and on the stems. Feel free to add texture to the stems using a dry brush and raw umber.

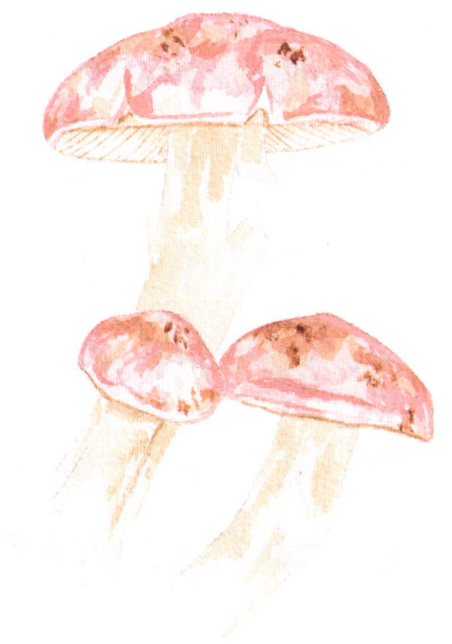 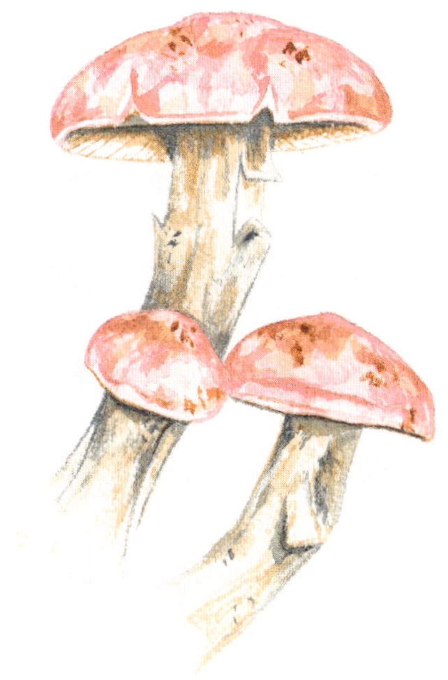

STEP 4

Go back to your permanent rose and raw umber mix and add another layer of darker value to the painting. Using a dry brush, start to add more texture to the mushroom caps and shadows along the bottom edge. Use the tip of the brush to create marks and dark spots on the caps, too. With raw umber, paint fine lines underneath the large mushroom cap.

STEP 5

Using a slightly more opaque mix of Payne's gray and raw umber, add more marks and texture on the stalks. Continue to build more texture with layers of washes. Dry brushing downward will also create some interesting effects on the stalks of the mushrooms.

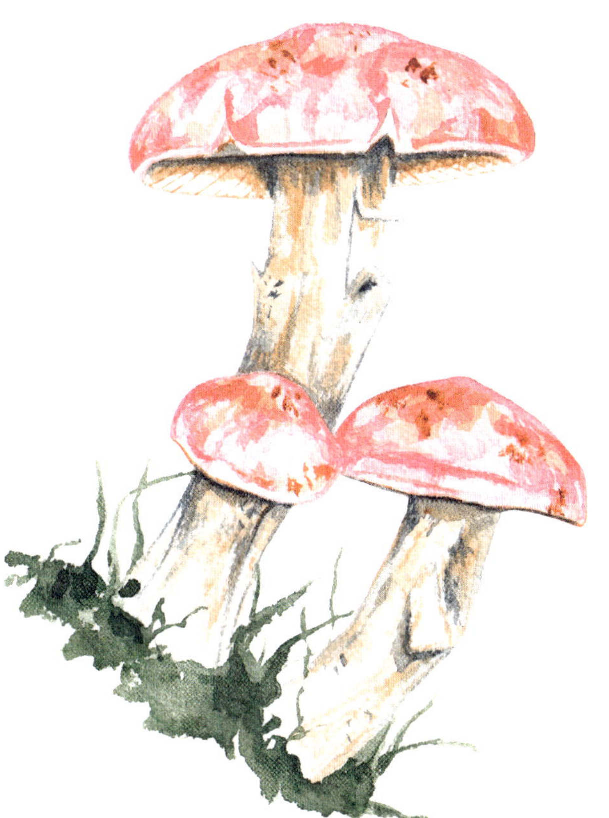

STEP 6 (OPTIONAL)

Mix sap green with a slight amount of Payne's gray. Using a wet brush, paint in the base of the mushrooms, mimicking the green moss and ground where these mushrooms would normally grow from. Using the tip of your brush, pull up wispy areas around the mushroom. Allow the watercolor paint to settle and move where it may for an easy way to create texture and interest in the greenery.

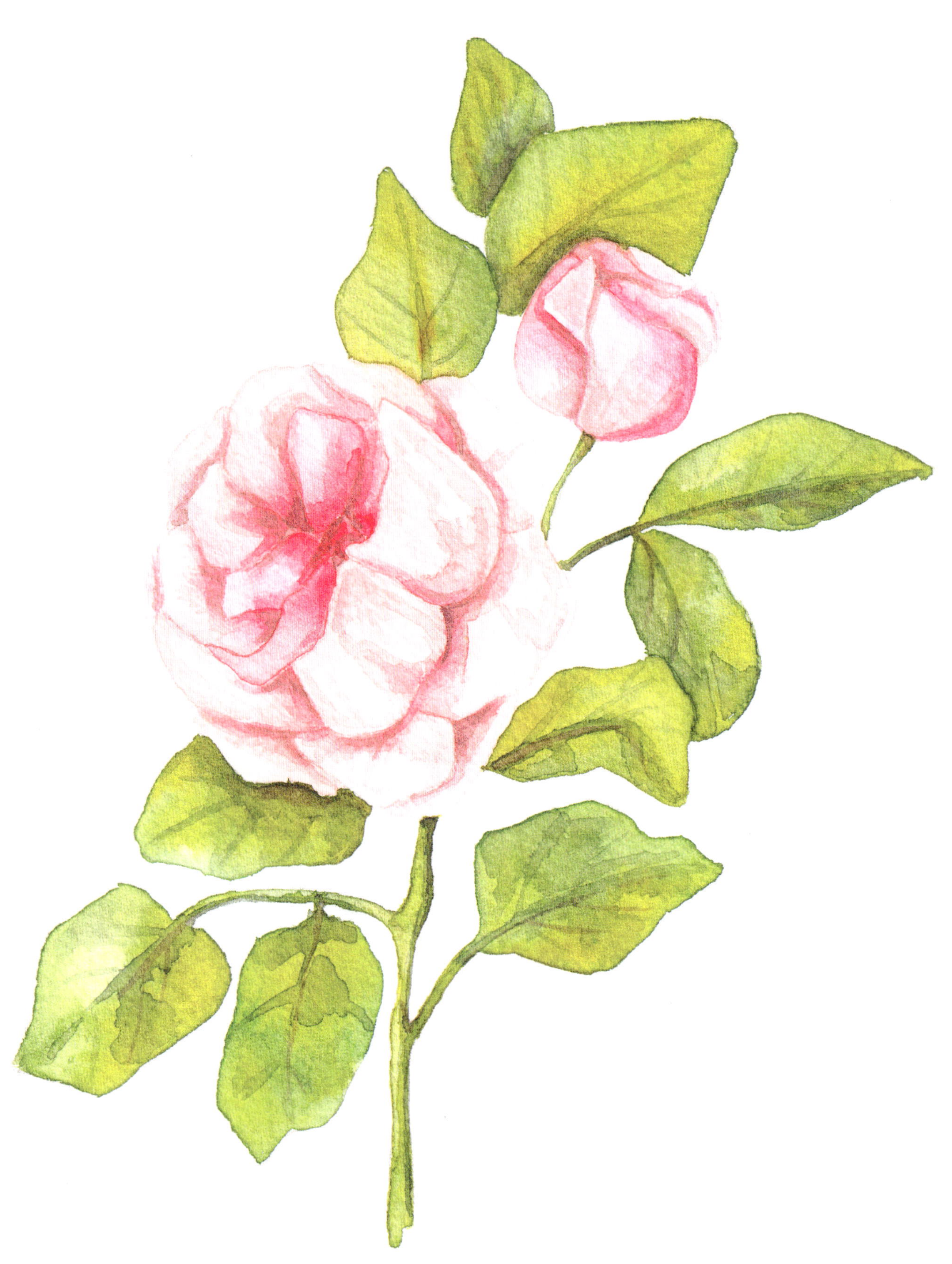

 alizarin crimson

 Winsor yellow

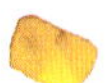 green gold

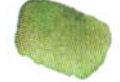 sap green

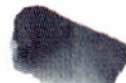 Payne's gray

floral bouquet

This simple bouquet requires you to paint each petal and leaf shape using wet-on-wet to build interest and texture without adding a lot of detail to achieve an illustrative-style painting. Take your time, use a small brush, and enjoy watching the floral piece come to life as you paint it. Patience and precision are what I recommend, along with a fine brush for painting each petal.

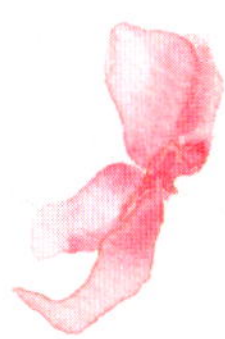

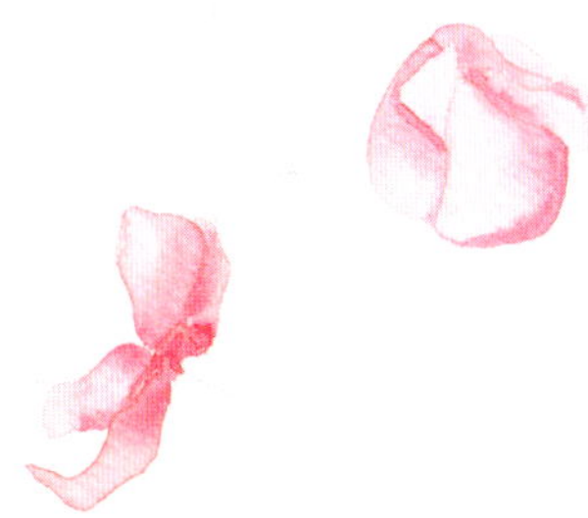

STEP 1

If desired, trace the template on page 133. Start by mixing a transparent mix of alizarin crimson and a touch of yellow to achieve a peachy pink tone. Paint the center of the larger flower first. Drop in a touch of alizarin crimson to darken the center of the petals. Using the lifting technique, while the petals are still slightly wet, lift away some of the paint at the tops of a few petals to create a highlight.

STEP 2

Paint the slightly open bud, using the same paint mix, working wet-on-wet, and letting the paint settle and create texture. Use the tip of your brush to add a slight amount of alizarin crimson to the edges of the petals while they're still wet.

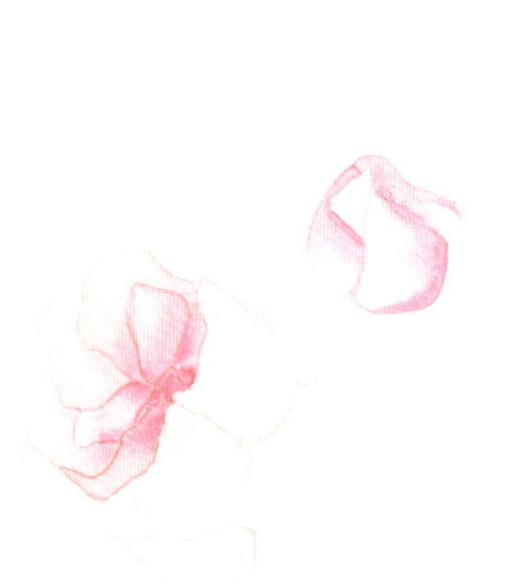

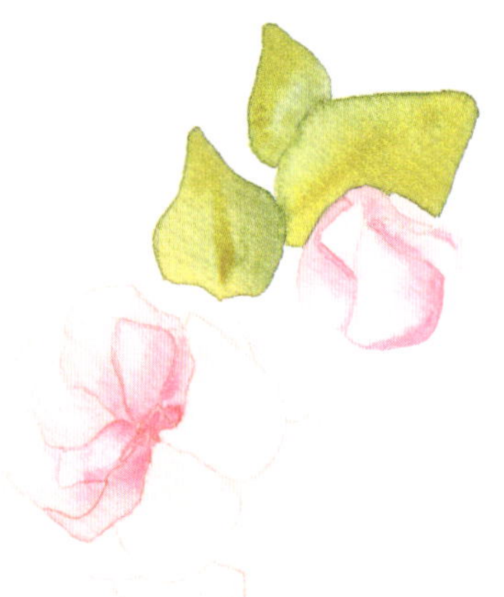

STEP 3

Paint the outer petals on the larger flower using the same mix of alizarin crimson and touch of yellow. Be sure to paint a variety of values from petal to petal. Lighten the petals gradually as you work from the center outward.

STEP 4

Mix a transparent puddle of green gold and a transparent puddle of sap green. Paint each leaf next to the bud starting with sap green. Next, while still wet, dab into the petal some green gold and let the colors mix and bleed into one another. Using a detail brush and green gold, dab into the wet leaf a vein if you choose.

STEP 5

Paint the stems and the rest of the leaves using the same washes of sap green and green gold. Remember to lift away paint if you want to create highlights on the leaves and dab in more paint wet-on-wet to create a darker value for shading. Let the watercolor paint flow and bleed to help create interesting texture in the leaves.

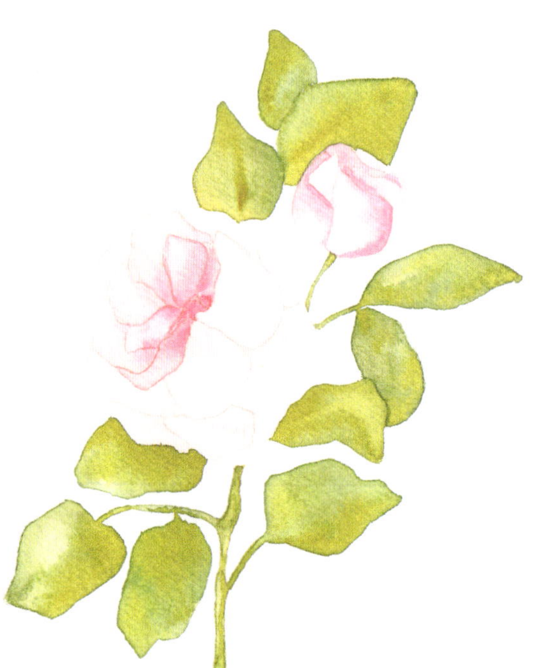

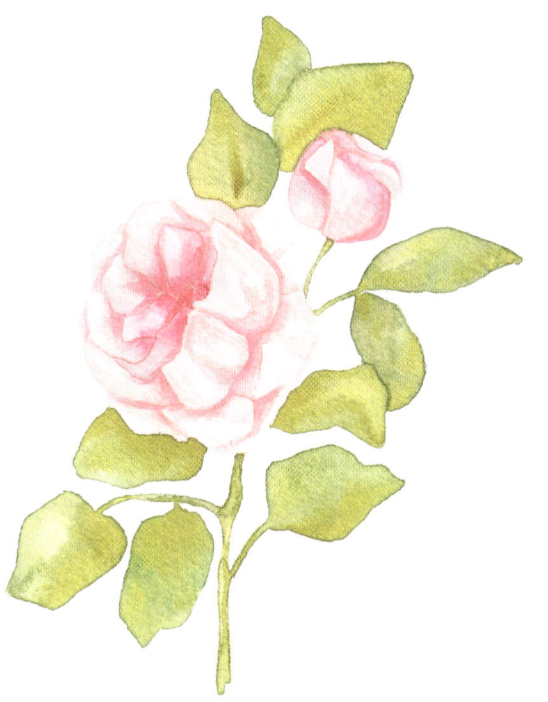

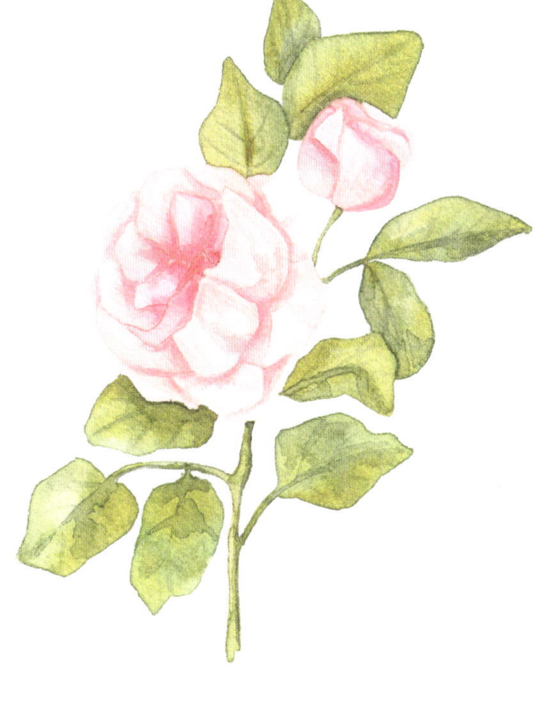

STEP 6

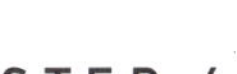

Using a small detail brush and the transparent paint mix of alizarin crimson with a touch of yellow, paint in a darker value where the petals meet. Use your pencil lines as guides and work wet-on-dry to slowly build your shadow layers. Also paint the parts of the petals where there is shadow cast from the petal above. A light touch and detail brush will be best to start to add details here.

STEP 7

Add detail to the leaves and stem. Mix a slight bit of Payne's gray into sap green to create a dark green and paint in shadows and veins in the leaves. Using a detail brush and wet-on-dry, paint in shadows and darker value of greens to create interest in the leaves.

STEP 8 (OPTIONAL)

Add a touch of Payne's gray to your floral color mix to darken it slightly. With a detail brush, paint in ever so slightly the darkest areas of the petals to really make your flower pop. The contrast of this darker tone will make the lightest value even brighter. Feel free to also use it in small areas of the leaves where you want to paint in a slightly darker value and shadow.

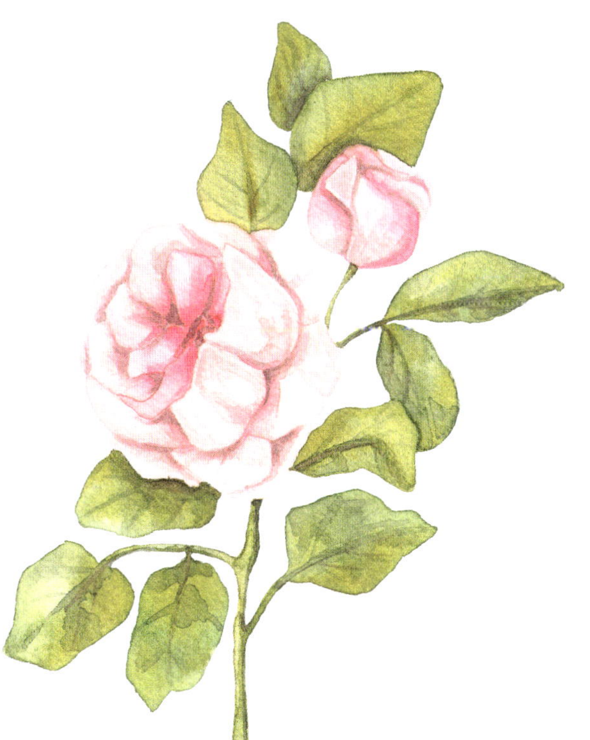

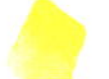 permanent rose

 Winsor yellow

 yellow ochre

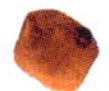 Payne's gray

burnt umber

a colorful moth

As I was researching moths for this book, I found a beautiful variety of colored moths and landed on this gorgeous pink and yellow one to paint. Using yellow, yellow ochre, and pink colors made me realize that I rarely use this color combination, and I had a lot of fun exploring this palette. The approach for painting this moth is to build layers, leaving some areas open and light, while painting dimension and depth with each additional layer.

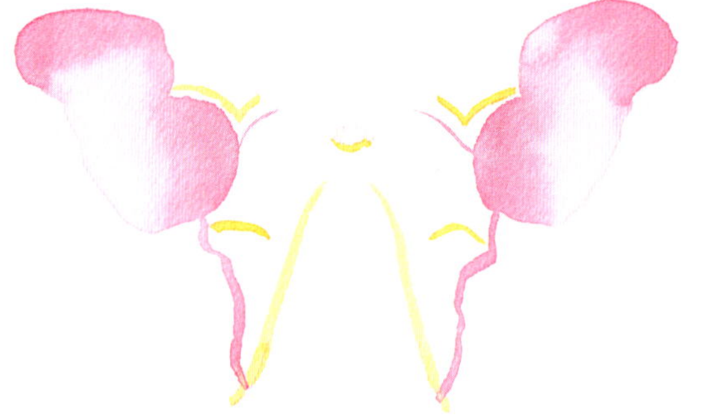

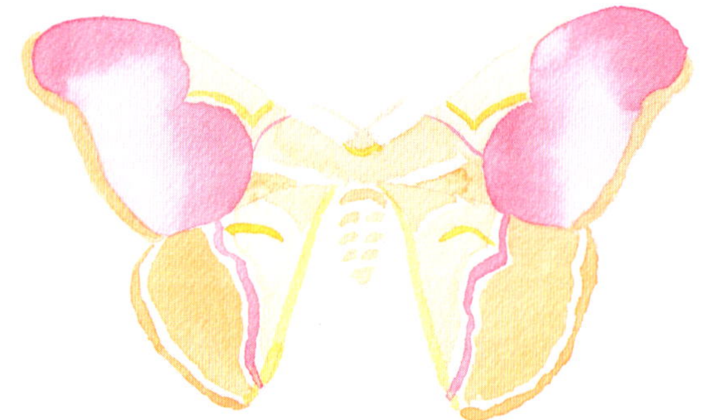

STEP 1

If desired, trace the template on page 135. Mix a transparent wash of permanent rose and paint the top wings of the moth. Using an opaque mix of yellow, paint in areas of the wing where you want to keep the wings bright, such as the outer edges and stripes.

STEP 2

Using a transparent wash of yellow ochre, paint in the rest of the wings and body of the moth, including the antennae. Use a more concentrated mix of yellow ochre in parts of the wings to paint variations in the moth.

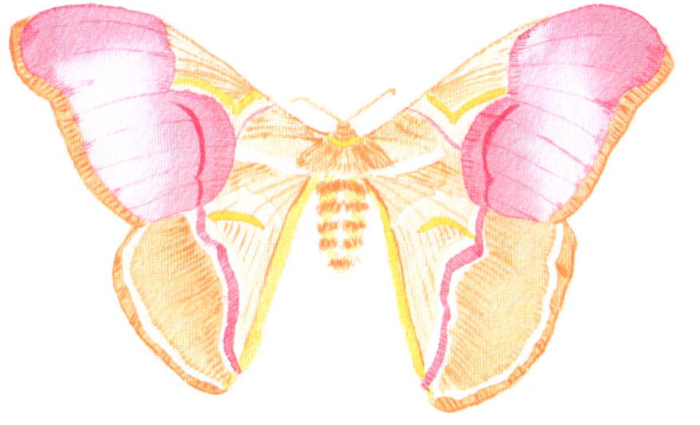 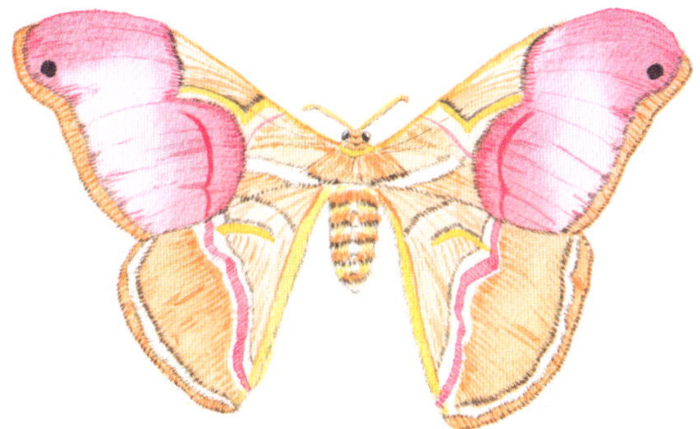

STEP 3

With a small detail brush and a very concentrated mix of yellow ochre, use short strokes, dry-on-dry, to paint in the fuzzy parts of the moth and veins. Focus on the edges of the wings as you paint short, fine strokes. Do the same with permanent rose to add depth and an extra value of color to the pink parts of the wings and veins. Take your time and paint short strokes, using the very tip of your brush with light pressure.

STEP 4

Here is where the moth really comes to life. Mix Payne's gray and burnt umber and use a detail brush to paint darker details in the moth's body and wings. Add layering in areas where veins come together in the wings. Paint in the eyes, leaving a touch of white, and paint the body using short strokes and light pressure.

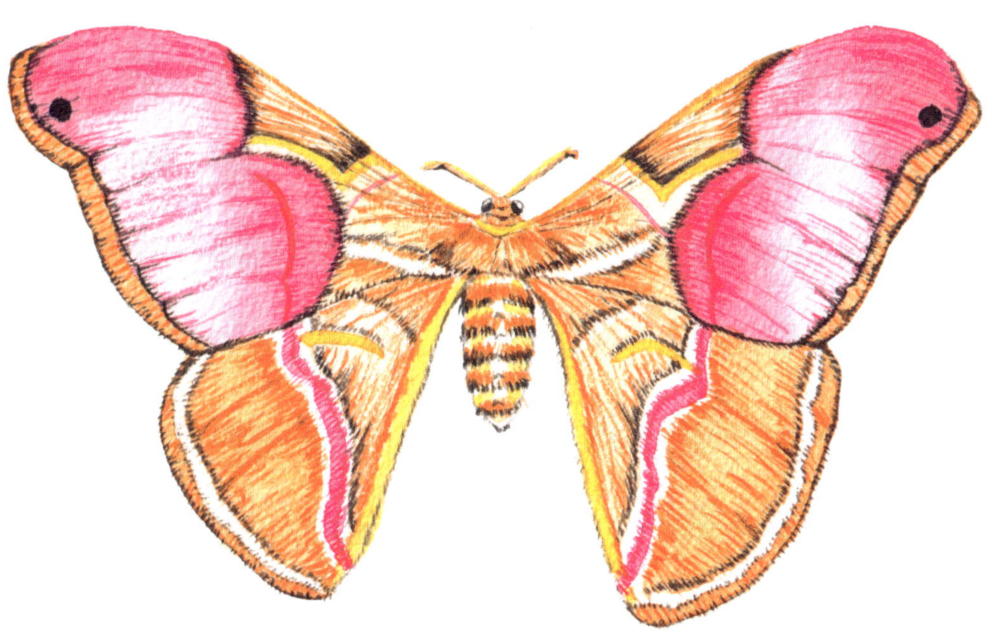

STEP 5 (OPTIONAL)

If you'd like to create more depth and texture in the moth, use a detail brush and dry brush even more layers of texture. Use the same color on top of the last layer to paint in even more strokes ranging from long to short and add more texture and interest. You can't go wrong with adding too many strokes on this furry moth.

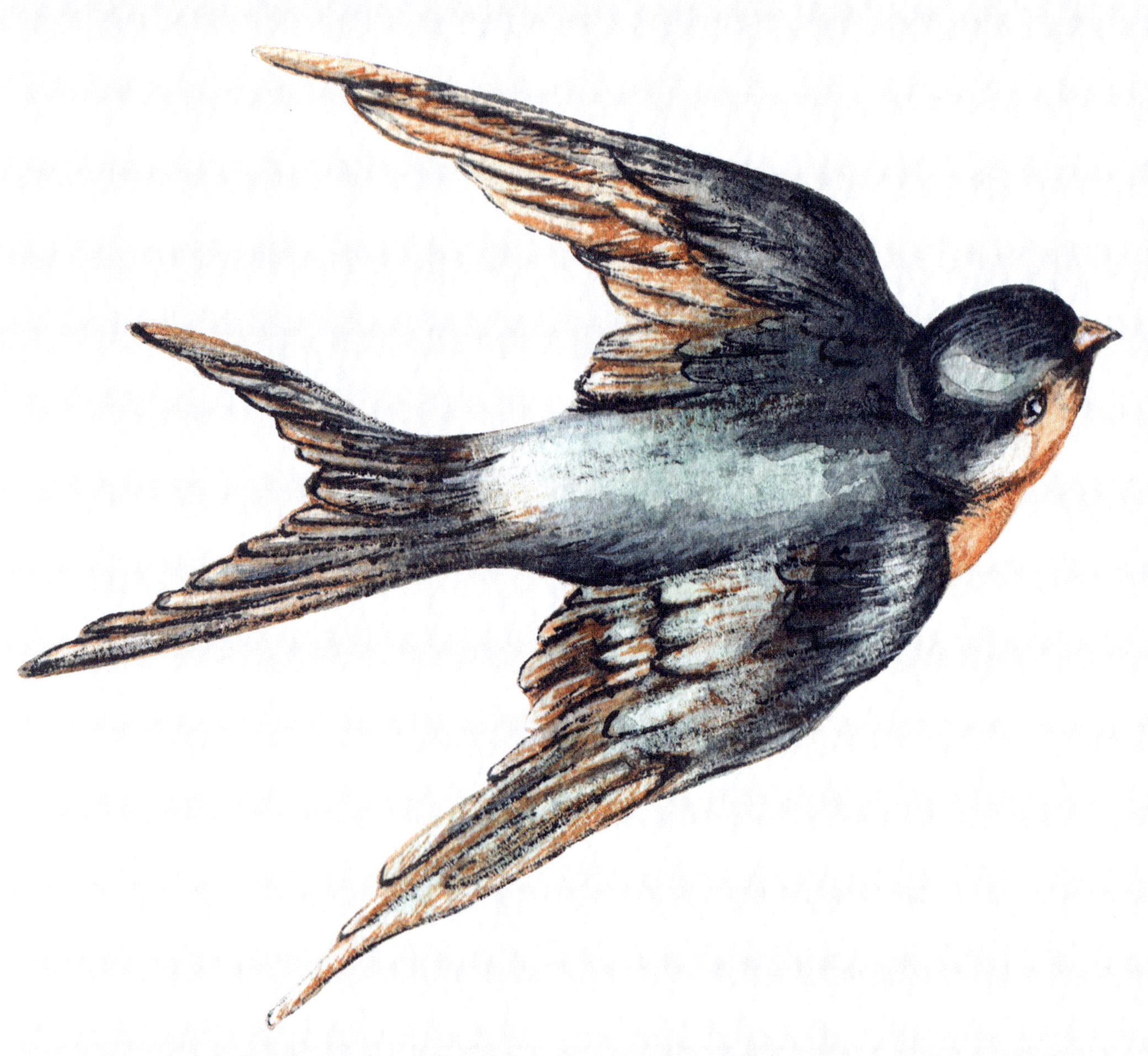

PAINT COLORS

 yellow ochre

 turquoise

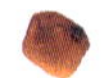 burnt umber

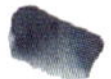 Payne's gray

white gouache or
white ink for
finishing touches

swallow in flight

I really loved painting this swallow and explored painting it a few different times. The position of the bird and shape of the wings is so graceful and makes me feel like it's soaring in the sky. Painting it with Payne's gray as the primary color made it even more exciting for me because Payne's gray is one of my favorite colors to paint with.

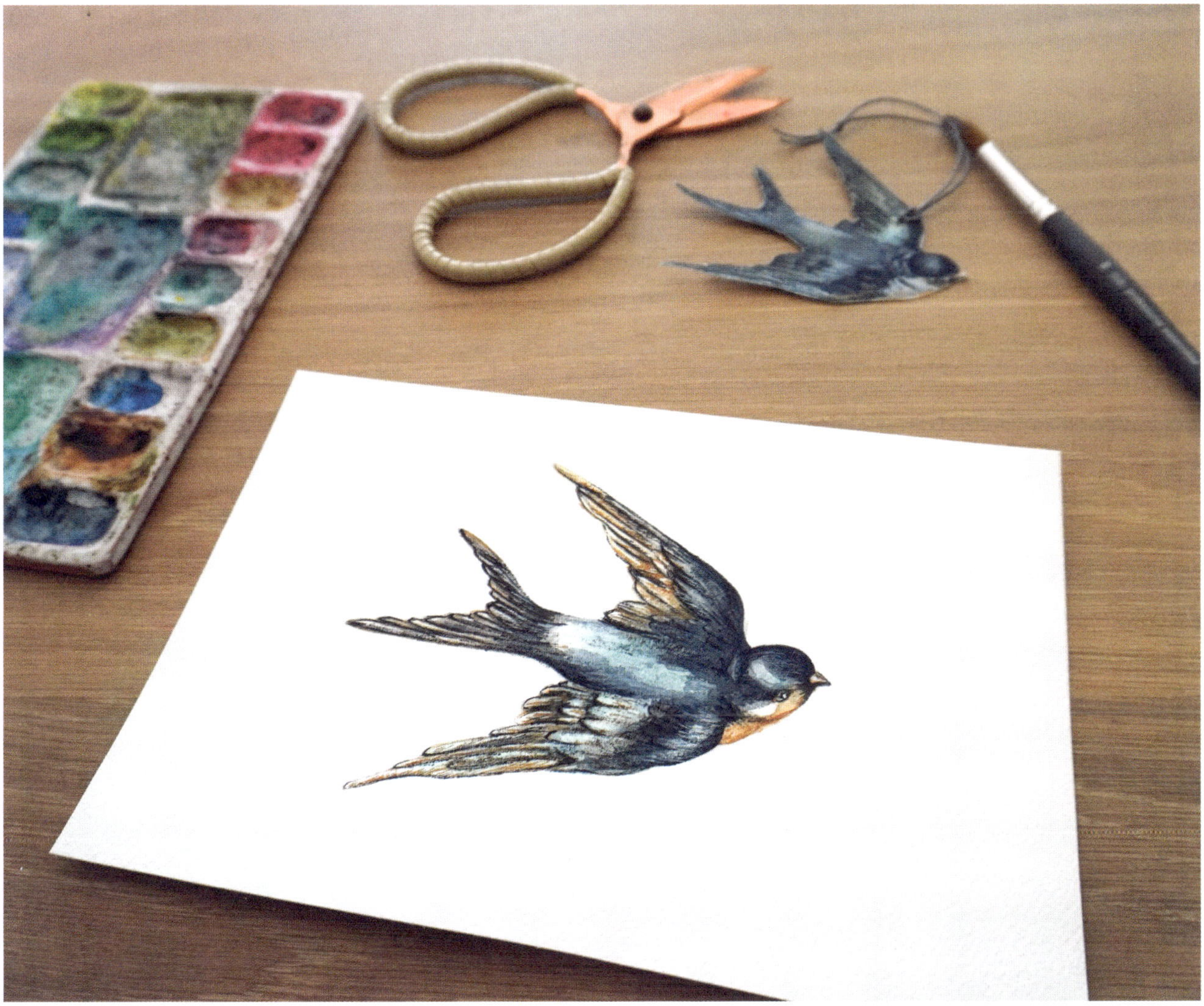

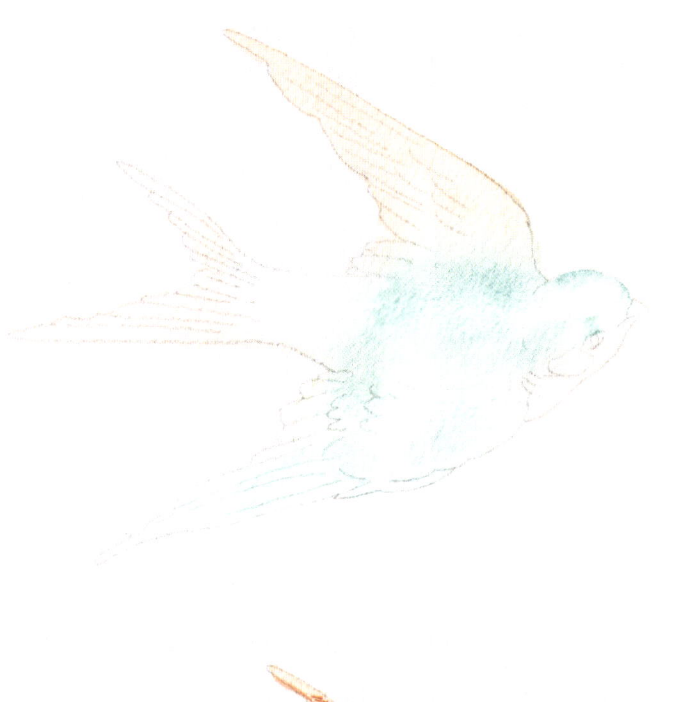

STEP 1

If desired, trace the template on page 135. Start with a light wash of yellow ochre on the wings, tail, and face. While it's still wet, using the wet-on-wet technique, blend a light wash of turquoise on the top of the head and on the front wing, letting it bleed into the yellow ochre. Let dry.

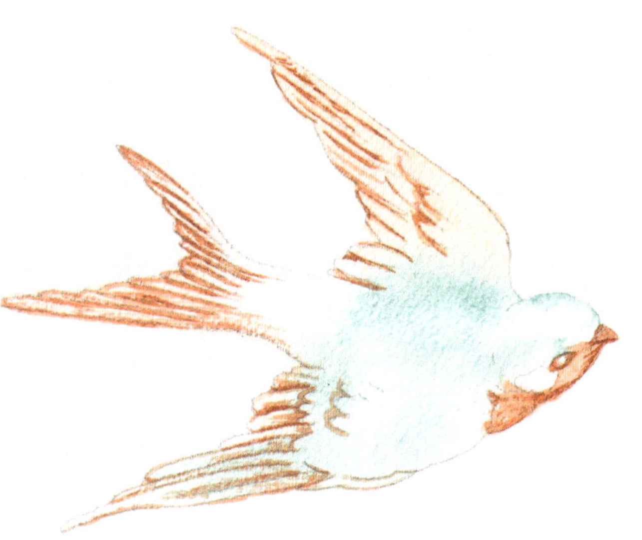

STEP 2

Add a light wash of burnt umber to the cheek and beak of the swallow. Use a small detail brush that is fairly dry and an opaque mix (higher paint-to-water ratio) of burnt umber to paint in the darker areas between the feathers, creating depth and definition to the bird.

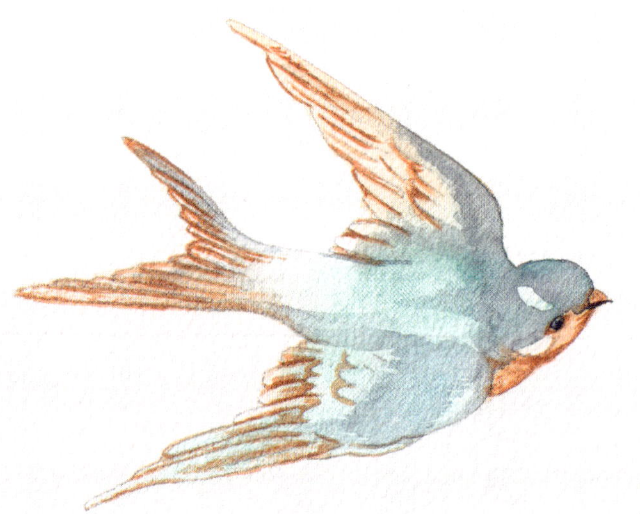

STEP 3

Mix a loose, transparent puddle of Payne's gray and layer this deeper value on the back and head. Let dry.

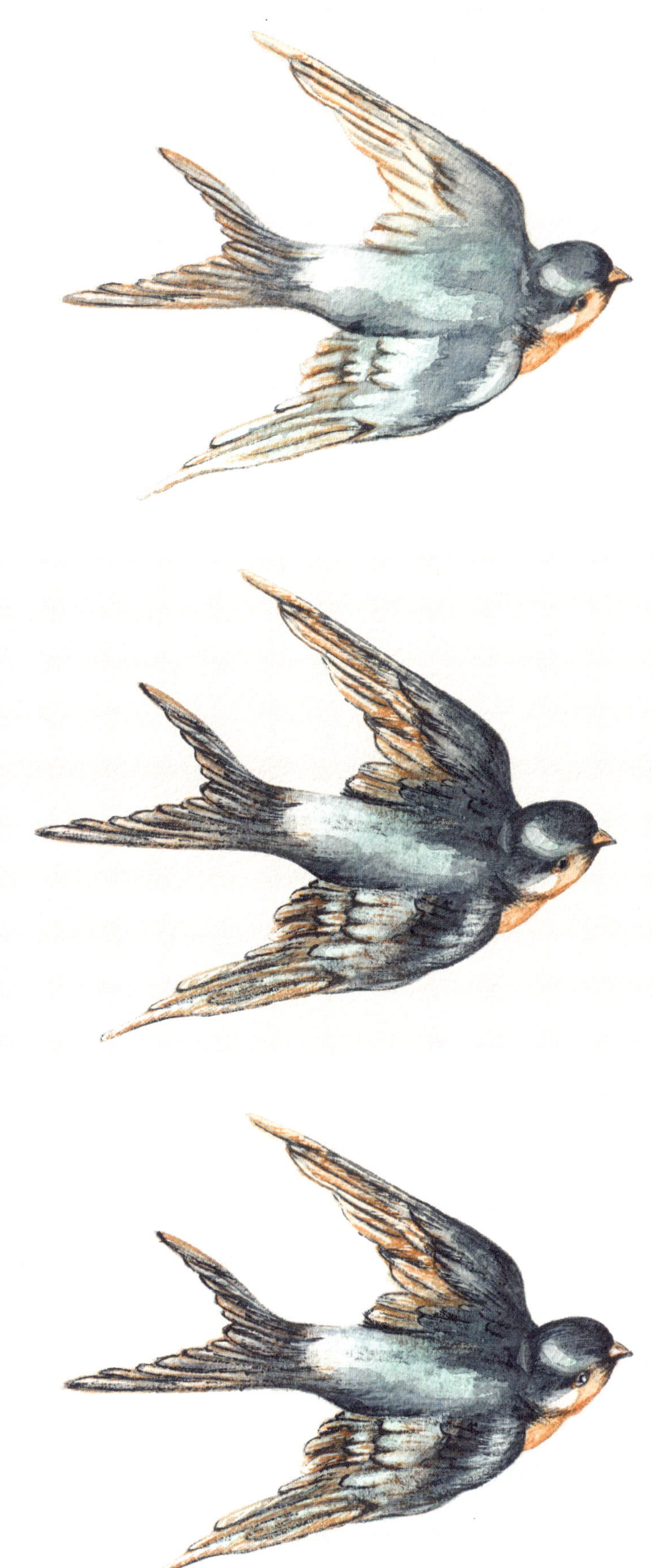

STEP 4

Repeat step 3 to paint another layer of depth to the top of the head and outline the body, the tips of the wings, and any other areas where you want to create more depth. Use a detail brush to paint the Payne's gray mix between the feathers, creating definition and even more depth. If you find the mix to be too watery, dab the tip of the brush on your kitchen towel slightly before putting your brush to the paper. Continue to use a fine detail brush to add a slight amount of Payne's gray to the eye and underside of the beak.

STEP 5

Take your time and use a very fine brush to dry brush some texture on each tail and wing feather, as well as the body. I used a highly pigmented puddle of Payne's gray and alternated with burnt umber. Add as many layers of detail here as you choose; focus on adding depth to the areas between the feathers using a dry brush and highly pigmented Payne's gray. As with any painting, you decide when it's done and how much detail you want to add.

STEP 6

When your swallow is fully dry, you can choose to use white gouache or white ink to define the white spot in the eye and add highlights to the parts of the head and body that you want to brighten. Use a clean fine brush for this step.

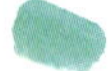 burnt umber

 turquoise

 alizarin crimson

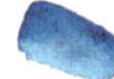 Winsor yellow

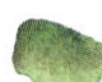 Prussian blue

sap green

dragonfly

This dragonfly painting will require a small detail brush and some patience. You have the option of adding details to the wings or letting the wings remain light and airy. This painting will include some fun color mixing to achieve custom colors as you build more color theory practice and confidence. I recommend that you keep your pencil drawing light if you intend to have the wings be light and airy. Otherwise, relax and enjoy bringing this dragonfly to life.

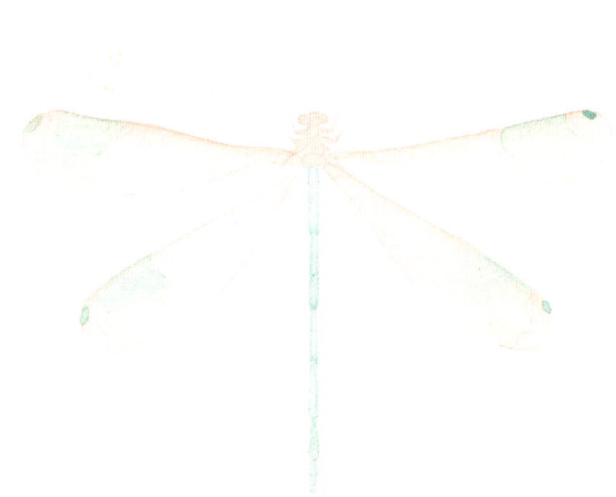

STEP 1

If desired, trace the template on page 135. Mix a transparent wash of burnt umber to paint in the body and wings of the dragonfly. When dry, you can choose to lightly erase the pencil lines of the wings to create a light and airy effect.

STEP 2

Mix a light wash of turquoise to paint in the abdomen of the dragonfly. Use this same mix to paint the edges of the wings and a small section toward the edges of the wings.

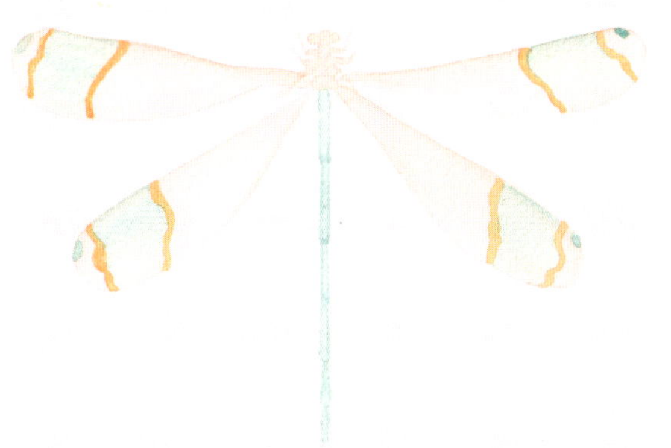

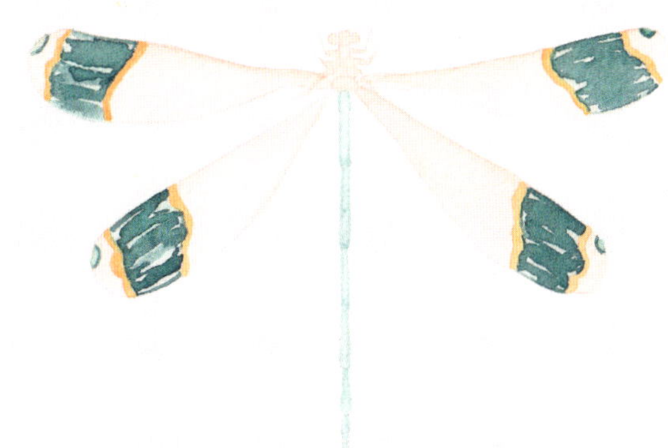

STEP 3

Mix equal parts alizarin crimson and yellow until you get an orange color that you like. Remember to use your scrap paper to test your mix. Paint in the lines on the wings that are on either side of the larger turquoise blocks.

STEP 4

Mix one-fourth Prussian blue, one-fourth turquoise, and one-half sap green to create a bold teal color. Paint in the areas of the wings between the orange parts. I left space to create some interest, but you can paint a solid area here if you choose. Use this same mix to outline the turquoise dots on the wings as well.

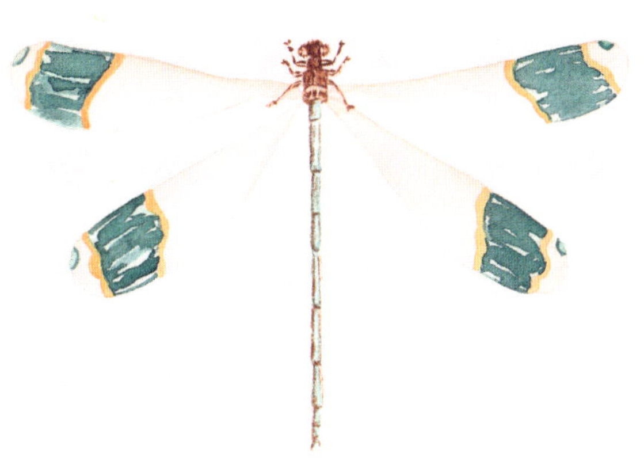

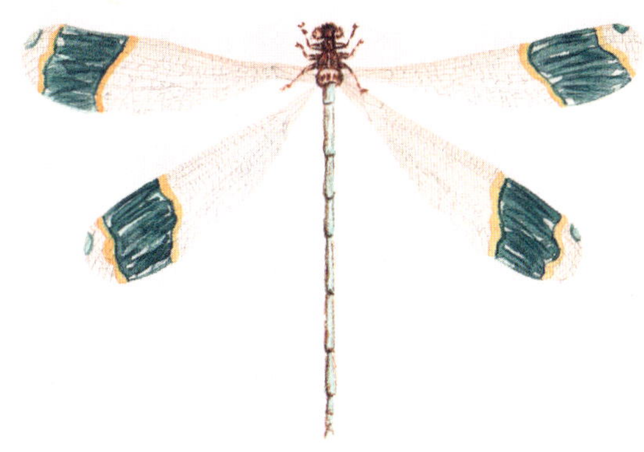

STEP 5

Mix an opaque puddle of burnt umber and use a mostly dry brush to dab in the furry details on the head, thorax, and legs. Paint in a shadow between each section of the abdomen, using the dry brush technique. When your piece is fully dry, erase the pencil lines around the wings if you haven't done so already.

STEP 6 (OPTIONAL)

If you like, use a freshly sharpened pencil with a fine point and lightly draw in the details of the wings to create a more in-depth finish. Add a darker value of the teal color you mixed to enhance the wings and shadows on the abdomen.

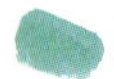 turquoise

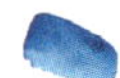 Prussian blue

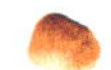 raw umber

 sap green

simple landscape

If you have yet to paint a landscape using watercolors, I think you'll really enjoy this painting project. Painting landscapes with an abstract approach is a really great way to practice using the wet-on-wet technique to create interest as you build value, which will draw the eye into different parts of this painting. Be sure to prop up your painting and step back frequently to see how it looks from a distance and to make sure you have painted a wide range of values.

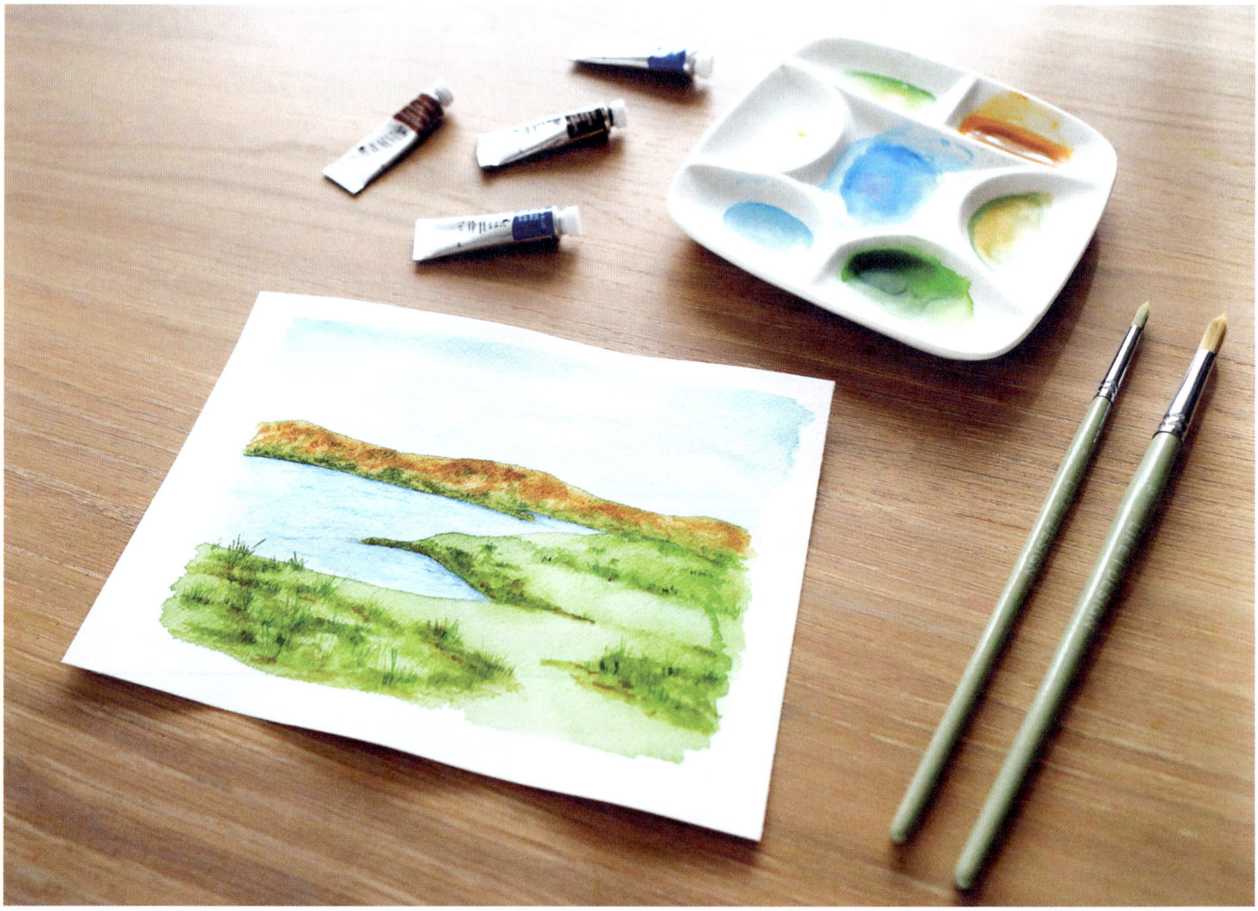

If desired, trace the template on page 137. Mix a puddle of turquoise, adding a dab of Prussian blue. Using a large clean brush, wet the entire sky, then paint it using the turquoise mix. Wipe off the brush and, using the lifting technique, lift away areas of the sky, exposing the white of the paper to mimic long puffs of clouds.

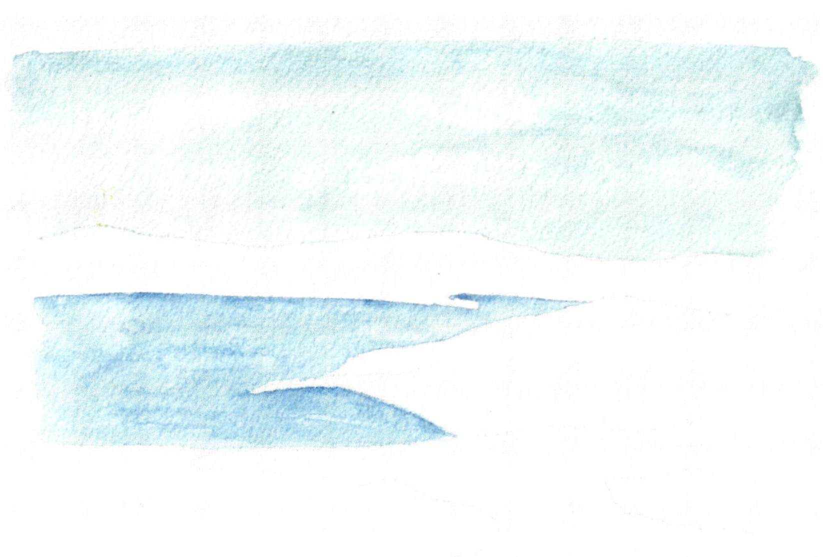

Mix a transparent puddle of Prussian blue and paint the water. Using the tip of the brush and the wet-on-wet technique, dab in darker values of this mix to the shoreline as well as very fine lines to demonstrate the slight waves in the water.

t i p ······ If you prefer a clean edge for this painting, before you begin, tape a border around your landscape. Carefully remove the tape when your painting is dry.

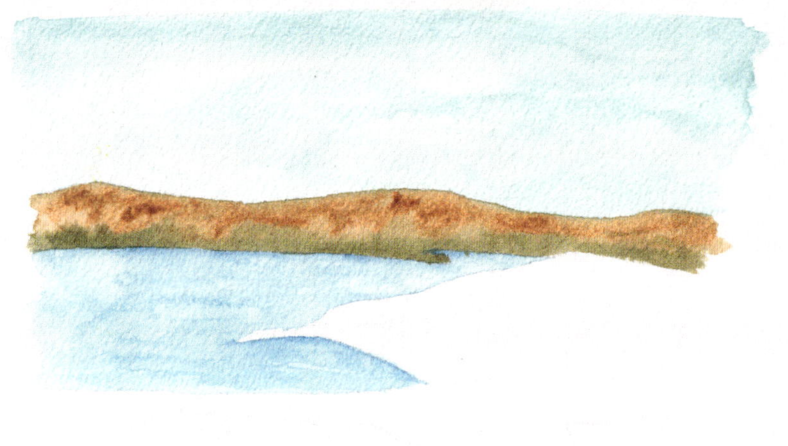

STEP 3

Mix two puddles of raw umber. Add a bit of sap green to one puddle to create a deep green color. Start with the pure raw umber mix and paint in the hills in the background. While they're still wet, dab the deep green mix on the base of the hills and let the colors mix and blend together wet-on-wet. Feel free to dab wet-on-wet to achieve variation and darker values across the hillside.

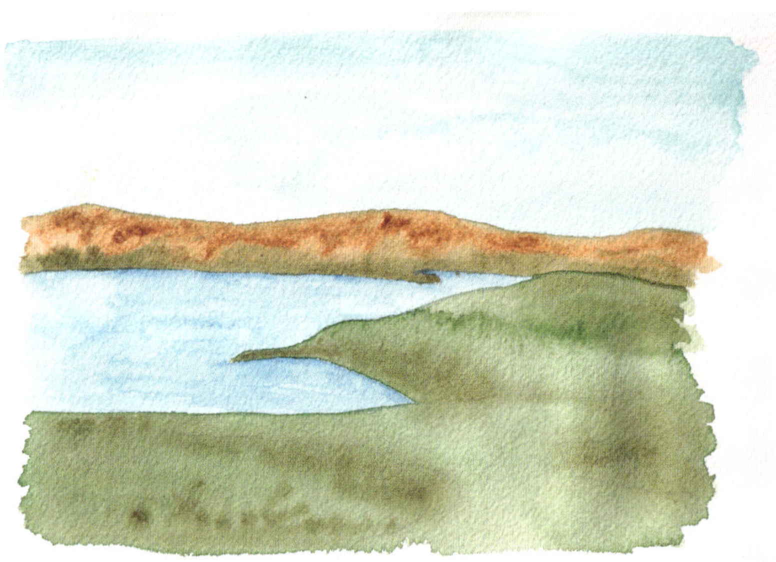

STEP 4

Mix a transparent puddle of sap green. Paint in the remaining grassy areas of the midground and foreground. Follow the pencil lines to drop in the deep green color you mixed in step 3. Work wet-on-wet here to achieve a range of variation between the greens.

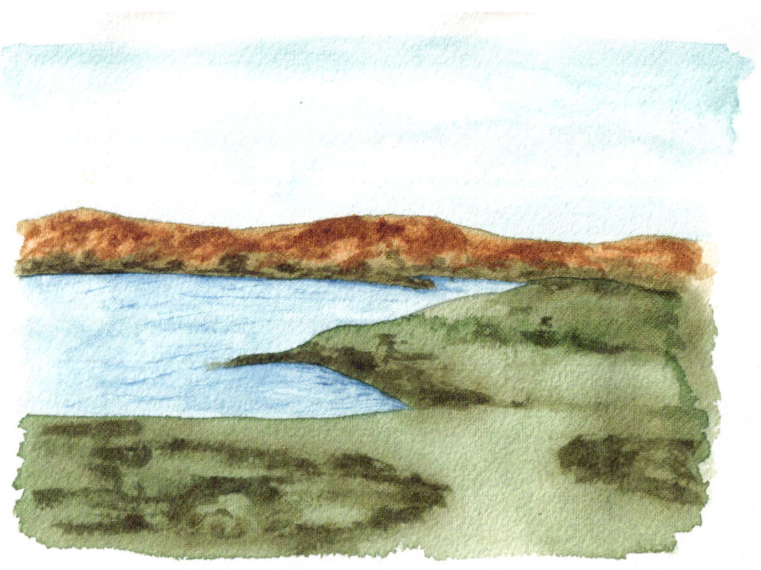

STEP 5

Here is where you add depth and interest to the landscape that will be most noticeable when viewed from a distance. Use a small brush and opaque mixes of the colors you used already and paint in a deeper value to areas such as the shoreline, fine waves in the water, and the hill in the background. This step creates contrast between the lightest values and the darkest values. Dry brushing also works great here to create some contrast.

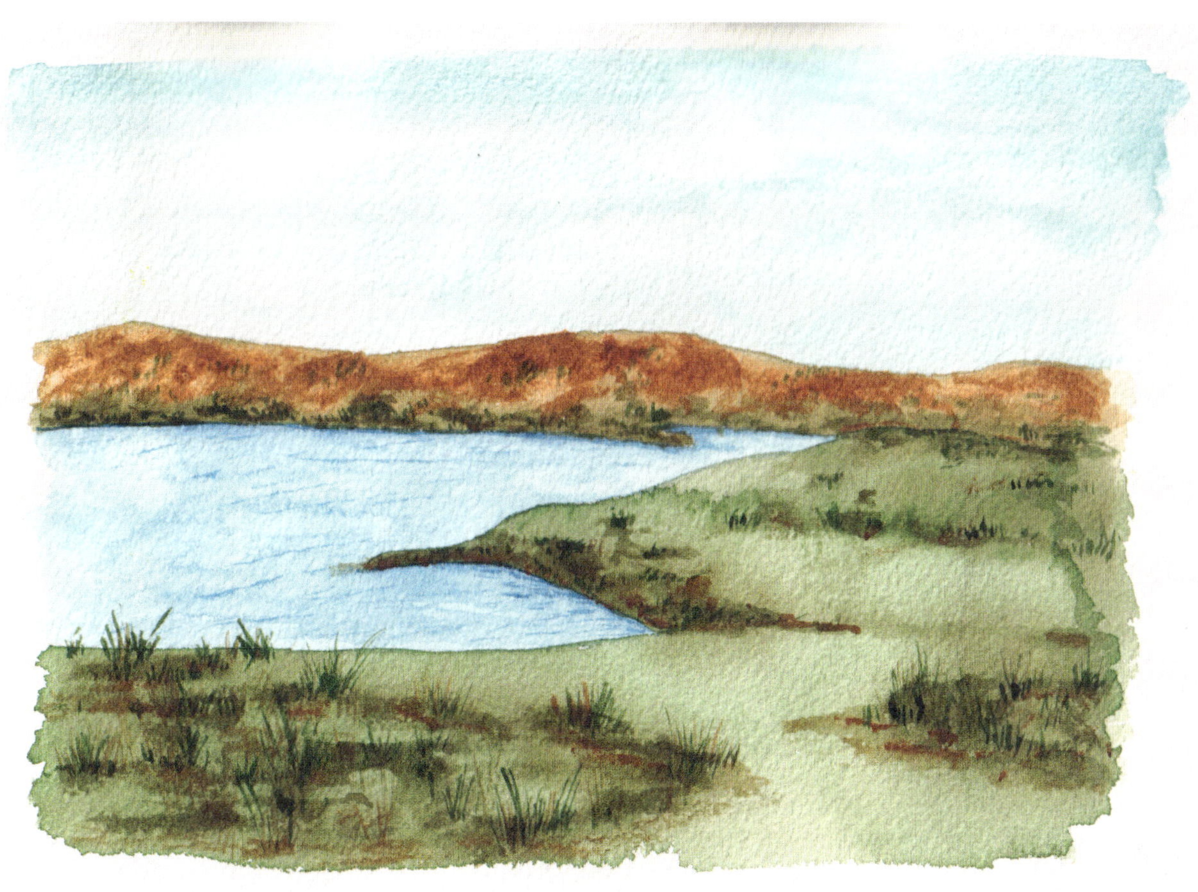

STEP 6 (OPTIONAL)

Using a mix of sap green and the deep green you mixed, along with raw umber and a fine detail brush, add fine grasses in mounds and clusters to the foreground. You can even go back once more and add more fine details using the detail brush and darker values in areas of the hills and grass.

tip ······ Most of us have an abundance of landscape photos that we've taken with our phones. Have a look at your saved photos to see if you can find a landscape shot that you've taken and try painting it! There's nothing better than painting a landscape that you've experienced firsthand.

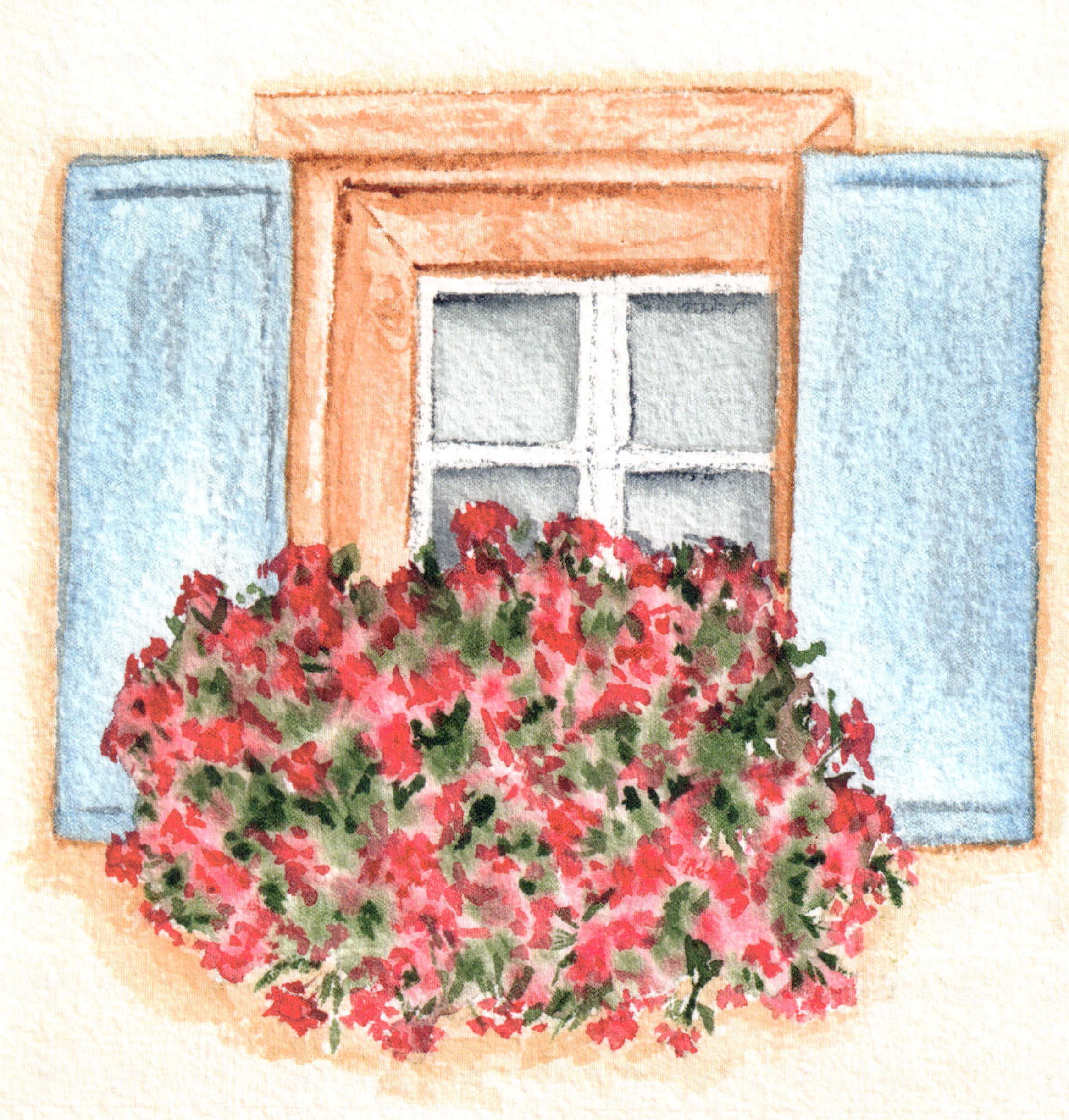

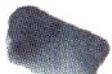 Payne's gray

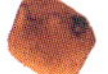 burnt umber

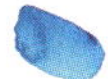 Winsor blue

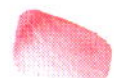 alizarin crimson

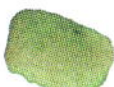 sap green

window flower box

I hope this painting inspires you to go through your vacation photos and paint a scene from one of your favorite places. We will be painting this large, full planter box in an abstract way that requires little detail and lots of wet-on-wet painting. This is also the first time we are painting very straight lines, but I don't want you to worry too much about your lines being perfectly straight. Embrace the wobbles and remember to use the tip of your brush as a guide.

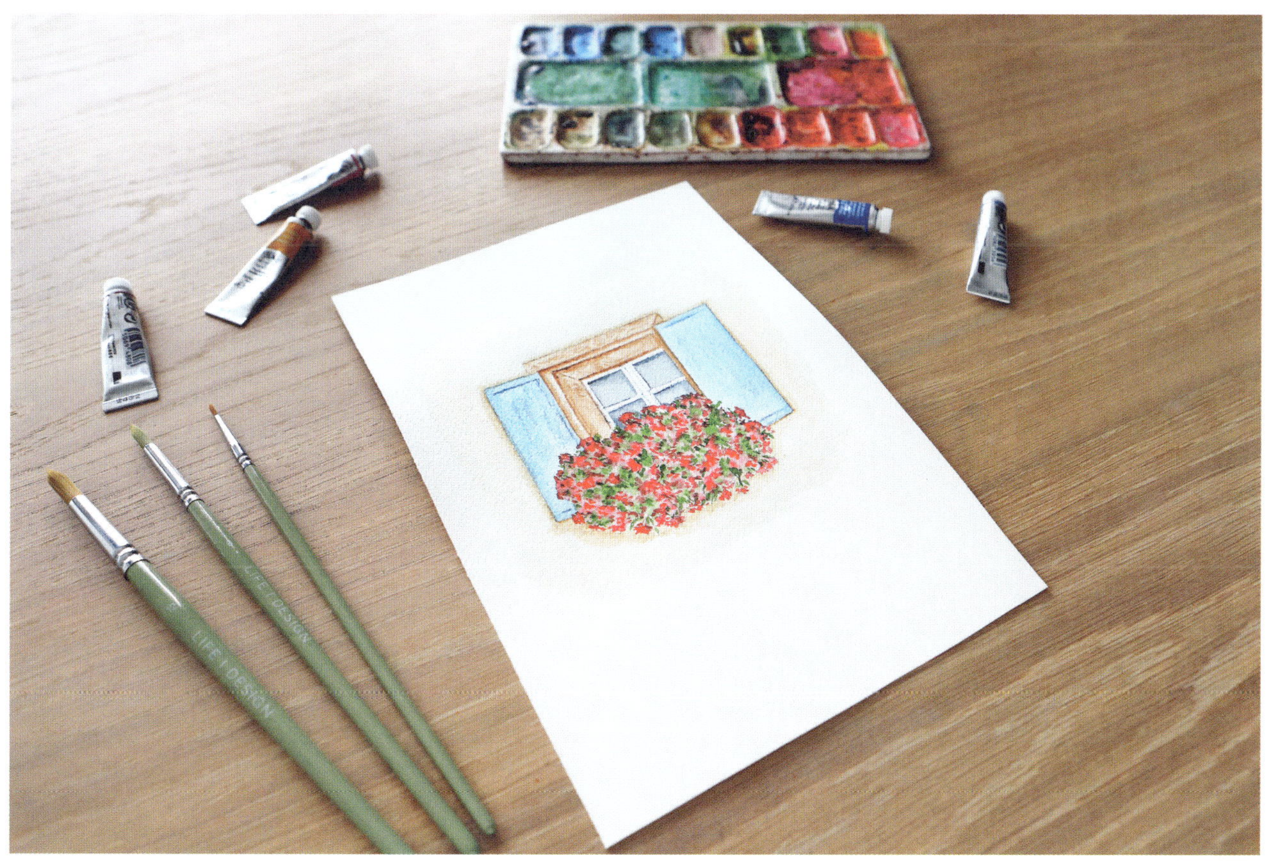

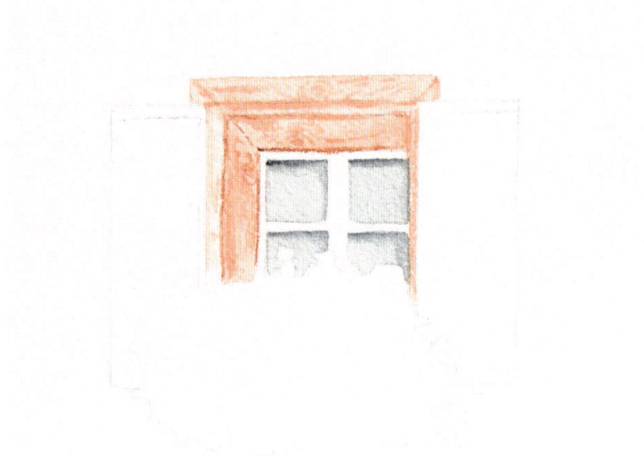

STEP 1

If desired, trace the template on page 137. Mix a transparent wash of Payne's gray and paint in each window glass. While the windows are still wet, use the tip of a small brush and a more concentrated mix of Payne's gray to paint in the shadows at the top and right of the window glass.

STEP 2

Mix a transparent wash of burnt umber to paint in the window frame. We will be using the white of the paper to keep the border of the windows white. As the window frame starts to dry, use a dry brush to paint in the lines of the frame and even add some details to imitate wood that is worn and discolored in spots. This will give the window character.

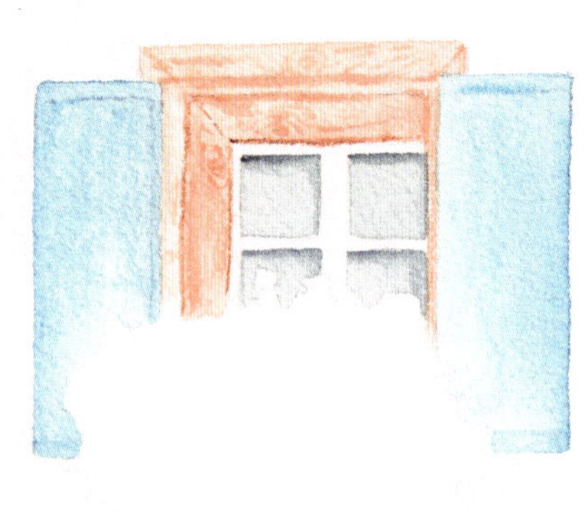

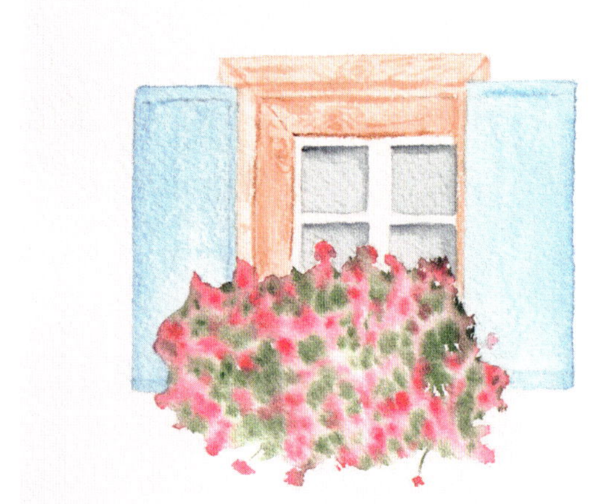

STEP 3

Mix a transparent wash of Winsor blue and paint in the shutters. As the shutters dry, use a dry brush and, with downward strokes, add in marks and texture to the shutters to suggest that they are weathered.

STEP 4

Mix a transparent wash of alizarin crimson and a transparent wash of sap green. Wet the area of the flowers and, with the tip of a small brush, begin to work wet-on-wet and drop in alizarin crimson in dots, allowing them to spread. Leave white space and use that white space to paint wet-on-wet with the sap green. As this section begins to slightly dry, feel free to paint in stronger brushstrokes to indicate more flowers and leaves. I like to tap the tip of my brush to give definition and start to create bulk in the flowers. Doing this will also help add a range of values.

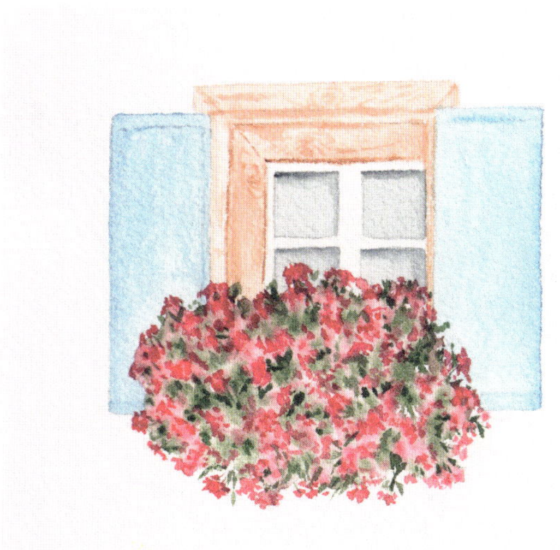

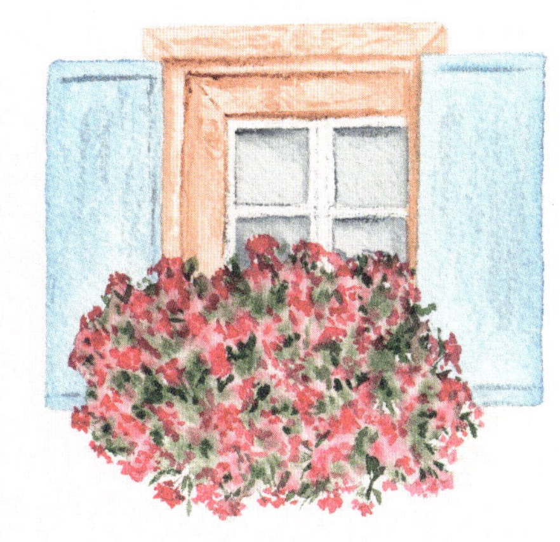

STEP 5

Go back to the same washes of alizarin crimson and sap green and start to paint more defined flowers and leaves. I like to tap or wiggle the tip of the brush to emulate clusters of petals and leaves. Feel free to add in as much detail as you like here.

STEP 6

At this stage, once the piece is fully dry, I like to go back and, using a fine detail brush, paint in a darker value of the same colors used around the window, frame, and shutters to create more depth and interest. I used a dry detail brush and Payne's gray to paint in the frame around the glass to give it more character as well.

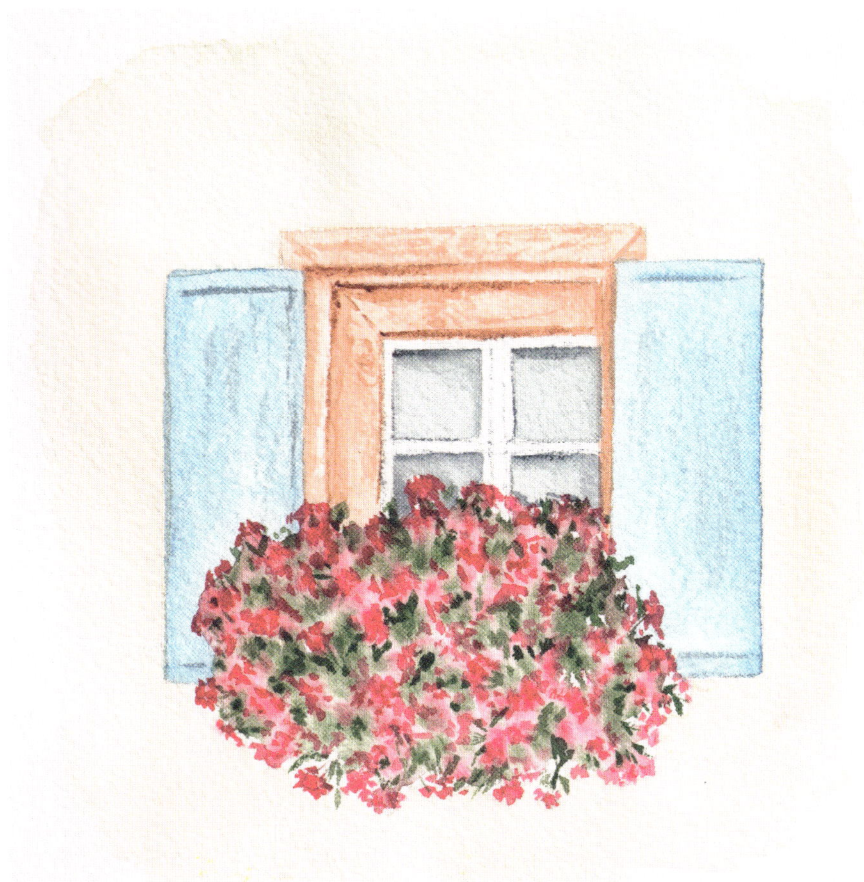

STEP 7 (OPTIONAL)

Using a large brush, paint in a very light wash of burnt umber on the background. Using a detail brush, paint this wash along the outside of the shutters, around the window, and below the flowers to add a slight shadow. This will ground the window so that it doesn't look as though it's floating.

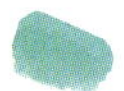 turquoise

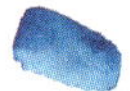 Prussian blue

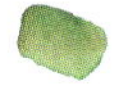 sap green

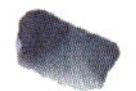 Payne's gray

 alizarin crimson

lamb in a field

I imagine this lamb is about ready to have his fluffy coat sheared. He was such a joy to paint, and I hope you paint him a few times and enjoy watching him come to life. We will be relying on wet-on-wet techniques for this one and will also be using the white of the paper to articulate his fur. Because you've already practiced painting a landscape (see page 90), the background on this one should feel a little familiar.

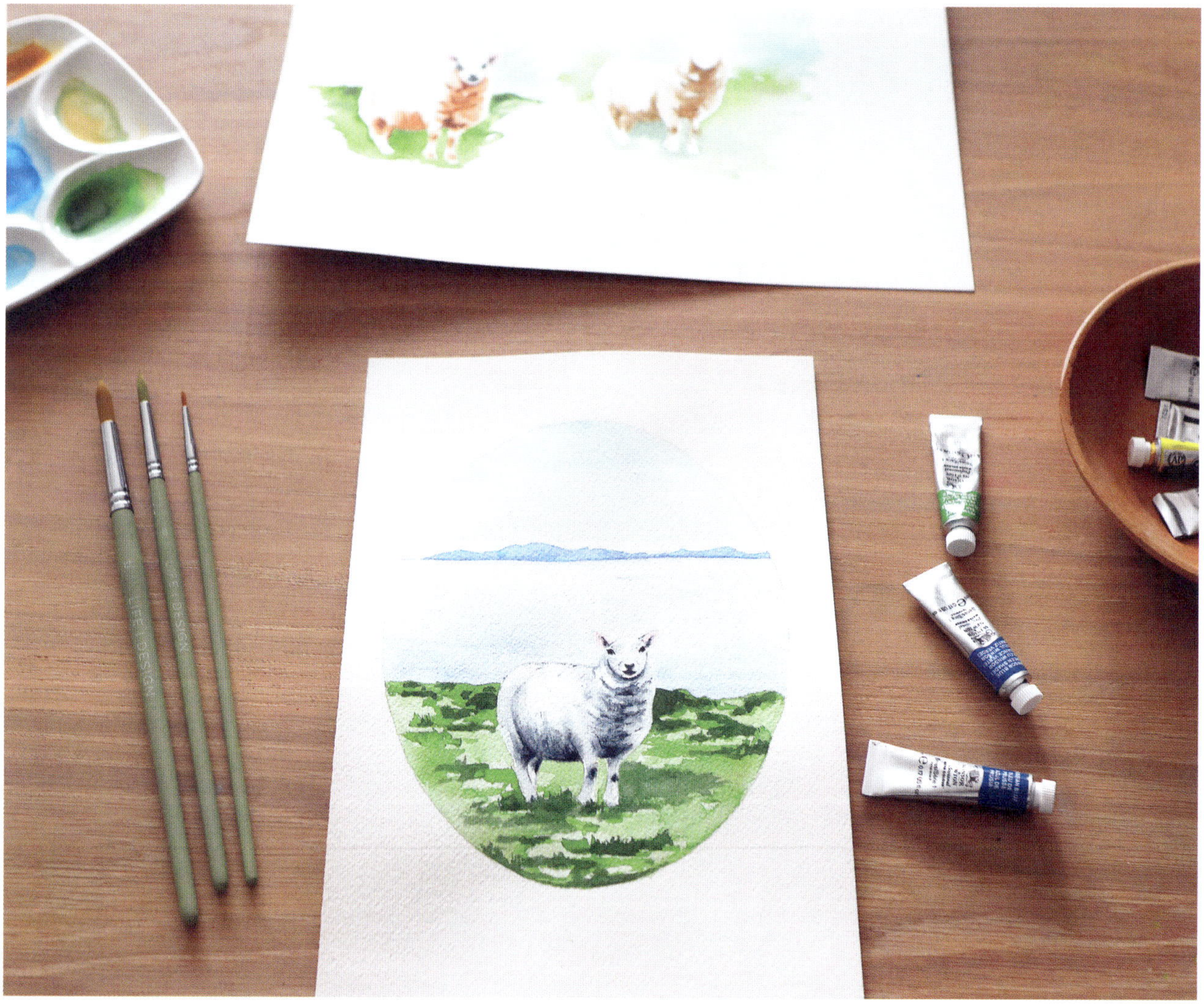

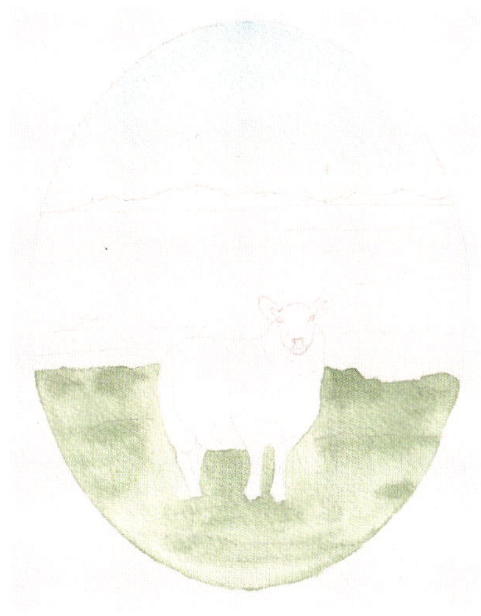 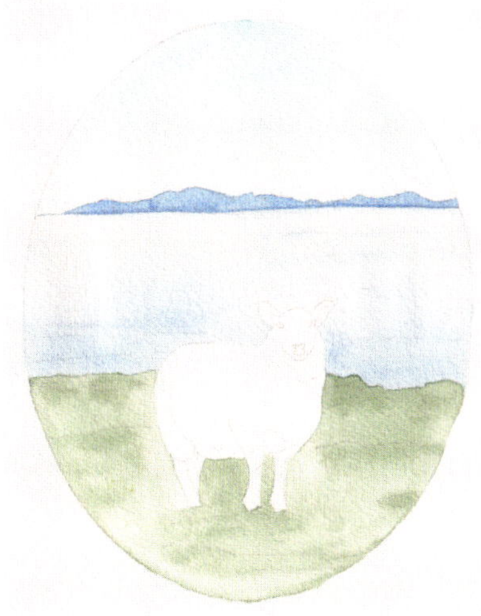 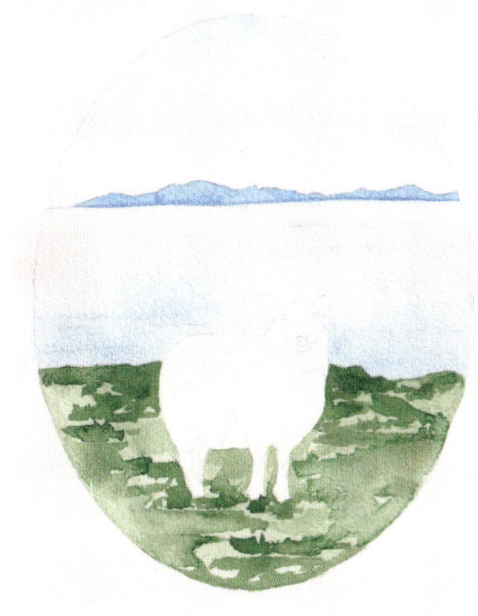

STEP 1

If desired, trace the template on page 139. Mix a very transparent puddle of turquoise with a touch of Prussian blue. Using clean water on your brush, paint a wet wash on the entire sky. Starting from the top of the sky, begin to paint into the wet layer with the blue. Use your brush to blend the blue paint until it is barely noticeable toward the mountain range line. Using the same technique, paint the grass with a transparent mix of sap green using wet-on-wet.

STEP 2

Mix a slightly darker version of the sky using more Prussian blue and paint in the mountain range that appears in the distance. Mix a transparent puddle of Prussian blue. Wet the paper with clean water; starting from the midground, paint in the water using the blue mix and working back and forth to imitate slight waves and movement in the water. As you work your way up toward the mountain line, the water should be lighter and fade into the mountain range.

STEP 3

Mix an opaque puddle of sap green; using a wet brush, paint in areas of the grass to create grassy mounds and add interest in the foreground as it begins to frame the fluffy lamb. Using a wet brush, start to paint in shadows and more texture in the grass. Use wet-on-wet to dab variations and texture in the paint, so that when the grass area is dry, it creates interest.

t i p ······ Make your hand more comfortable and steady by rotating your paper as you use the tip of the brush to paint in the lines of the oval and to paint clean edges.

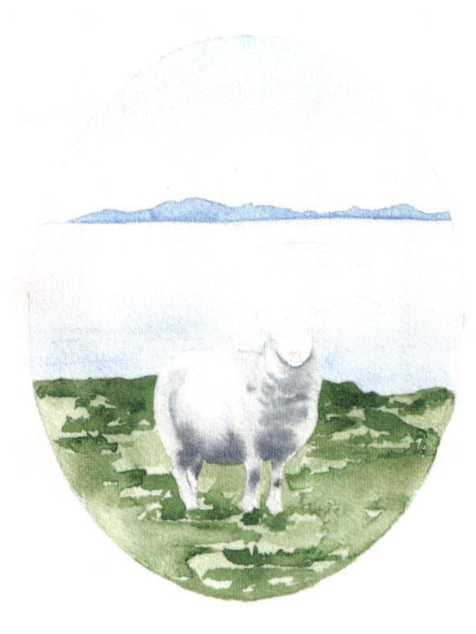

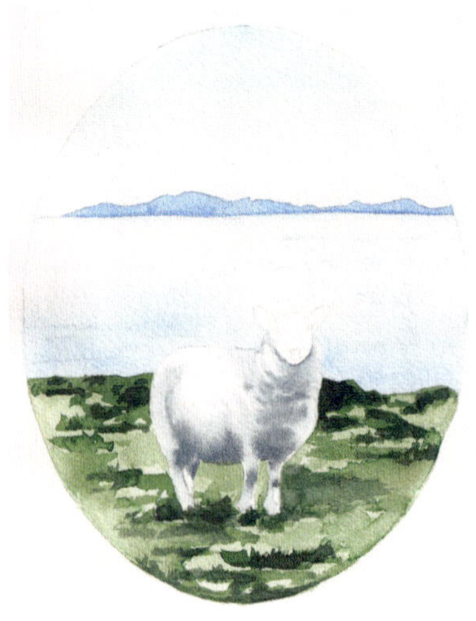

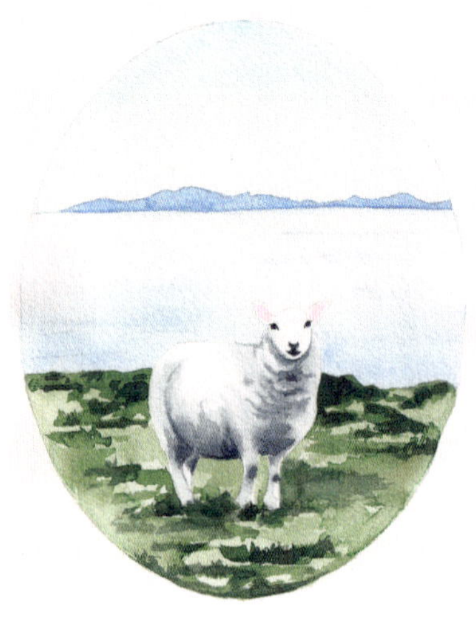

STEP 4

Make sure your painting is completely dry before this next step. Mix an opaque puddle of Payne's gray as well as a transparent puddle. Using a small brush, paint the body and legs of the lamb with clean water. Dry your brush slightly before dipping it into the transparent mix of Payne's gray, then dab the areas of the lamb that are to be shadowed as you use the pencil lines to guide you. Use the opaque mix of Payne's gray to drop in wet-on-wet a darker value under the face, between the front legs, the underbelly, and the hind legs. Take your time here and use a detail brush to help you drop more paint precisely where you need to create shadows in the lamb.

STEP 5

Time to finish up the grass. Add a slight bit of Payne's gray to the sap green to mix a darker green. Use a smaller brush to add more depth to the foreground, focusing on darkening areas that are already the darkest value in the grass section of the painting. Adding a variety of values will give depth and dimension, especially when viewing the painting from afar.

STEP 6

Painting the face of the lamb requires a detail brush and a little bit of patience. Start with the pinks of the ears. Mix a transparent puddle of alizarin crimson; using a detail brush, paint the inner ears. While that is drying, using the same detail brush and an opaque mix of Payne's gray, paint in the nose and eyes. Lastly, paint another darker value to the shadows of the lamb's body.

STEP 7 (OPPOSITE)

Time to add the finishing details to the face and body. Use an opaque mix of Payne's gray and a detail brush to paint in the center of the ears. Use a transparent mix of Payne's gray to add slight shadows to the face and any final touches to the body, darkening the areas that are most shadowed. Feel free to use a detail brush and dry brush some texture in the fluffy body.

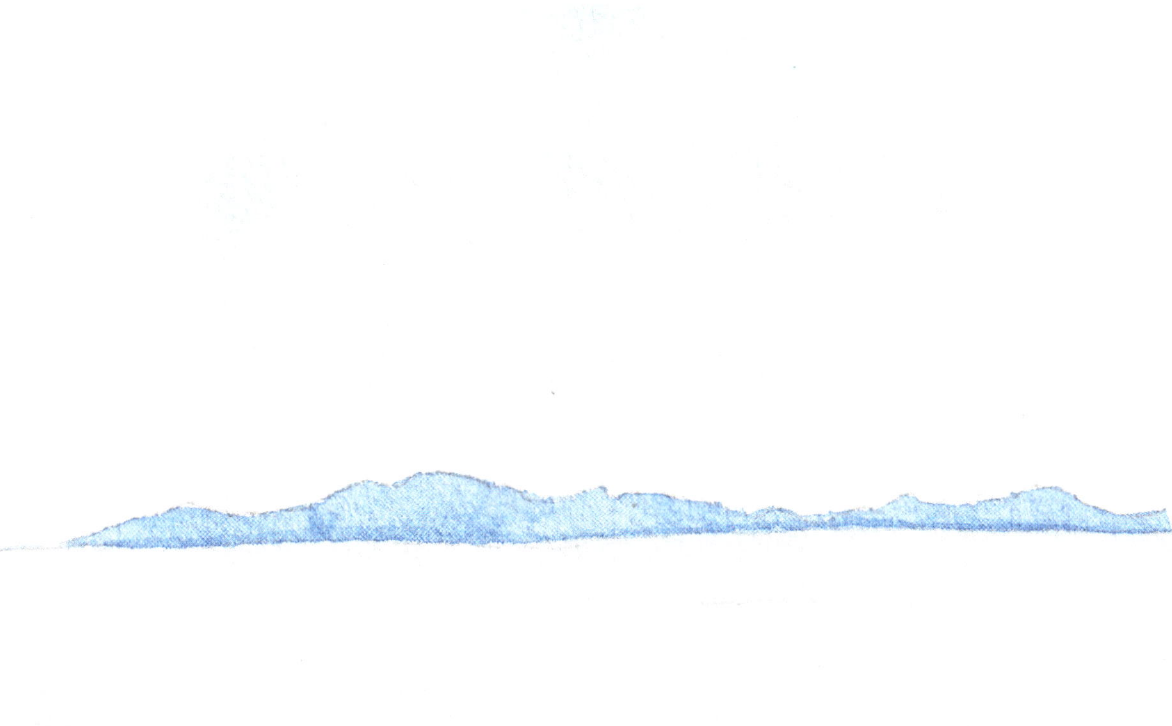

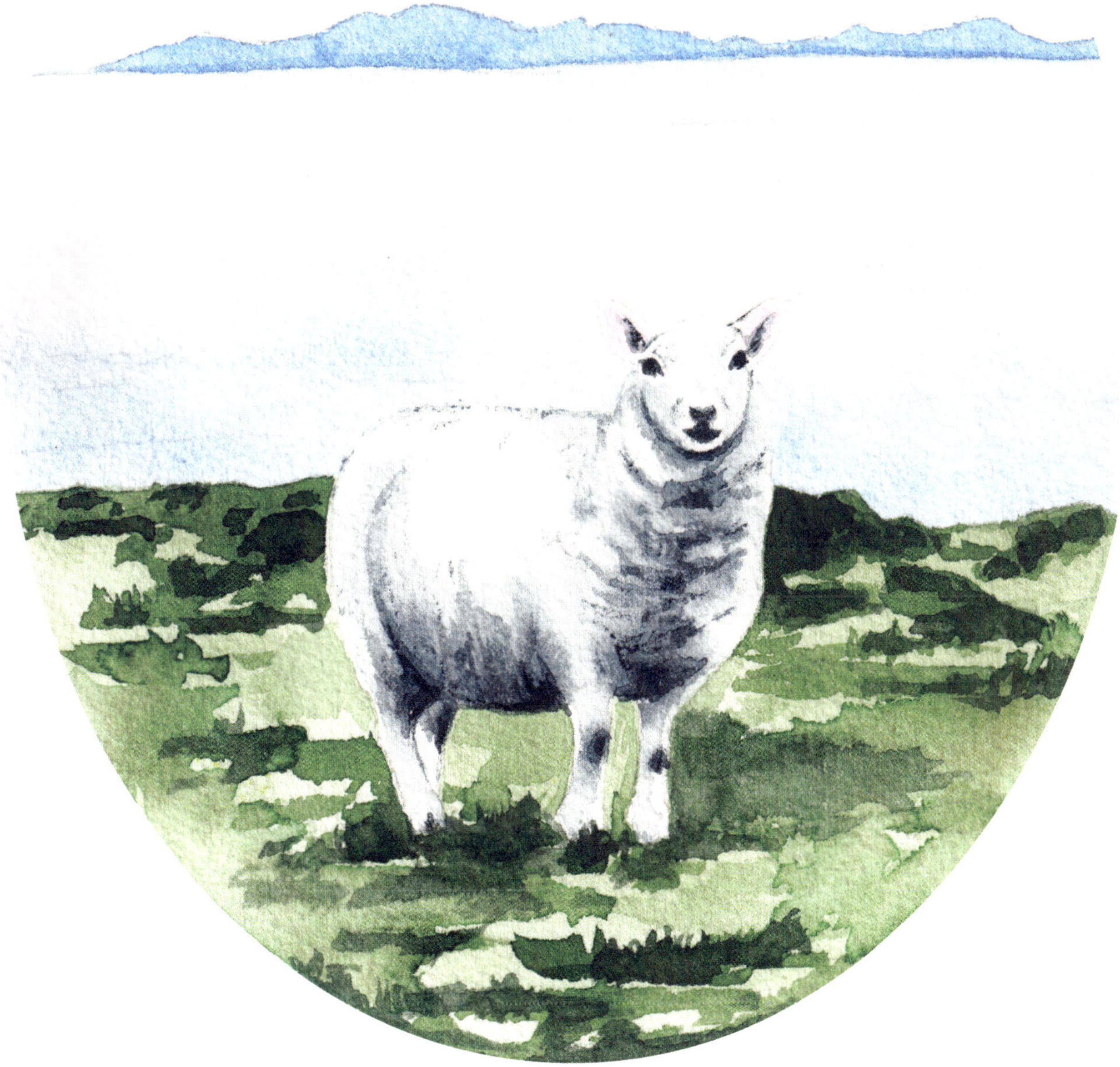

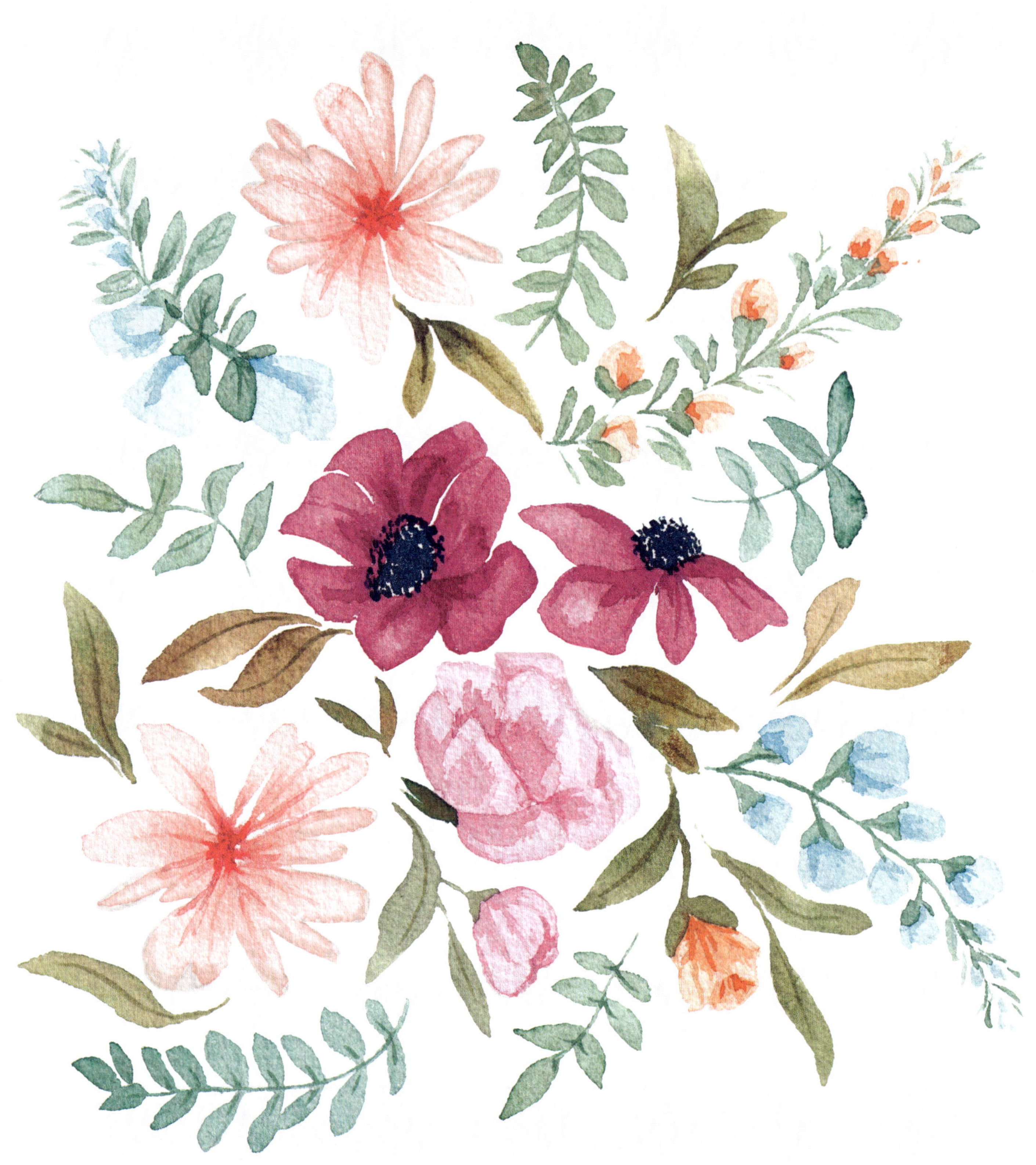

 alizarin crimson

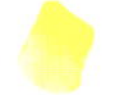 Winsor yellow

 permanent rose

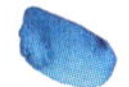 Winsor blue

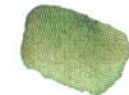 sap green

 raw umber

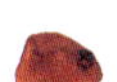 burnt umber

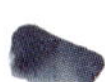 Payne's gray

whimsical florals

For this final painting project, I really want you to have fun with color and with painting something that is less realistic than some of the other motifs we have explored. Perhaps you'll be inspired to give this to a special person as a way to celebrate all of the practice and growth you've experienced while painting your way through this book. I left room between the florals in case you want to add more leaves. The main thing is that you have fun with this one, let the blooms happen, work wet-on-wet, and watch these florals come to life.

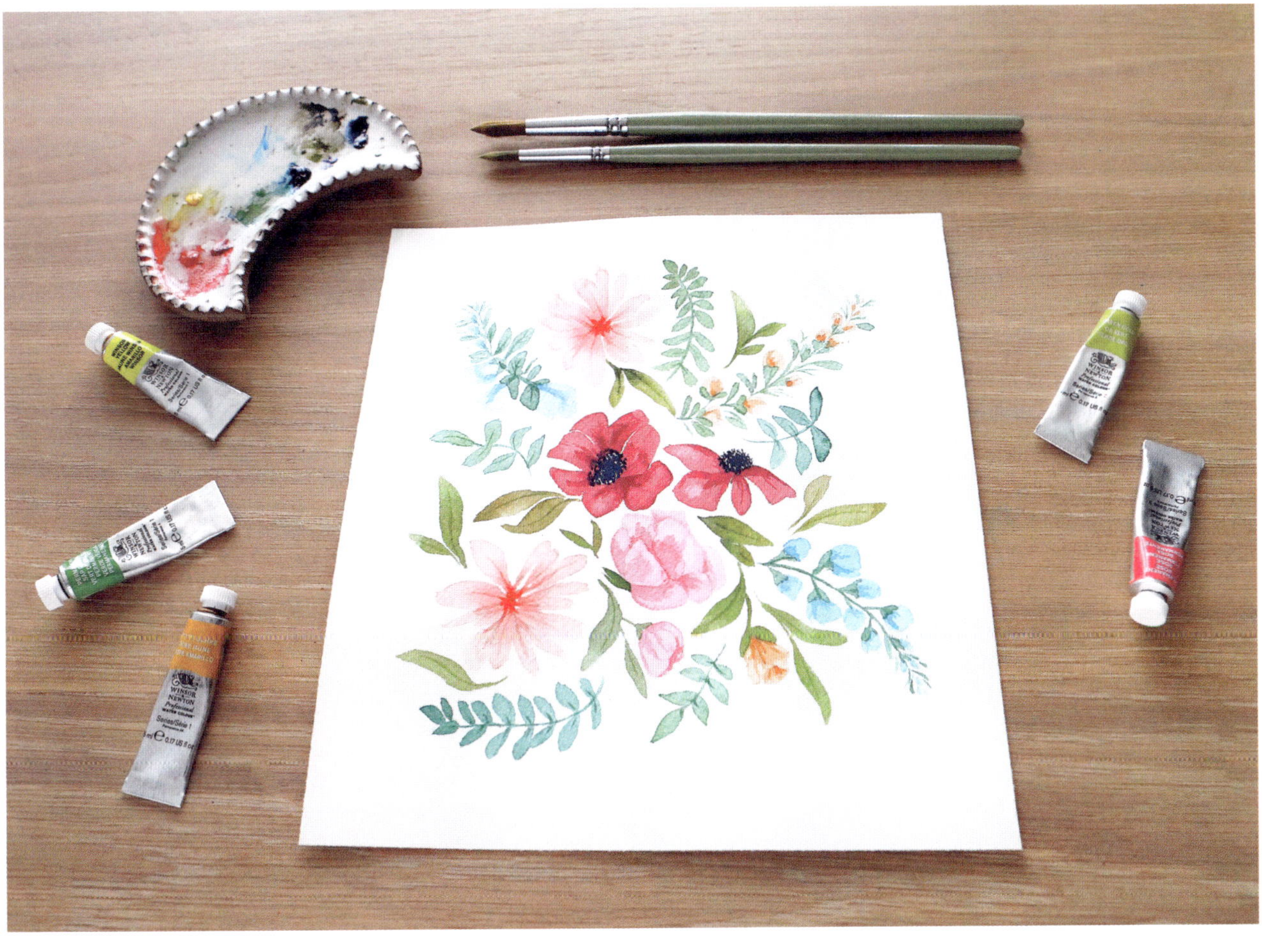

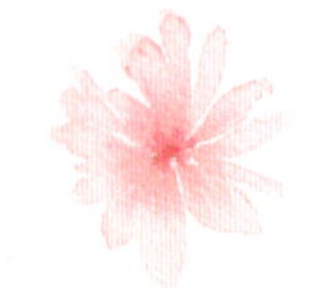

STEP 1

If desired, trace the template on page 133. Mix a very transparent puddle of alizarin crimson and add a touch of yellow to achieve a peachy-pink tone. Paint in the two starburst flowers. While still wet, use the tip of your brush and an opaque amount of alizarin crimson to drop in the centers of the flowers. Let the watercolor move and bloom to add interest to the petals.

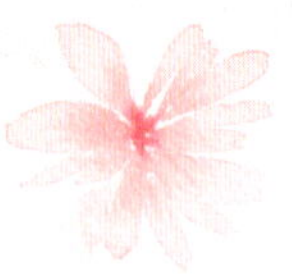

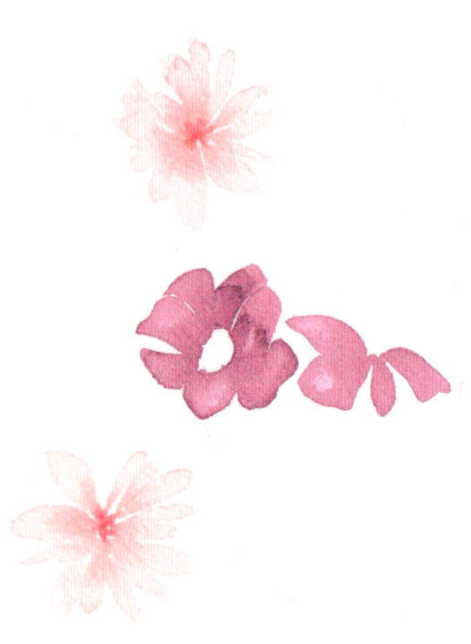

STEP 2

Mix permanent rose with some Winsor blue to achieve a reddish-purple tone. This mix should be opaque with a little more water so that your puddle is loose and has movement. Paint the two center flowers working wet-on-wet to add a deeper tone close to the center of the petals. Leave the very centers unpainted for now.

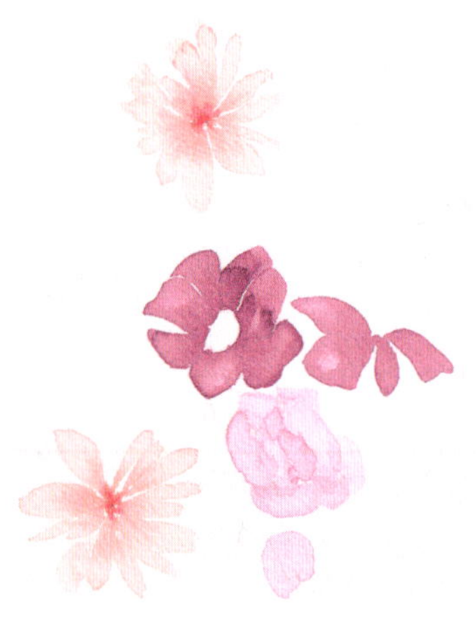

STEP 3

Mix a transparent wash of permanent rose and paint the lower two flowers. We will be adding a darker value to these florals, so feel free to paint this first layer lightly.

t i p ······ For the lighter florals, I paint just inside the pencil lines so I can erase them when the paint is fully dry and the piece is complete.

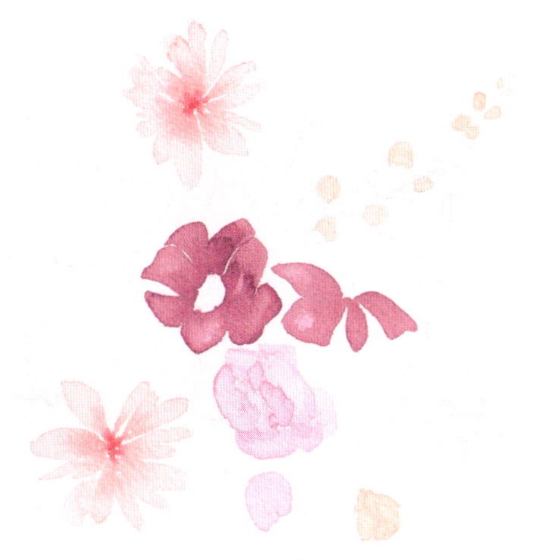

STEP 4

Mix a transparent wash of yellow and paint in the single lower flower as well as the trailing flowers at top right.

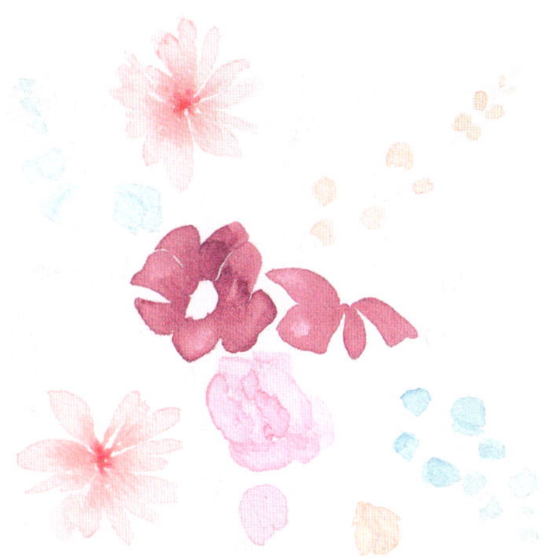

STEP 5

Mix a transparent wash of Winsor blue and paint in the flowers of the outer trailing stems to complete the first layer of florals.

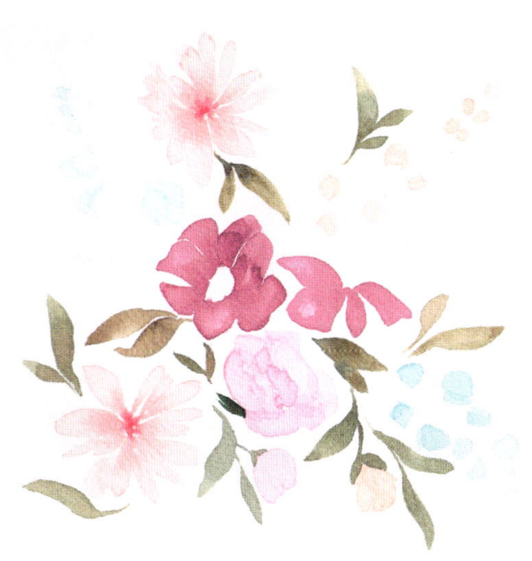

STEP 6

Mix up three puddles of green for the leaves. I mixed sap green with raw umber in one puddle, sap green with burnt umber for the second, and sap green with a touch of Payne's gray for the third. Using your variety of green mixes, paint all the supporting leaves. As you paint each leaf, feel free to drop in wet-on-wet one of the other greens that you mixed up. Doing this will create a nice, cohesive variety of leaves that frame the florals.

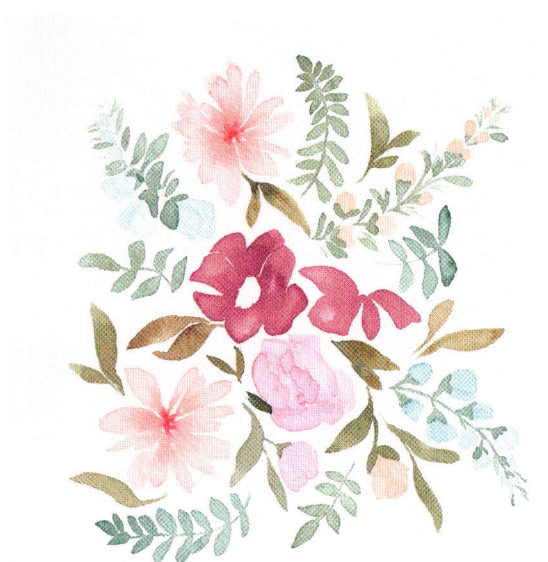

STEP 7

Mix a puddle of sap green and Winsor blue until you achieve a greenish-blue. Mix a second puddle that has more blue than green in the mix until you've achieved a bluish-green. Use these two mixes to paint in the remaining leaves.

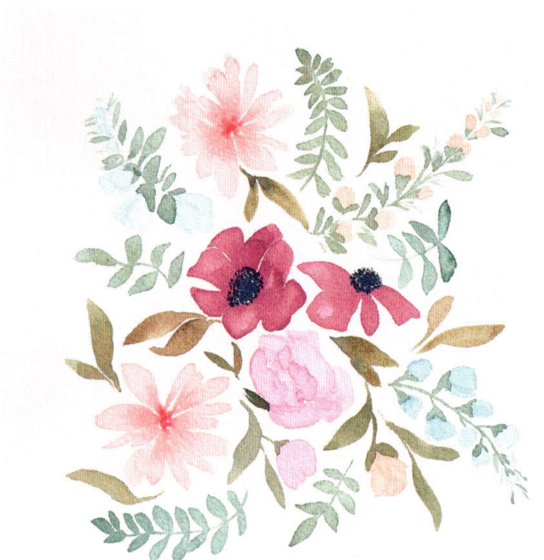

STEP 8

Mix an opaque puddle of Payne's gray and use it to paint in the center of the flowers we left empty. Use the tip of a detail brush and dab in wet-on-wet to create dots clustered in the center.

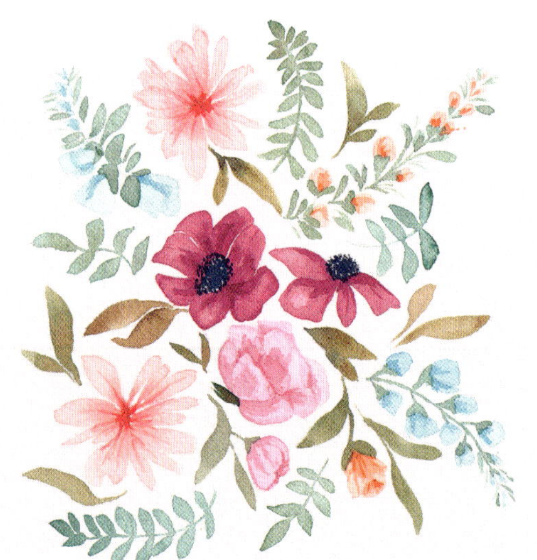

STEP 9

Use colors that you mixed for each flower to paint some details on the petals and shade the centers of the flowers. Feel free to add veins and create depth by layering your brushstrokes and allowing the paint to puddle and dry. Remember to use the same color to add your layers—i.e., more yellow to the yellow flowers—and use the layering technique we learned in chapter 3.

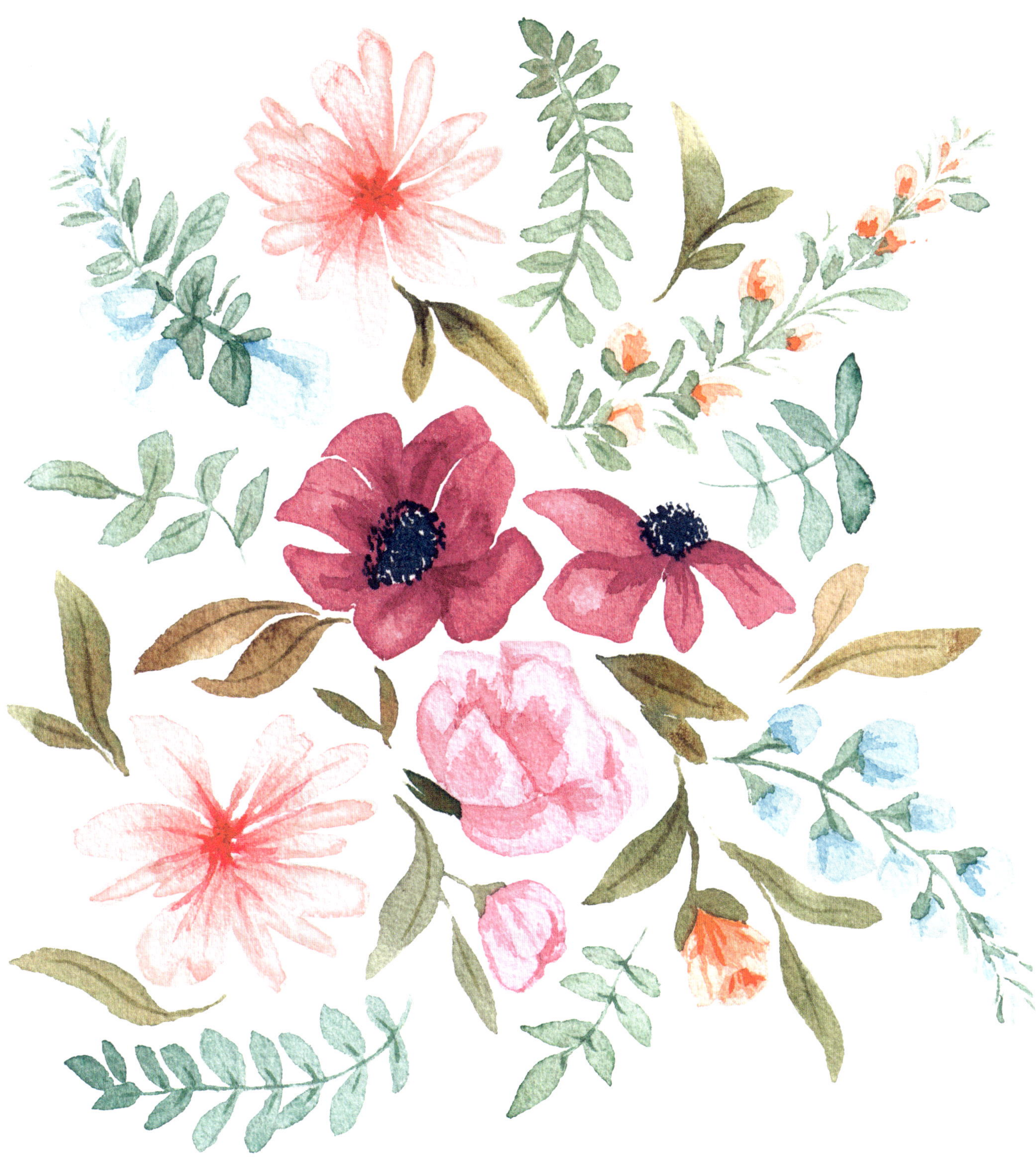

STEP 10

Use the greens you mixed for the leaves to add a
deeper value to some of the leaves. Using the layering
technique and wet-on-dry, add veins with a small
detail brush.

t i p ······· When your painting is fully dry,
use an eraser to carefully remove
any pencil lines that you have not
painted over.

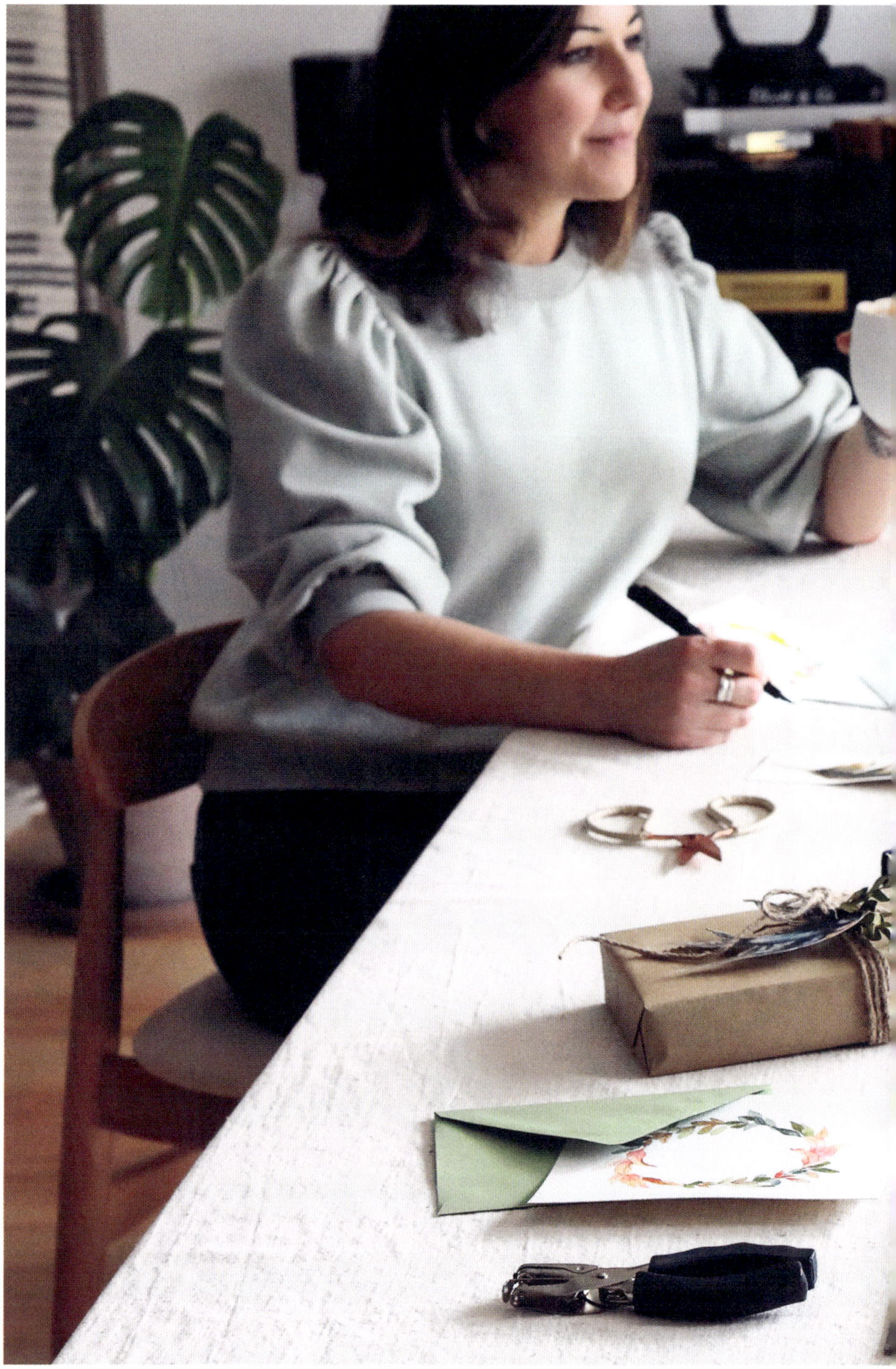

7

PAPERCRAFTING

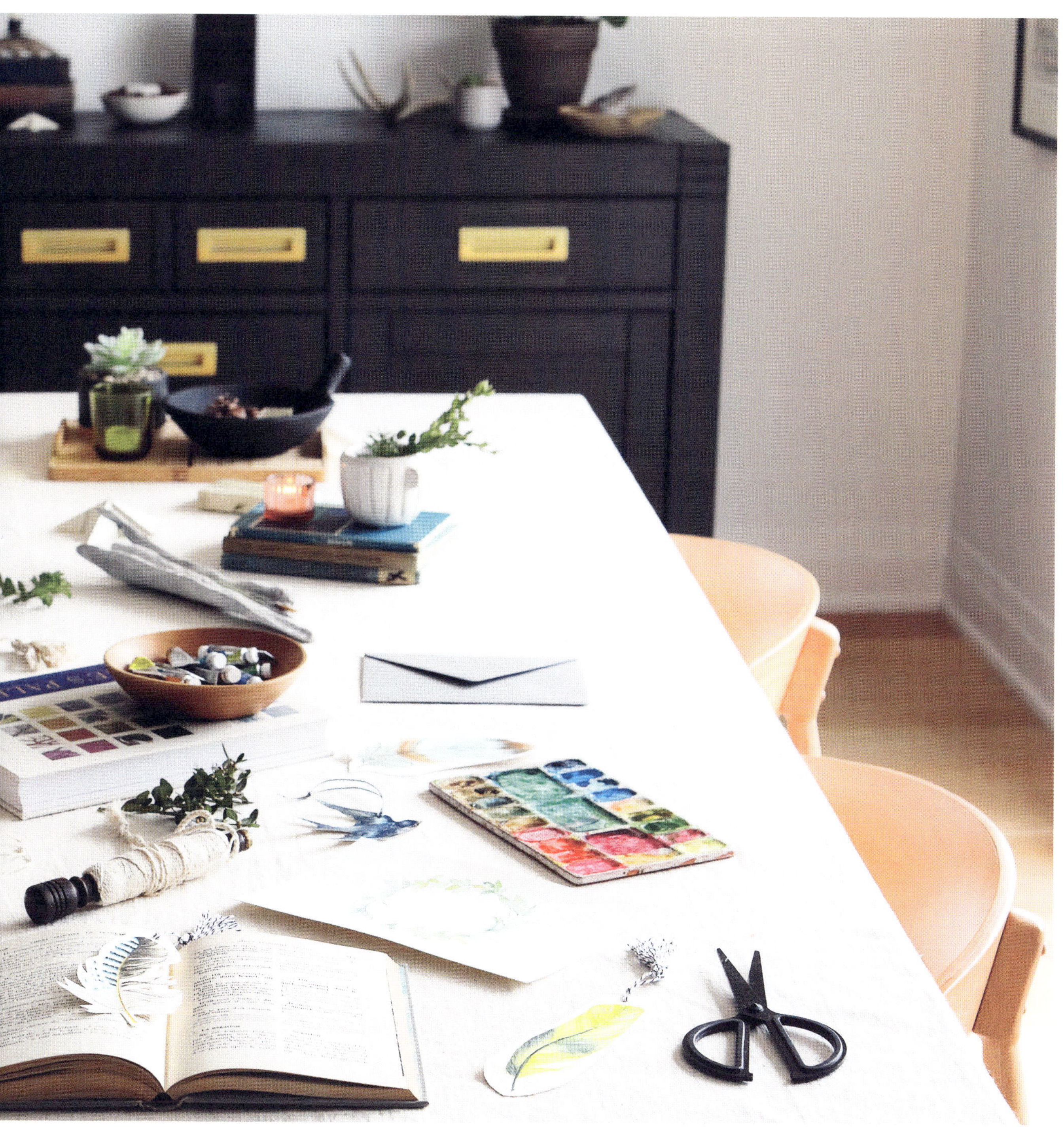

By now you should have stacks of watercolor paintings and are probably looking for things you can do with everything you've painted. Let's get creative with a few of these paintings and have fun with paper projects that I know you're going to love. I hope these projects help inspire you to use your paintings in unique ways and that you even share them with friends and family. You may be feeling apprehensive about sharing your work, especially if you're just beginning your watercolor journey, but sharing your artwork is inspiring to others and may even give them the courage to try as well.

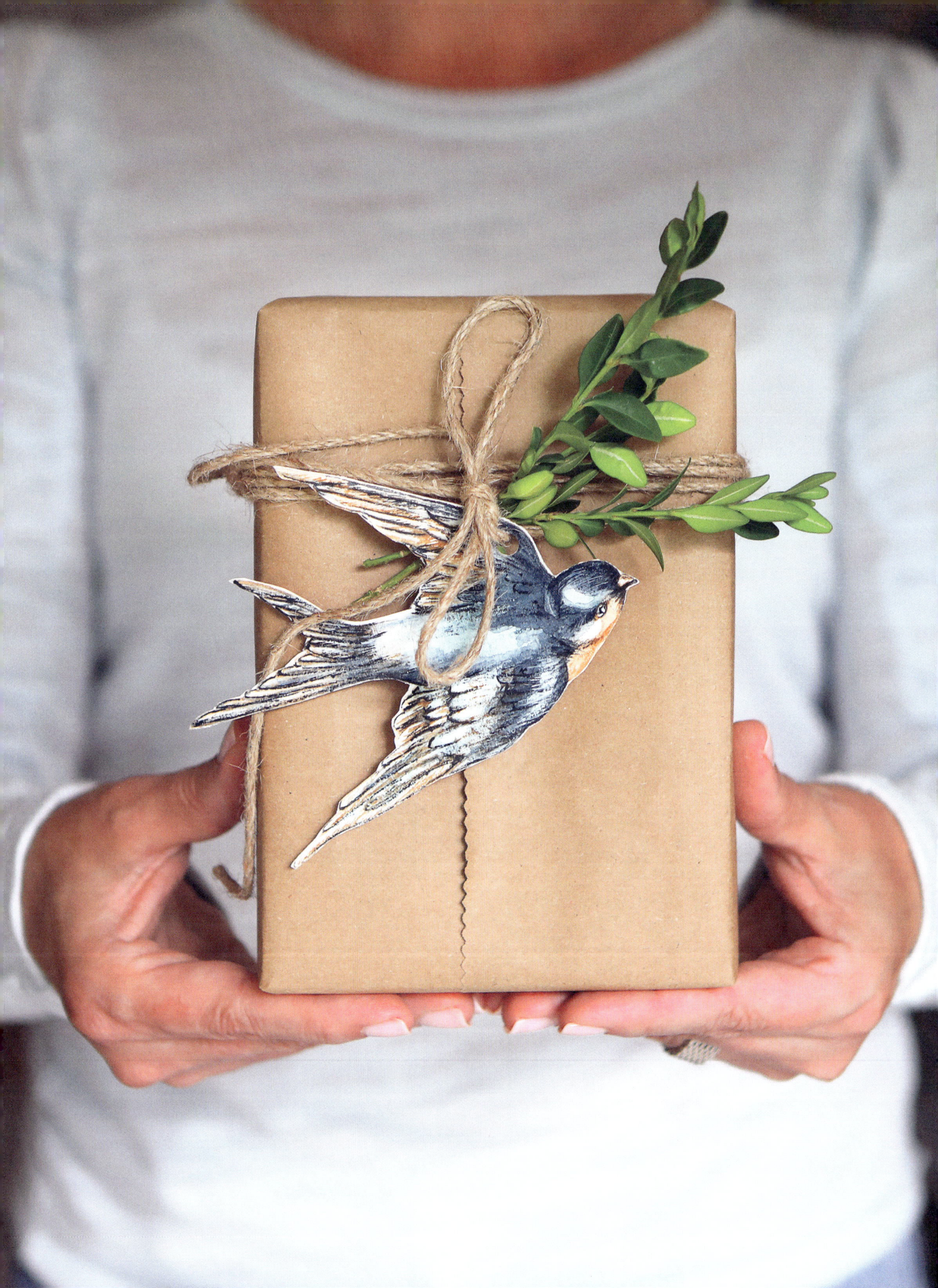

gift tag

Using art and creativity in areas of my everyday life is something that I hope to pass on to you with these paper projects. Let's have fun turning the swallow we painted into a very special gift tag that you can use to impress your friends and family. It really livens up a simple kraft paper–wrapped gift—especially when combined with a bit of greenery from the garden.

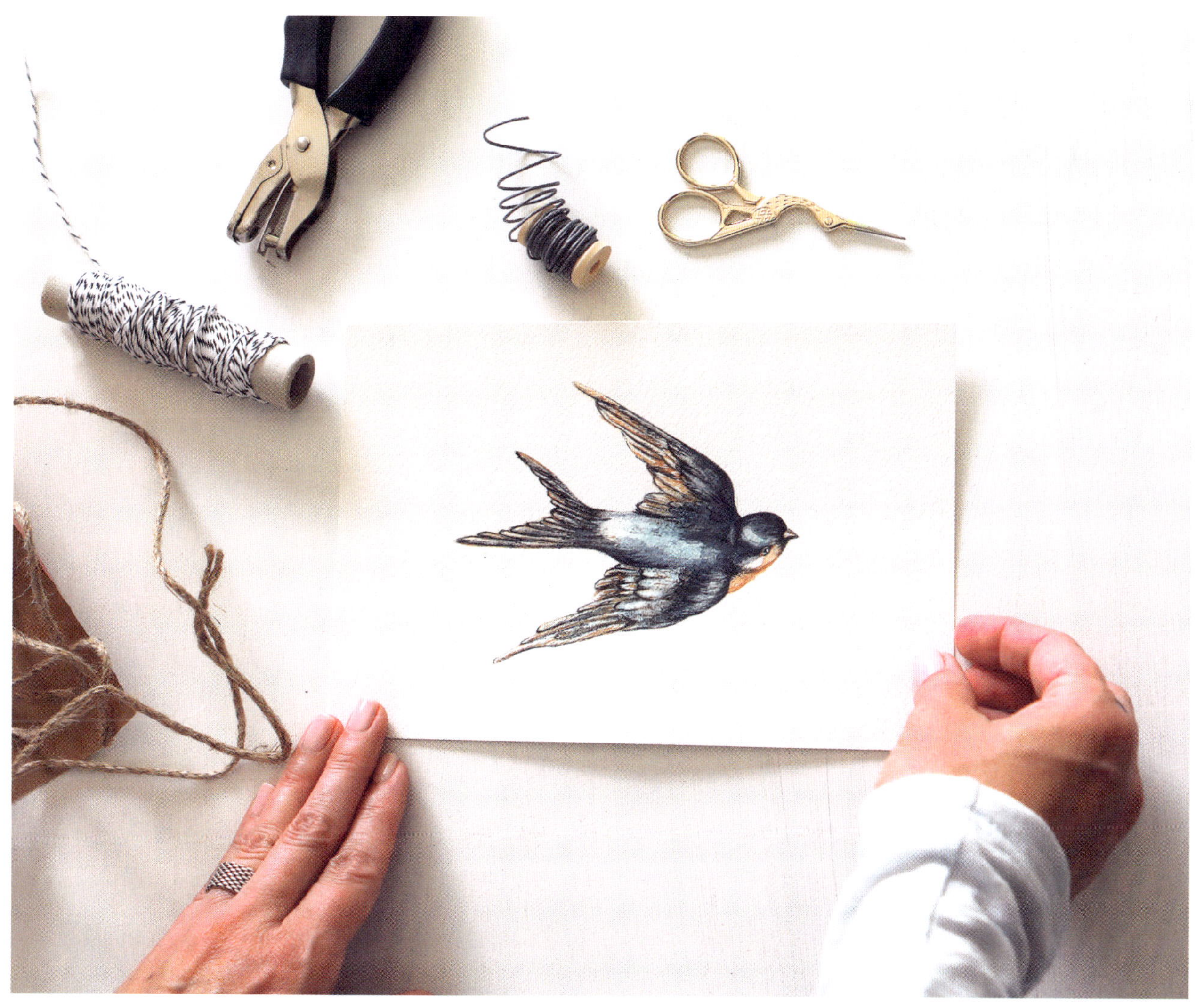

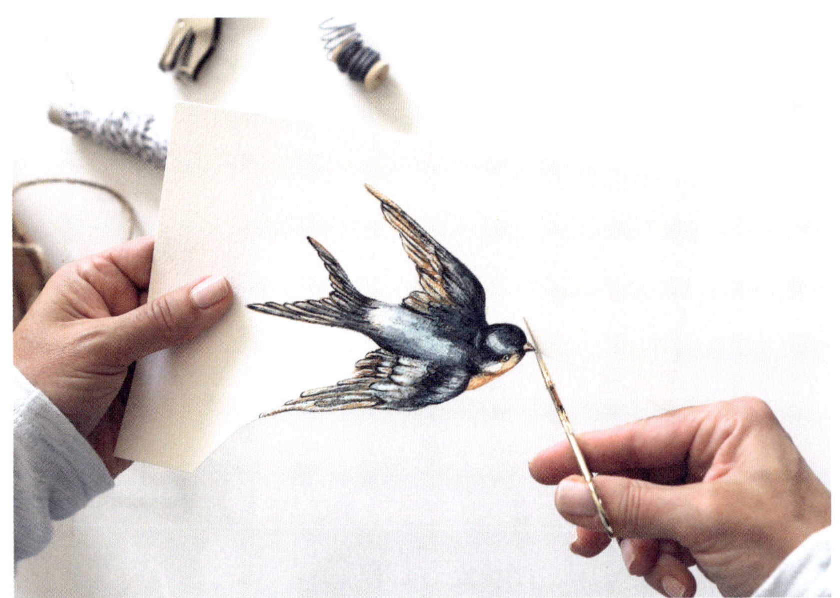

Carefully cut out the swallow that you painted.

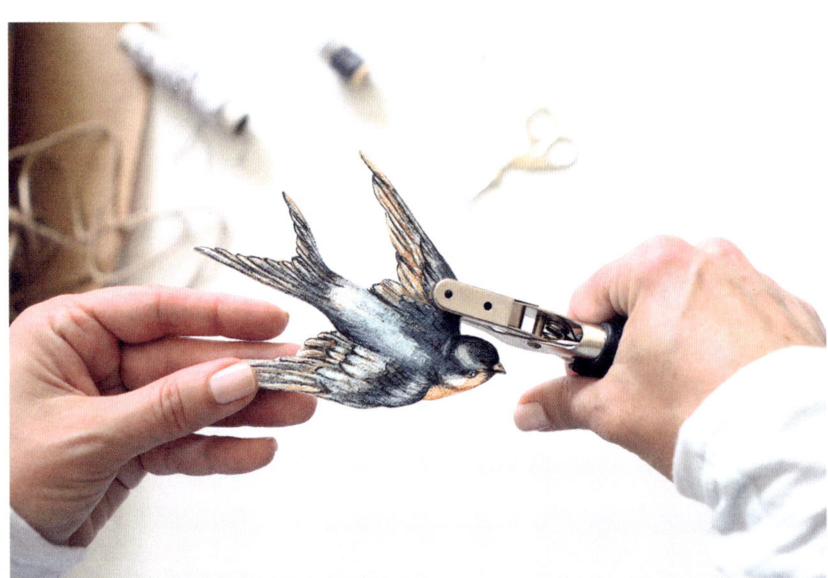

With a small hole punch or a threading needle, punch a hole at the top of the upper wing.

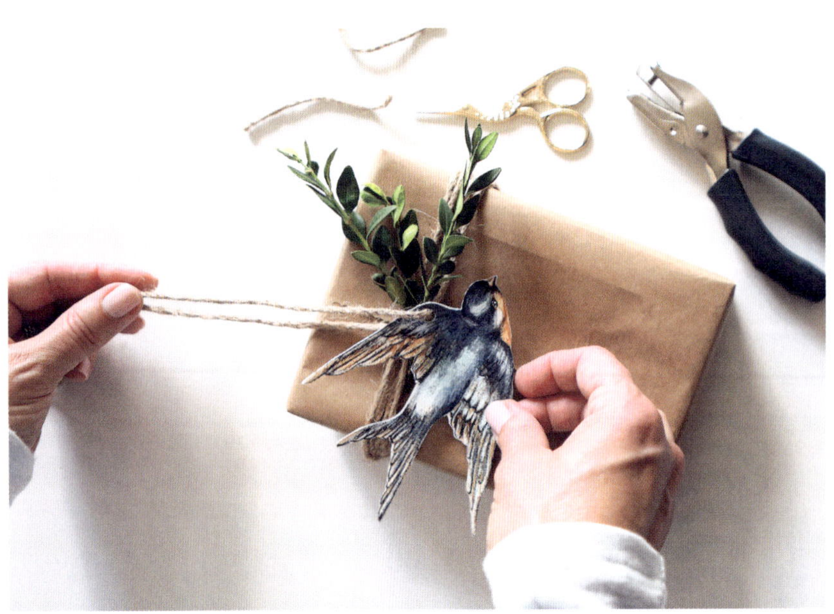

Cut a piece of the twine or ribbon long enough to wrap around your gift and leave it untied. Then feed the ends of the string through the hole punched in the wing of the bird. Carefully tie a knot at the end of the string and then tie a bow.

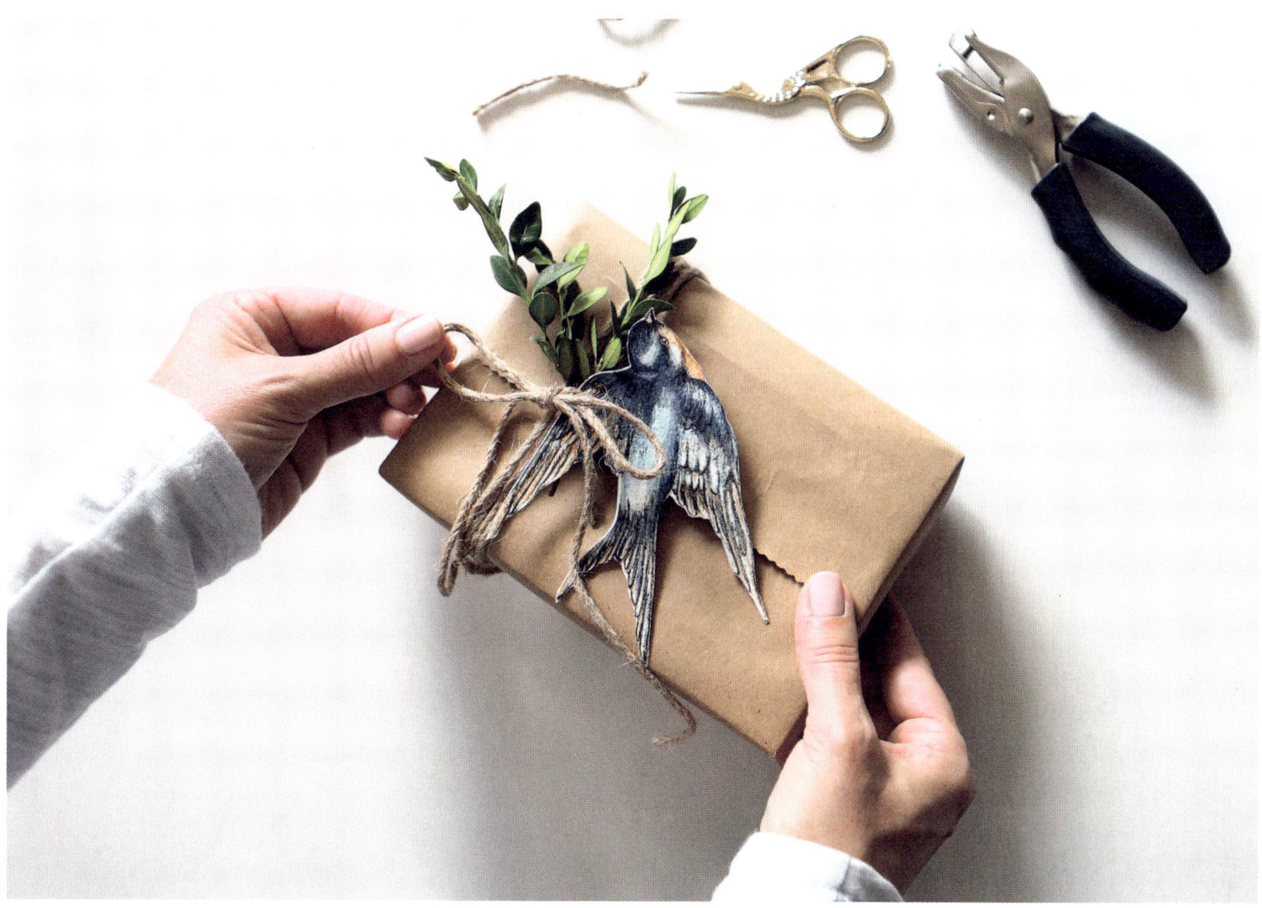

Tuck a sprig of greenery into the knot for an extra-special touch.

more ideas

Here are some other ways you can create beautiful, unique wrapping.

- Choose another painting to cut out for the gift tag, such as the Colorful Moth (page 82) or the Apple on a Stem (page 64).

- Tie the package with ribbon, yarn, metallic cord, or bakery string.

- Cut paintings you don't love into rectangles to create abstract painted gift tags.

- Instead of a sprig of greenery, personalize the package with a feather, dried flowers, or a small ornament.

- Wrap a gift in a painting, or even a sheet of watercolor paper you used to practice brushstrokes if you don't want to sacrifice a finished painting.

tip ······ If you choose to write a message on the back of the gift tag, do so before you attach the tag to the gift!

113

bookmark

If you're anything like me, you have stacks of books that you are reading, browsing through, or perhaps using for painting reference. I am always looking for bits of paper to tuck between pages that I want to find easily later. I started making these feather bookmarks a few years ago and have been gifting them to fellow book lovers too. Their shape and beauty are the perfect thing to mark your page with, and to open to, when looking back at the spot they hold in your book. Have fun with making tassels or even finding interesting ribbons to loop through the holes at the top.

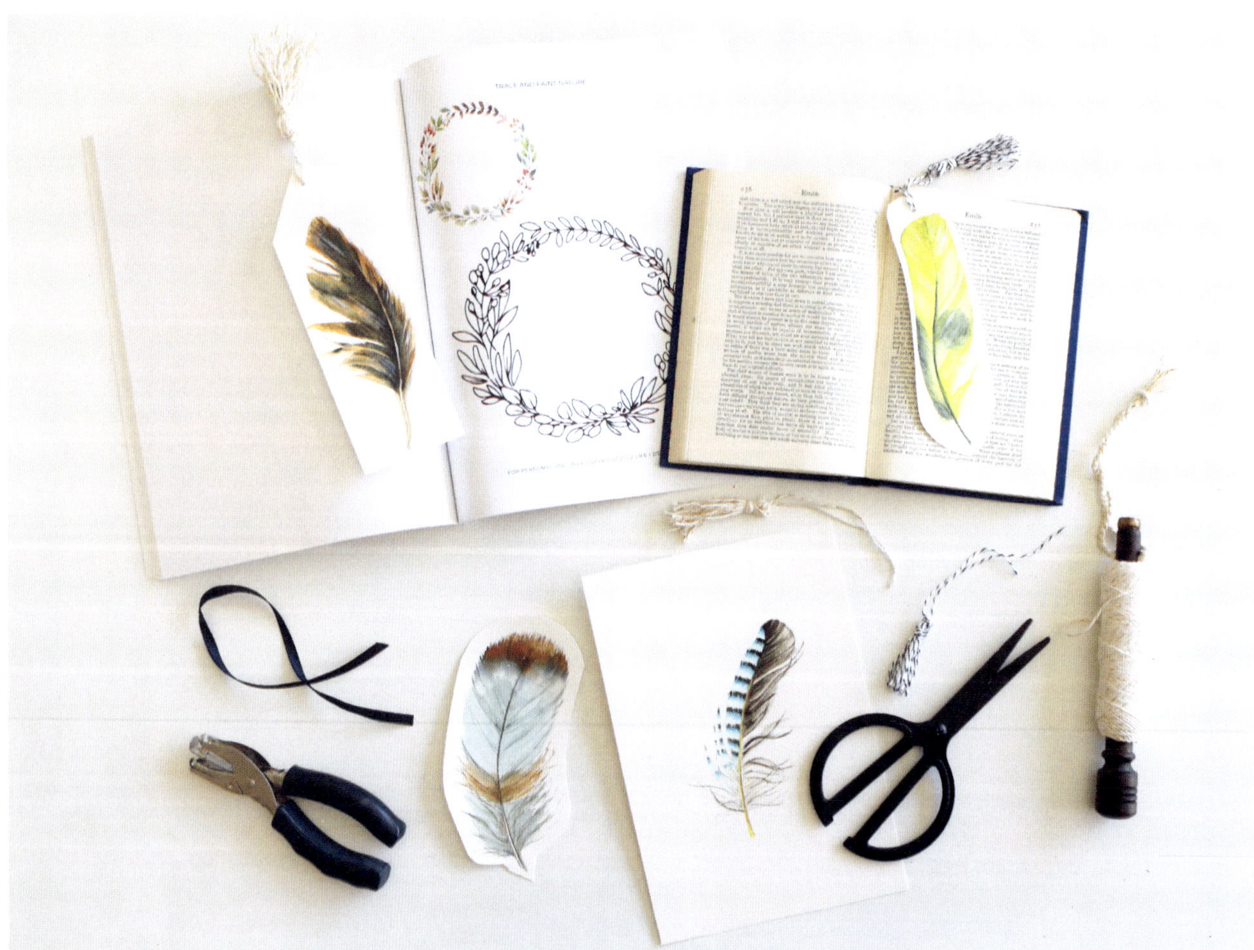

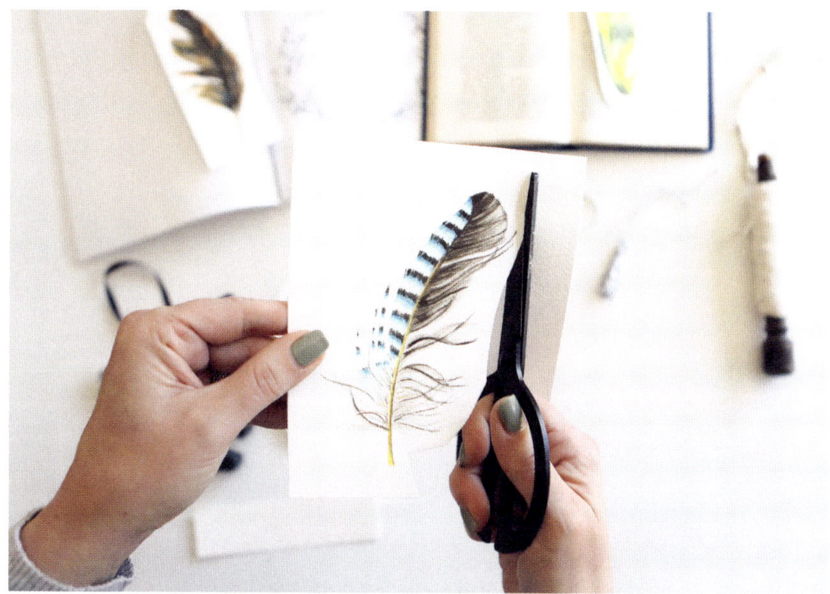

STEP 1

If desired, trace the template on page 131. Paint a few versions of the feather painting. You can also research some new feathers and try your hand at painting them. Carefully cut out the feather, leaving a small border around it. Leave a larger border at the top of the feather so there's room to punch the hole.

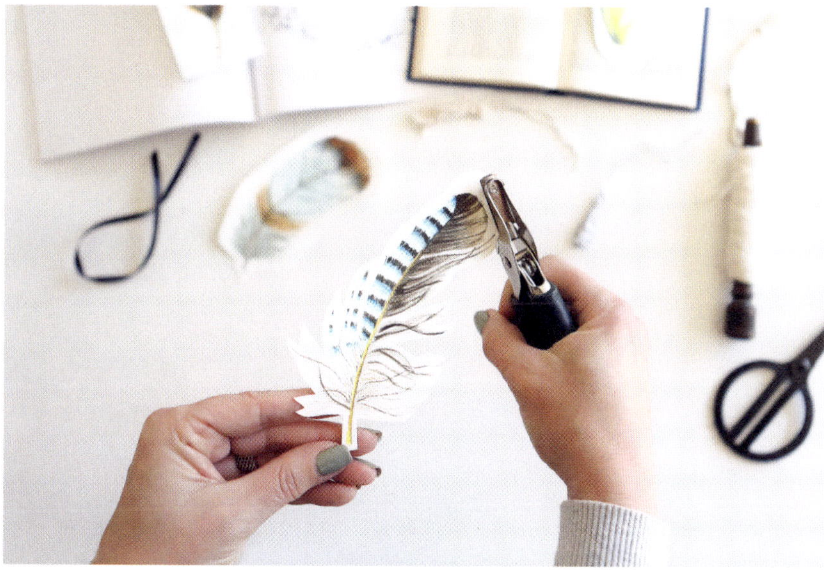

STEP 2

Use a hole punch to punch a hole at the top of the feather. If you don't have a hole punch, try using a needle to create a hole in the feather followed by a pencil or pen to increase the size of the hole.

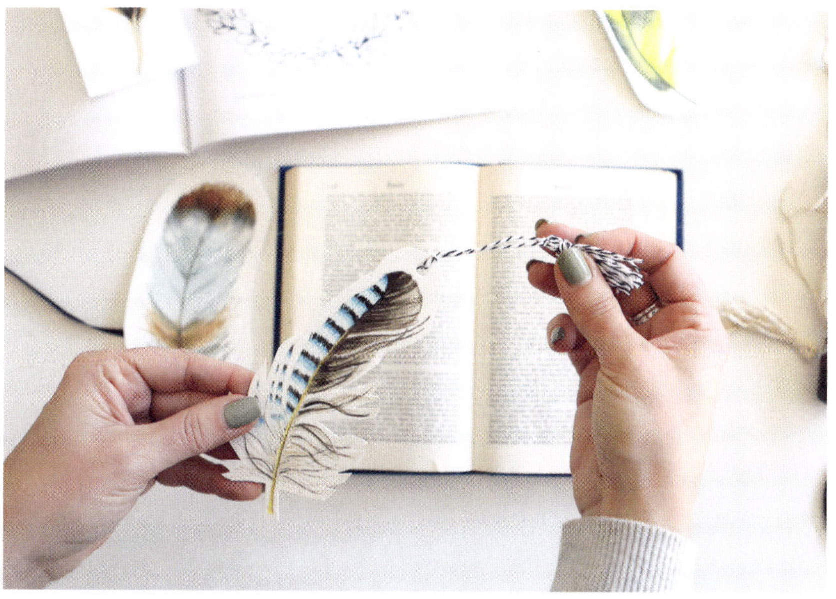

STEP 3

Choose thread, string, or even a tassel to thread through the hole. Knot the string and secure it in place.

tip ...... Write a message or an inspirational quote on the back of the feather using watercolor paint or a felt-tip marker.

ruler

watercolor paper—size should be as wide as the envelope and double the height

envelope of your choice (I am using 7¼ x 5¼ inches [18.4 x 13.3 cm])

greeting card

Making greeting cards has to be one of my favorite excuses to paint with watercolors. It's by far the easiest way to share your paintings with others. Keep it simple by using folded watercolor paper and purchase envelopes at your local craft store or online. Once you start gifting others your greeting card creations, you may never go back to store-bought cards. You can buy premade watercolor cards and envelopes, but making your own is quick and easy and less expensive.

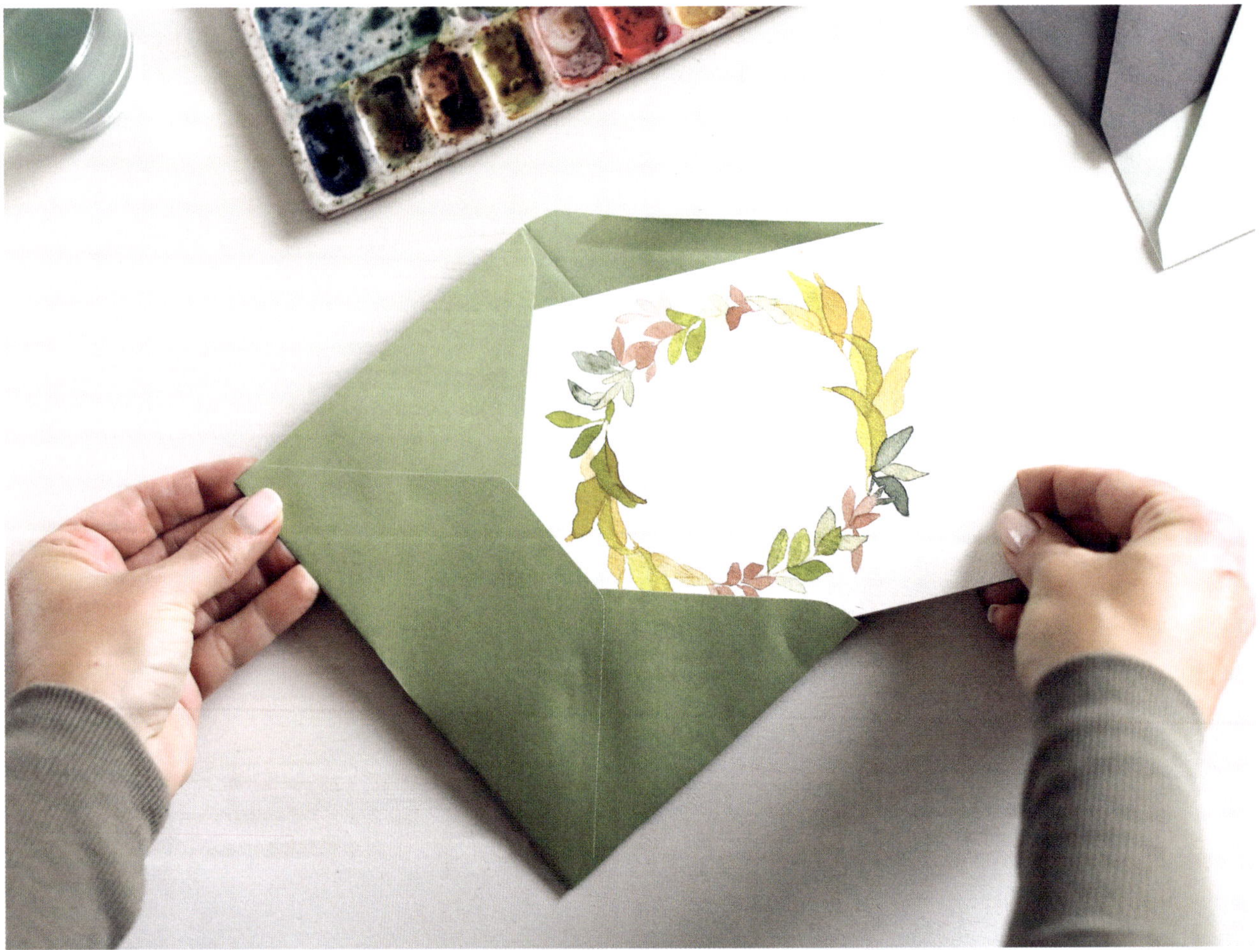

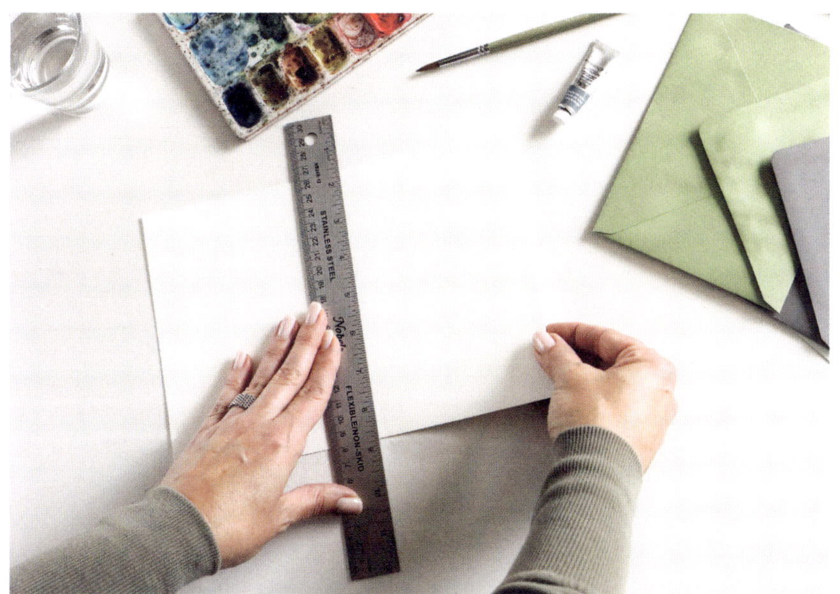

STEP 1

Measure the center of your watercolor paper at the longest end of your paper. Score the center of the watercolor paper using a ruler and the back of a watercolor brush. This will give you an indentation, making it easier to fold the paper at the end of the project.

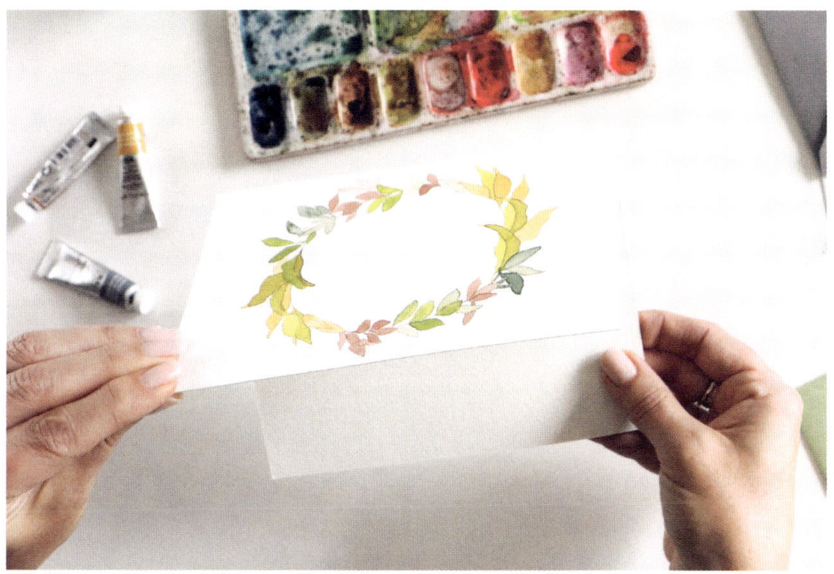

STEP 2

Paint the Leafy Wreath (page 60) or other design using the colors of your choice. When your wreath painting is dry, fold the card using the indentation and your ruler to give the paper a sharp edge.

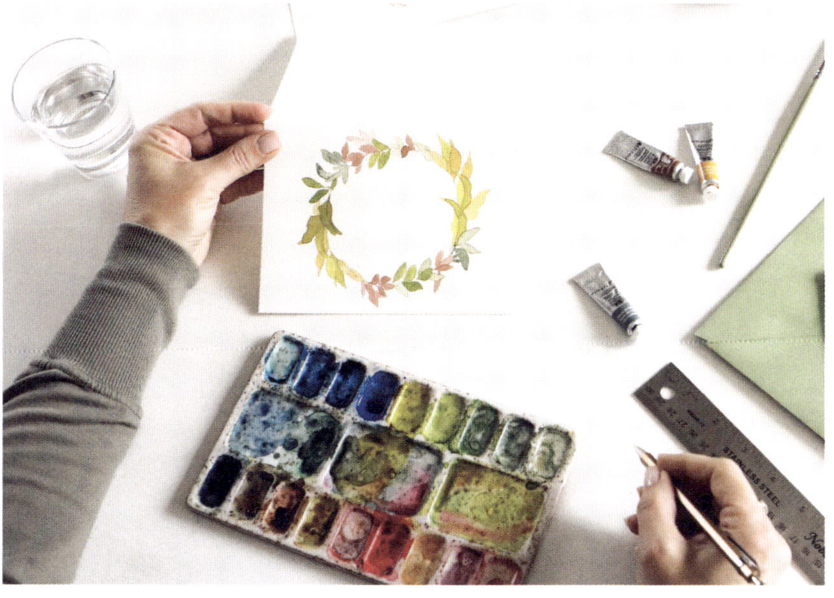

STEP 3

Write your message inside the folded card. Put it in the envelope.

t i p ······ If you choose, you can also paint on a piece of watercolor paper and attach it using double-sided tape or a glue stick to a card that fits the envelope of your choice.

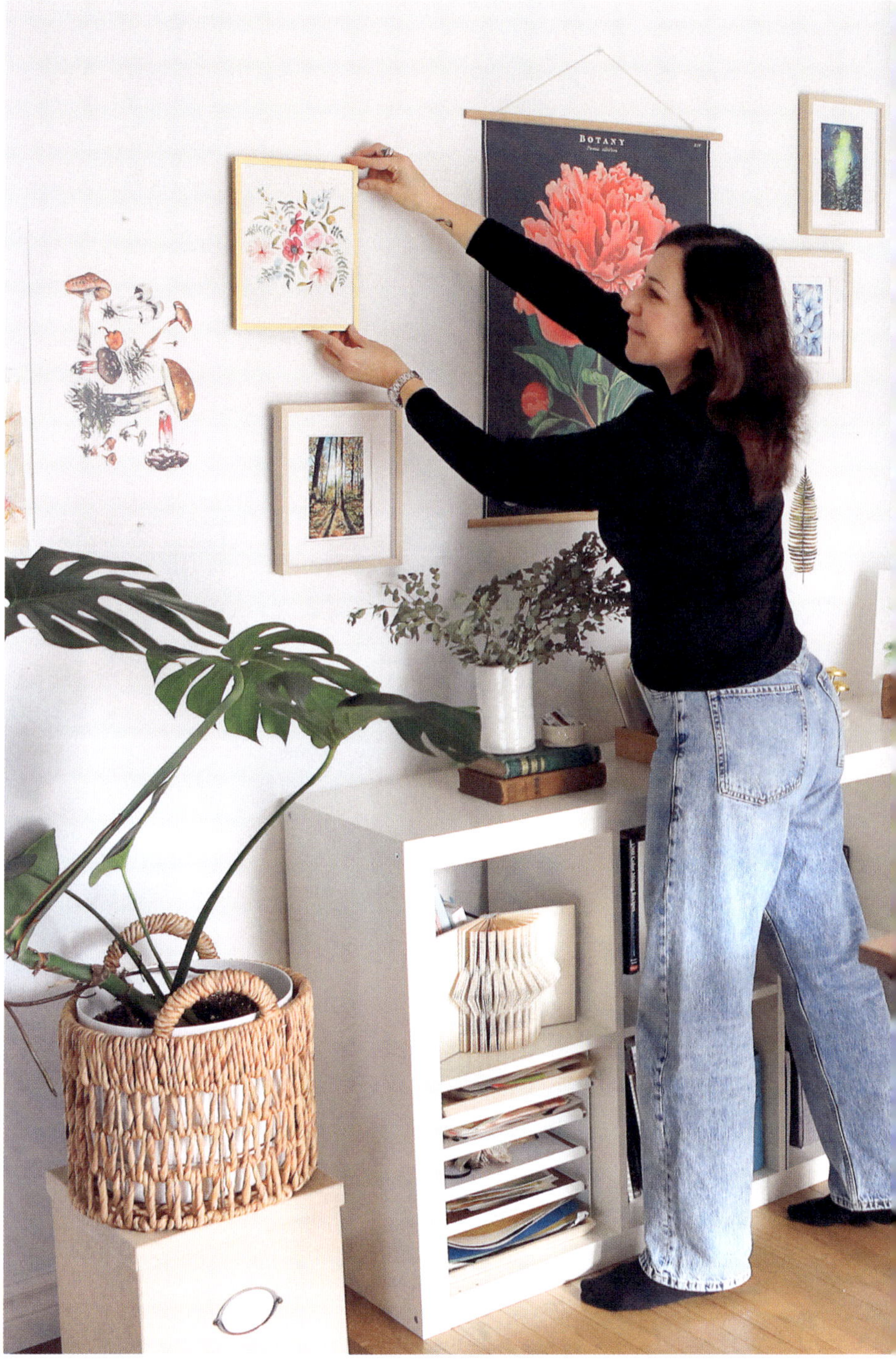

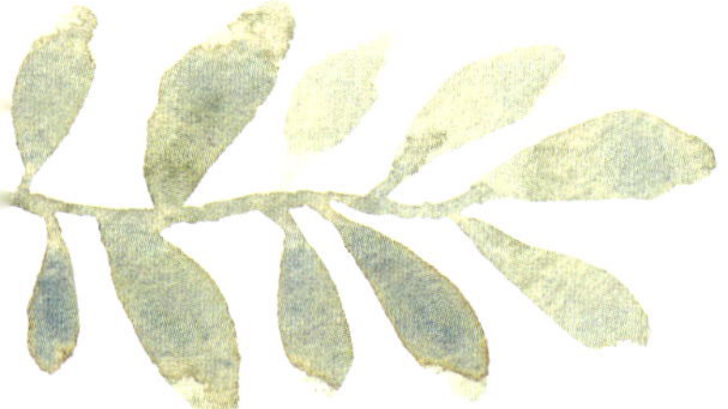

8

BEYOND PAINTING

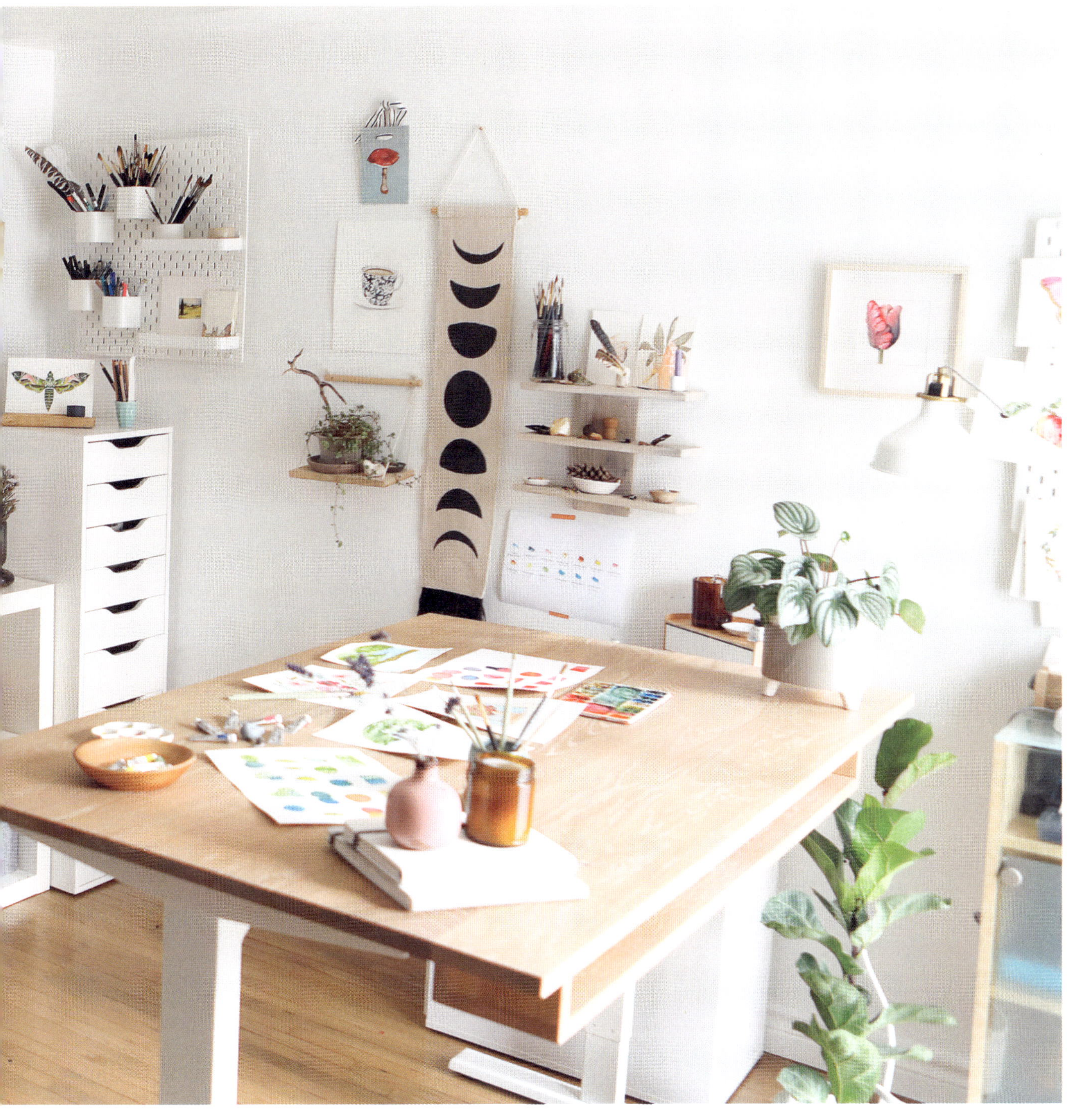

Let me start off by saying, "Congratulations!" If you've made it this far in the book and have practiced all my methods for using watercolor paints, then you are well on your way to really honing your watercolor skills and confidence. I hope at this point you're starting to own the title of "artist" or even maybe "watercolorist" and feel proud of all that you have learned and painted. Now it's time to have fun with the paintings that didn't turn out so well and to celebrate the ones that surprised you and are frame-worthy.

WHAT TO DO WITH PAINTINGS YOU DON'T LOVE

This fun and empowering exercise that I teach in my Watercolors Made Simple online class has become a favorite of many students. It's one that can help you clear some clutter from your painting desk and really focus in on parts of a painting that you didn't notice before.

Enjoy making new art, including abstract art from these new cuttings, and let them inspire more practice. The more you can connect to your new watercolor skills and have a relaxed approach to your art, the more joyful and fulfilling the experience will be. Chances are, you'll want to continue to paint and explore even more.

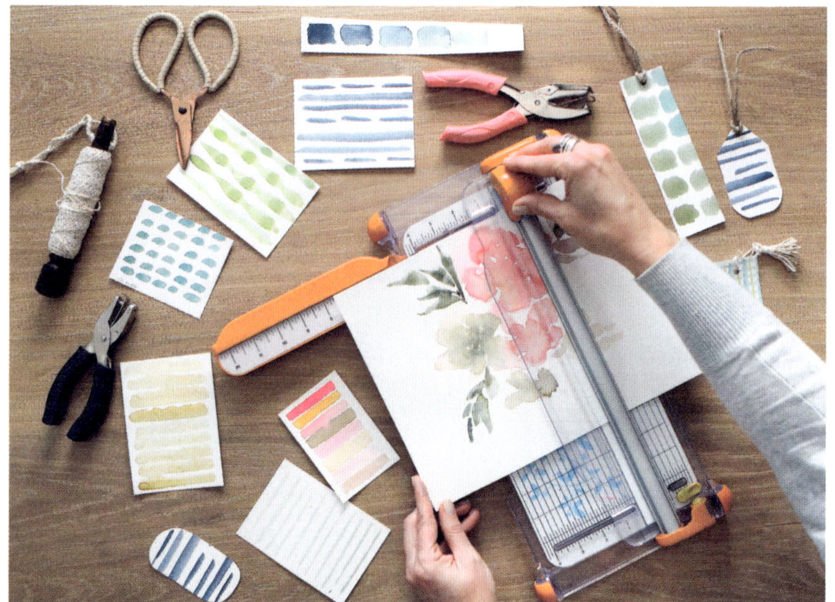

STEP 1

Gather up some paintings or practice sheets that you're okay with cutting up. (Hint: Use the practice sheets from the beginning chapters.) Then grab a paper cutter, or scissors and a ruler, and cut up that sheet. You can approach this step in two different ways. The first is to just cut the sheet into quarters and observe how each quarter now holds a unique section of the painting. Or you can look for unique textures, washes, and color blends and cut out those areas into shapes, such as squares or rectangles.

STEP 2

Turn your new cut pieces into bookmarks (page 114) or gift tags (page 110). Use them as a tool to continue to grow your observational skills and knowledge around how watercolor paint moves, dries, and behaves. You can even put the pieces into your sketchbook for future reference when working on a painting.

HOW TO PROTECT WATERCOLOR PAINTINGS

Because dry watercolor can be activated with water, we need to protect all our hard work and our finished paintings. I recommend you use a spray sealant, fixative, or varnish to protect your work. Even if I will be framing a painting behind glass, I use a spray to ensure that the painting is protected and lasts a long time.

When looking for a spray, choose one that offers UV protection and is nonyellowing. There are sprays that have a gloss finish, a matte finish, or a satin finish.

Whatever finish you choose, the method of application is most important.

It's better to spray multiple light coats of sealant rather than one heavy coat. You want to ensure that you don't overly wet the painting or it will start to run and bleed. Allow each coat to dry before spraying the next. I recommend three to five light coats to ensure even coverage. Taking the time to protect your paintings means they will last for years to come.

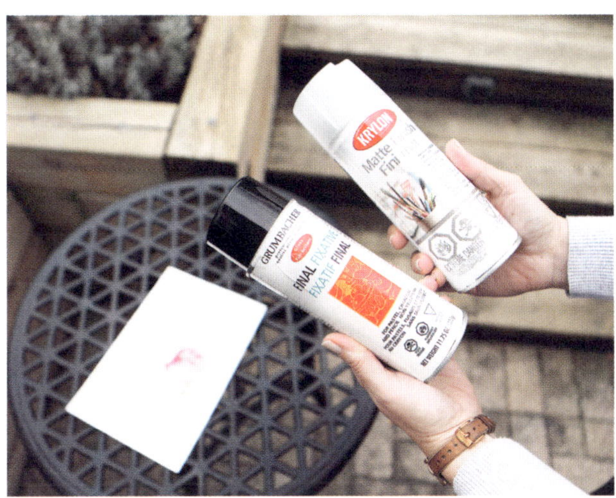

Spray sealants are widely available and come in different finishes.

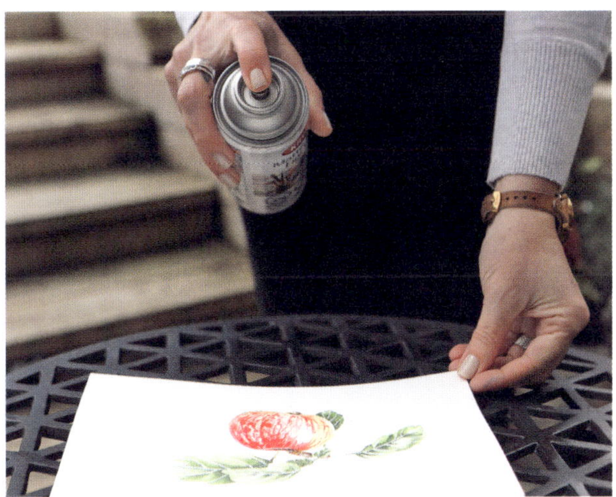

Due to the toxic nature of spray varnish, spray outside if possible or, at the very least, in a well-ventilated room.

FRAMING YOUR PAINTINGS

It's time to celebrate your favorite paintings. I encourage you to frame paintings you love and hang them where you and others can enjoy your hard work. Look for fun and unique ways to frame and hang your paintings and really be proud to display your art.

You'll be surprised at how much framing a painting can really change the way you look at your artwork. A white mat border frames paintings in a unique way and can easily create focal points. I love searching for vintage frames in secondhand shops to give my paintings a unique look and feel. Other times, I use simple frames that help keep the focus on the art. Here is where you can express your personal style and have a lot of fun with framing your pieces.

Get creative. Use different papers as backgrounds to mount your paintings. I cut out feathers that I painted and glued them onto old vintage book pages, then mounted them onto black cardstock. It creates a completely different look and feel.

Use your framed paintings as gifts or create a gallery wall in your painting area for an extra boost of inspiration. Most importantly, celebrate the ones that make you happy and excited to sit down and paint again and again.

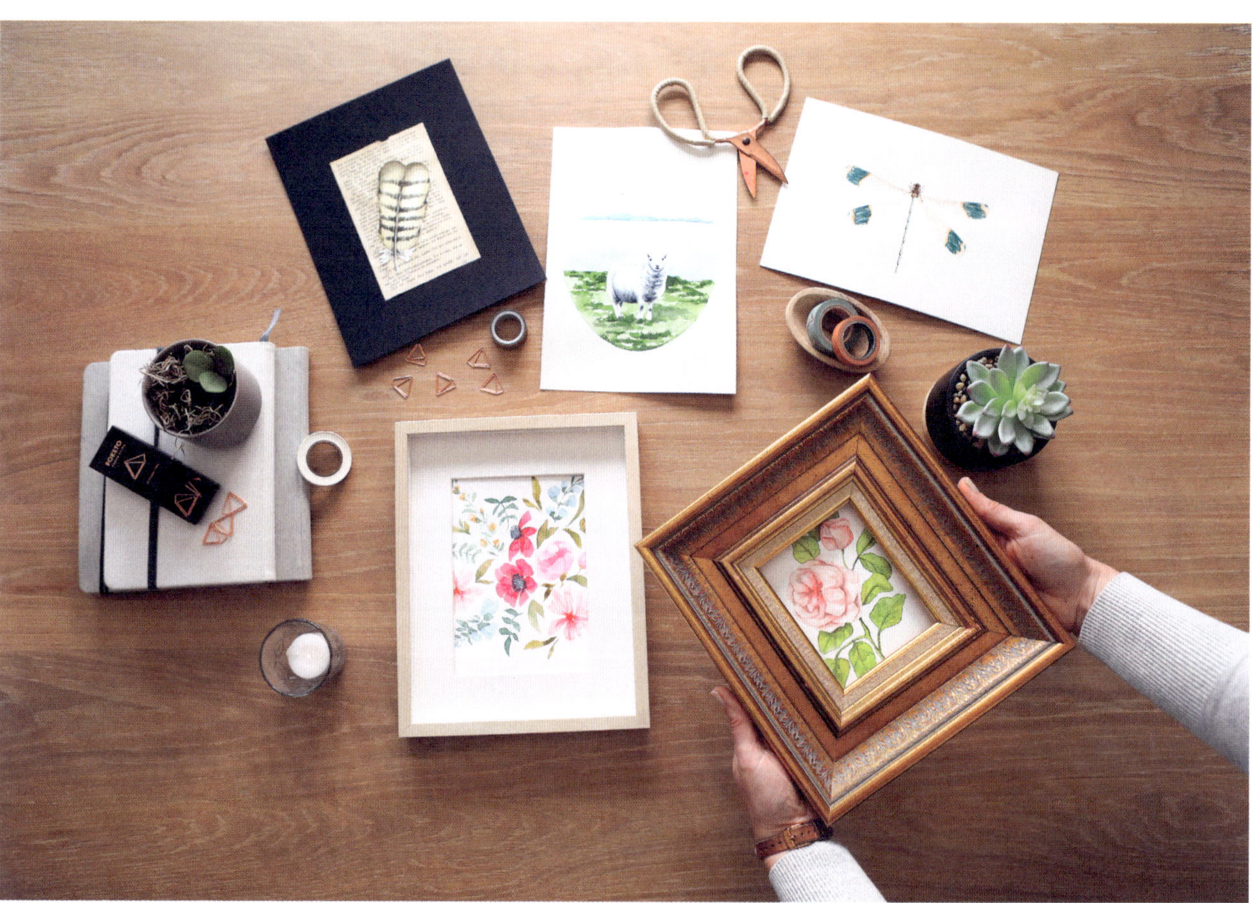

Have fun trying out a variety of mats and frames to showcase your work.

t i p ······ Before you frame your painting, don't forget to sign and date it.

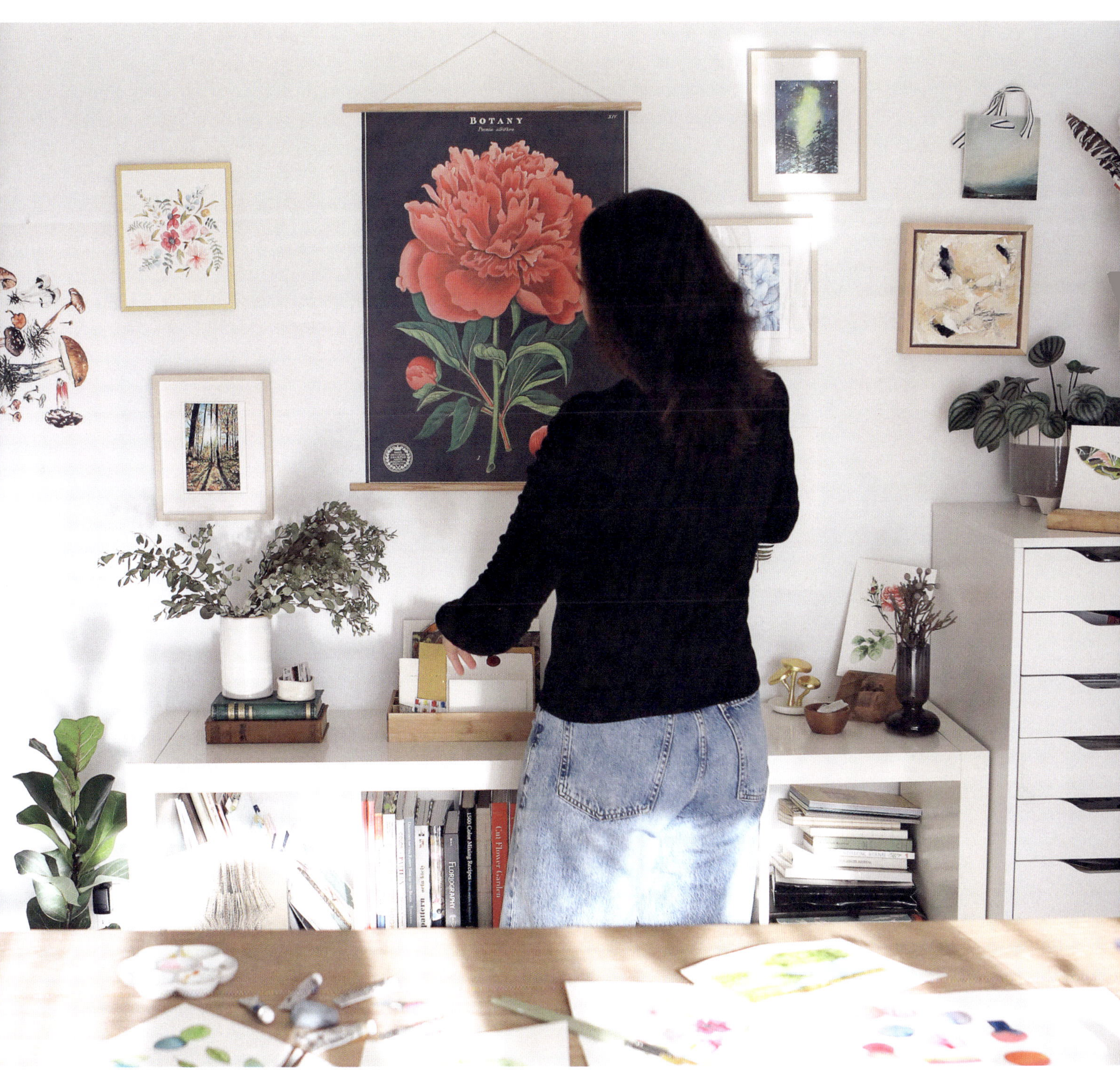

My studio walls are filled with my paintings. They help me stay inspired to paint!

NEXT STEPS

Now that you have learned and practiced foundational watercolor techniques, and you've painted all the projects in this book, I want you to take a moment and really let it all sink in. Learning something new and stretching yourself out of your comfort zone requires a lot of energy and courage. Painting and making art is very much like openly expressing a personal side of yourself. It can make you feel a little exposed as your creation is out in the world for everyone to witness and perhaps even judge—this includes self-judgment.

Remember that your art practice is just that… it's *yours* to embrace and enjoy. I want you to paint because you are called to paint and there's a part of you that needs to be expressed through the practice of picking up a brush and putting it to paper.

Release yourself from perfectionism. Embrace the imperfect marks, blobs, and mishaps that you will no doubt experience as you practice and explore watercolor. I still experience painting sessions that don't go well; and yes, it doesn't feel great when it happens, but know that every single time you sit down to paint, you connect to a side of you that will be energized by watching beautiful brushstrokes of color come to life. That is a lovely experience that we as artists get to enjoy over and over again. Aren't we lucky?

Don't push yourself when you feel tension in your art practice. We have all been there, done that. Sometimes when we are tired, stressed, not feeling well, or distracted, it'll be reflected in our painting session. I recommend that you step away from your art practice, take a walk in nature, enjoy a yummy meal, play music, and let your senses be filled with colors, shapes, imagery, and other forms of art. When you take these moments to fill up your creative energy bucket, you will return to your art practice more relaxed and with more ideas. Give it a try the next time you feel tension in your art practice. You'll be amazed at what a creative break can do for you.

Thank you for spending this time with me on your watercolor journey. I hope that you continue to practice, grow, and enjoy painting using my favorite paint medium. Remember to paint imagery that you are drawn to and use colors that you love, and you'll enjoy your watercolor painting practice even more.

For now, keep exploring, practicing, and growing your watercolor skills and confidence.

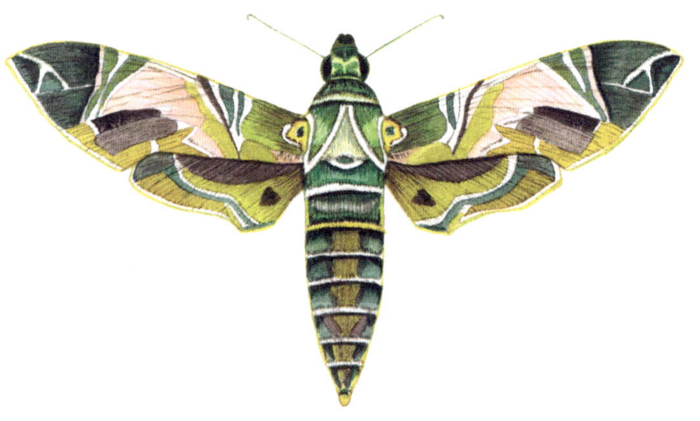

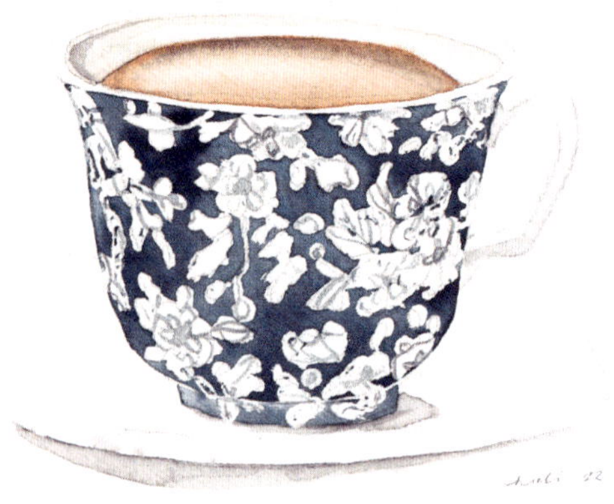

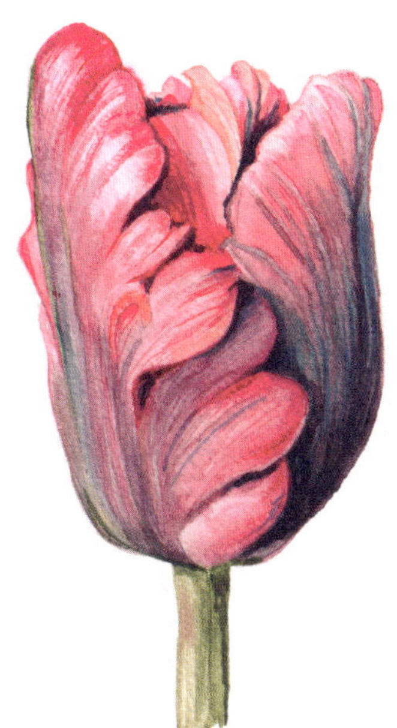

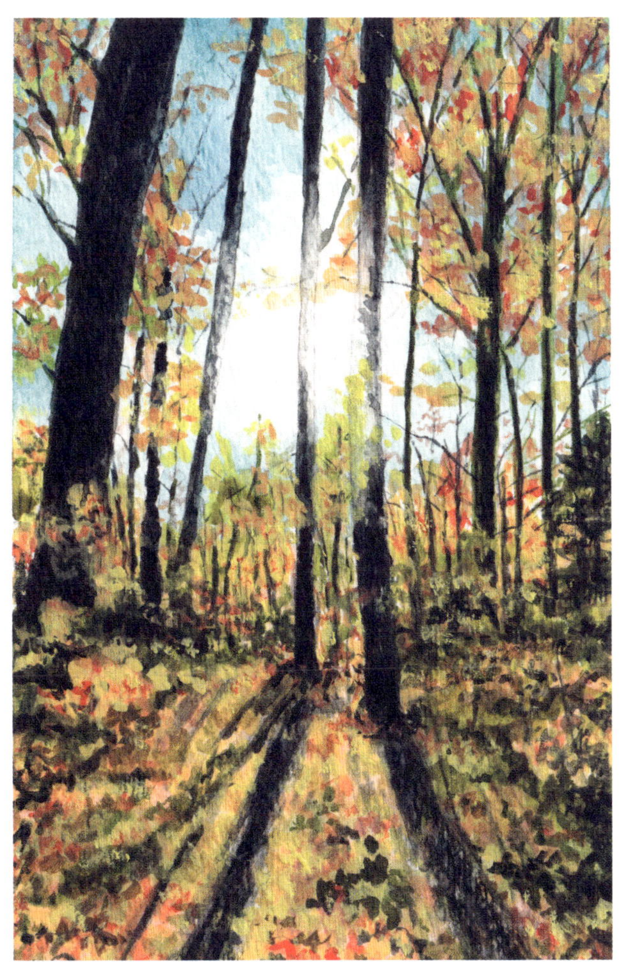

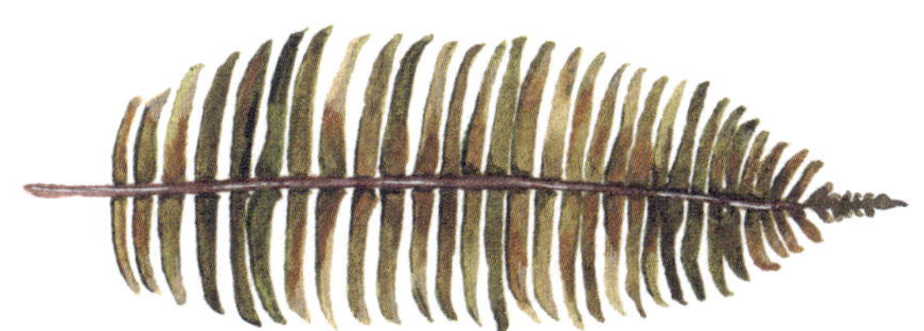

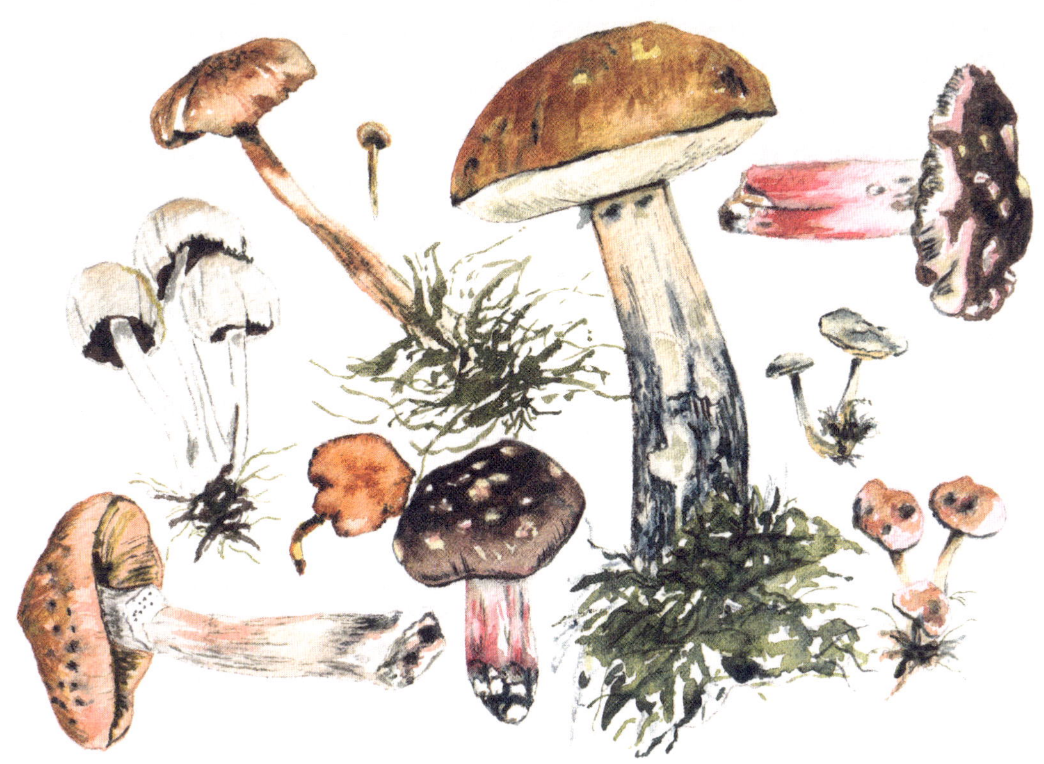

TRACE-AND-PAINT TEMPLATES

I have provided templates of all the projects in the book that you can use to jump-start your paintings. **Scan the code below to download the full-size templates.** Here are a few ways that I recommend you trace these line drawings.

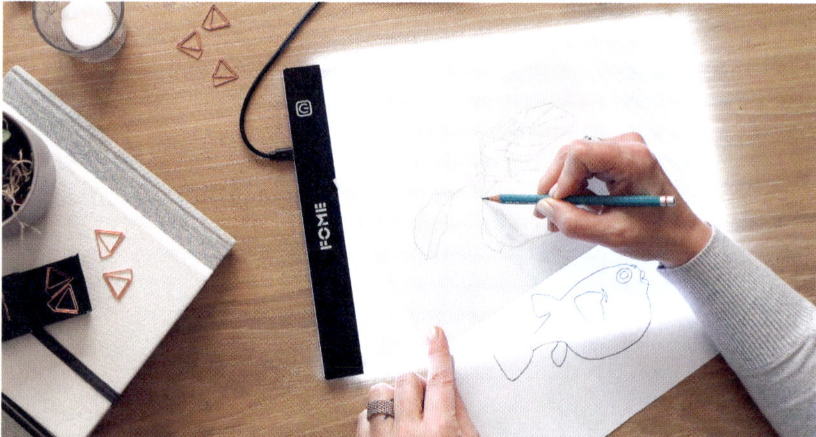

Light box method

Place the drawing directly onto a light box and lay a fresh watercolor sheet on top. With the light on, lightly trace the line drawing onto the surface of your watercolor paper.

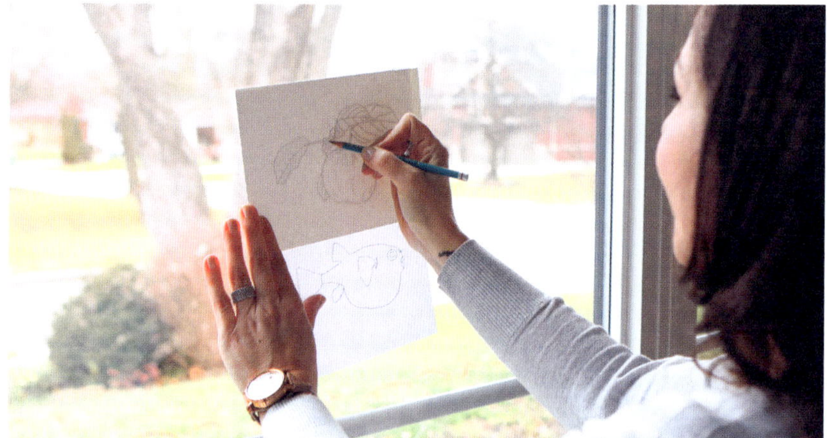

Window method

If you don't have a light box, you can do the same thing with a window. You don't need a sunny day to do this, simply some light to shine through so you can see the lines to trace using a pencil.

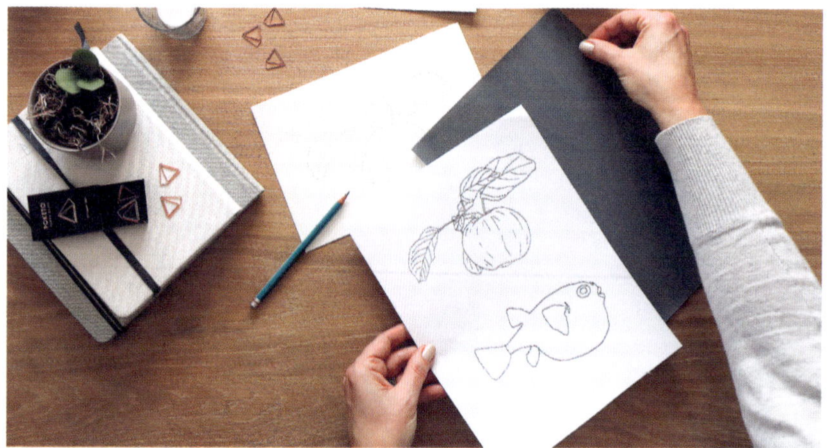

Transfer paper method

Another way to transfer the line drawing is to place a sheet of graphite transfer paper onto watercolor paper. Next, place the page that you want to trace onto the transfer paper. Press down firmly as you trace the line drawing that you want to paint.

SCAN TO
DOWNLOAD

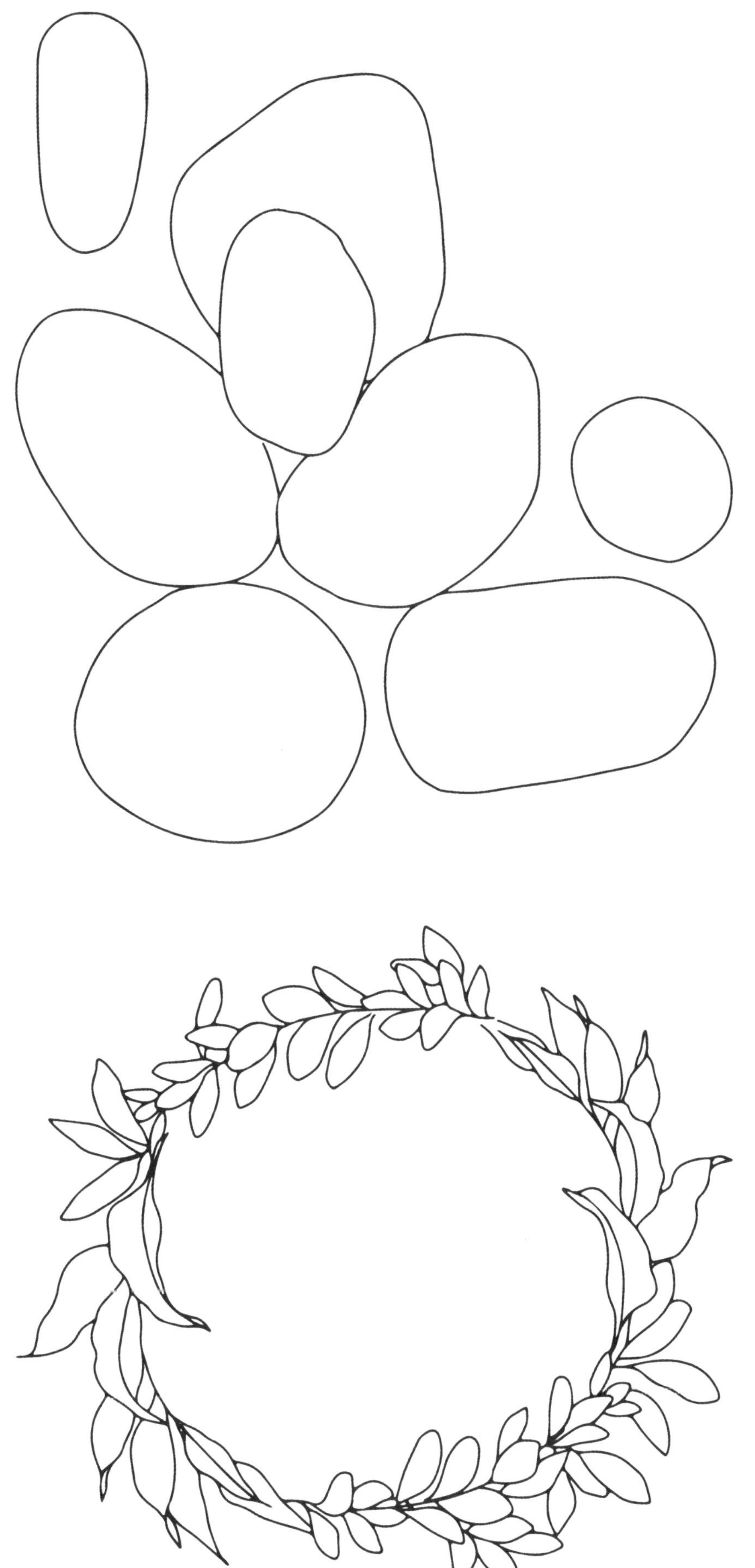

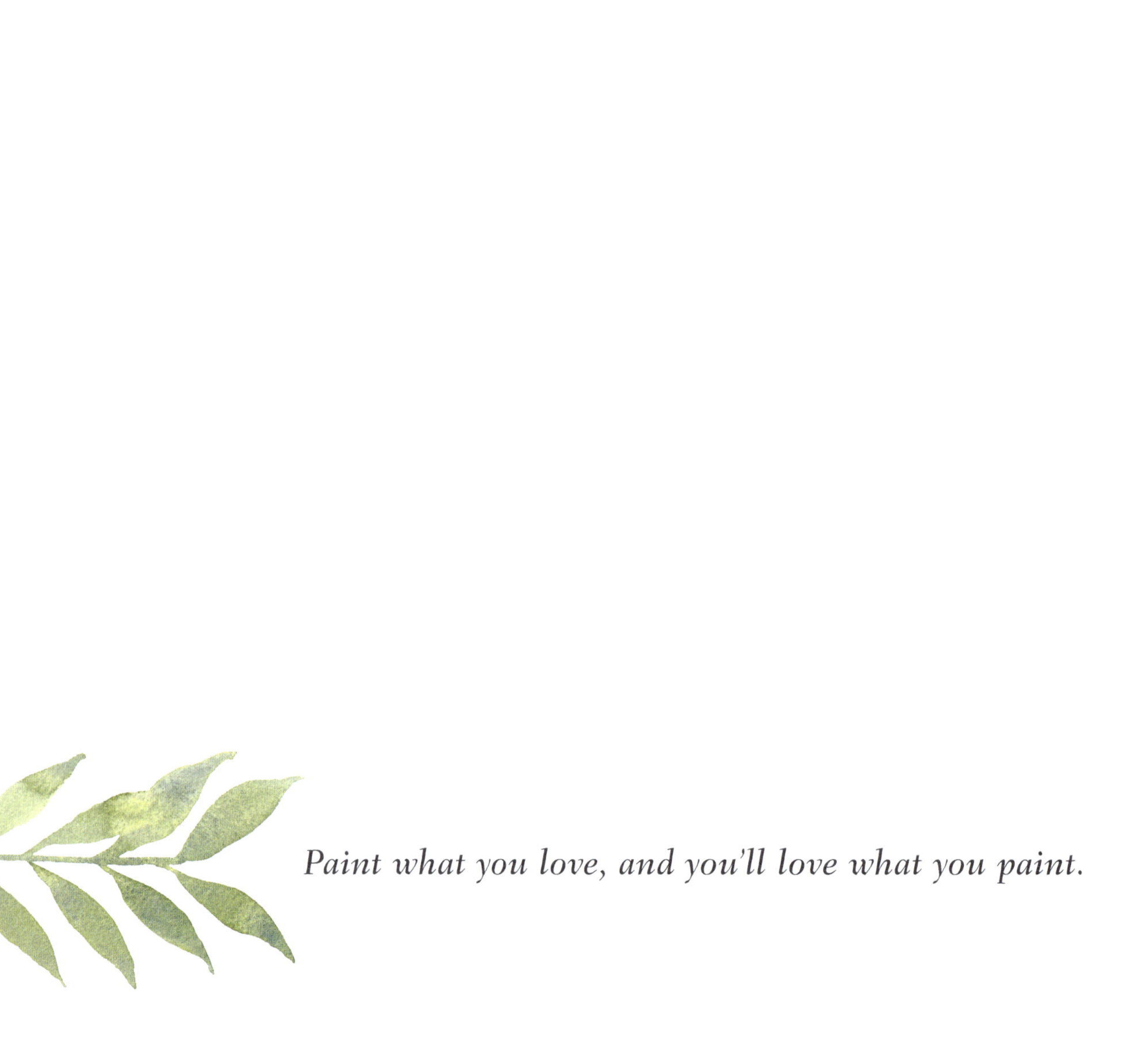

Paint what you love, and you'll love what you paint.

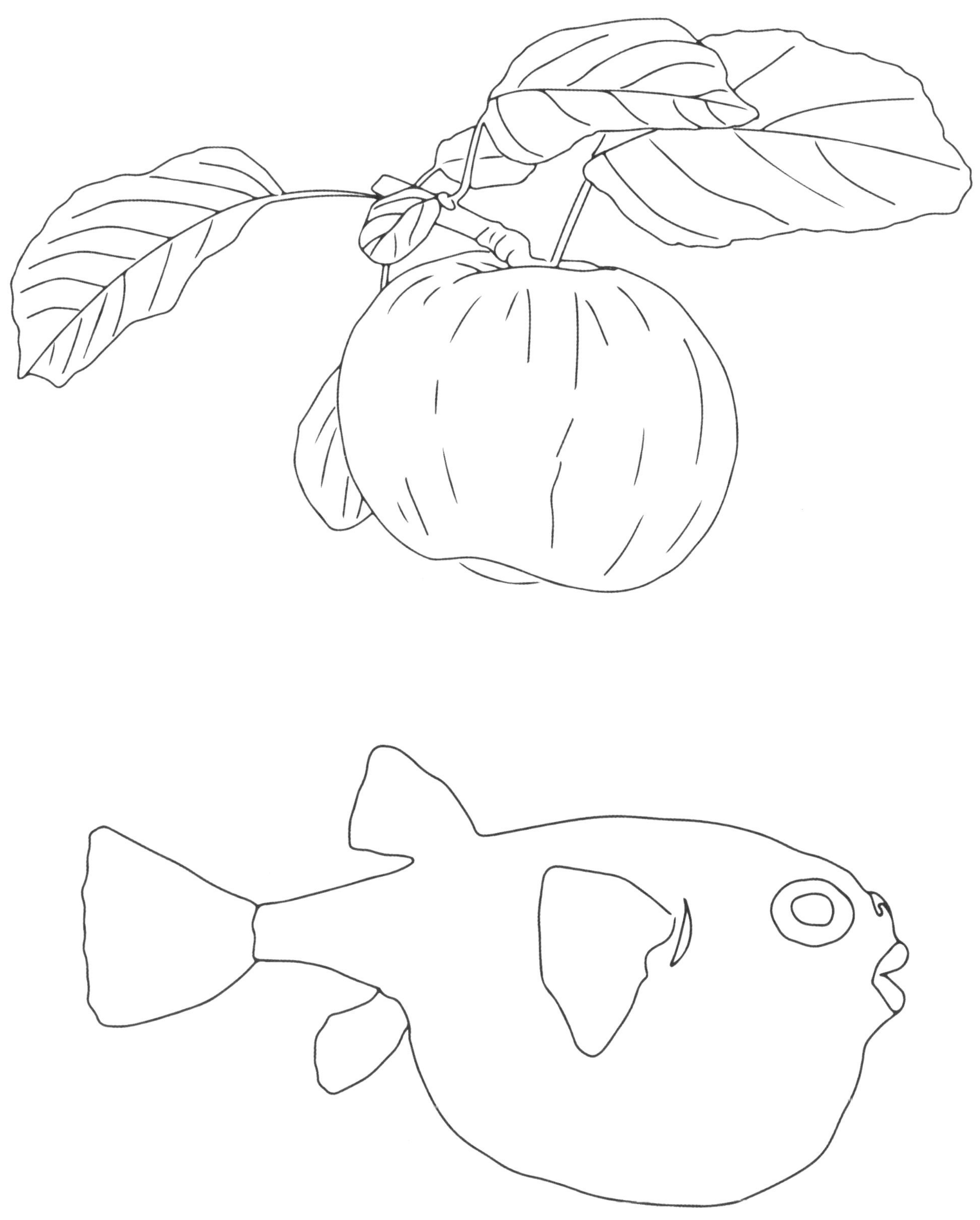

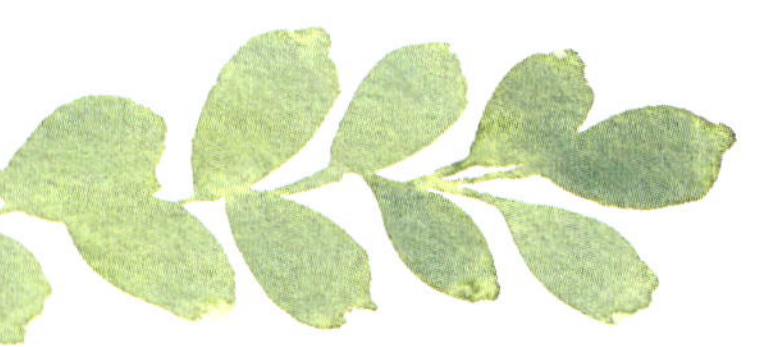

Every time you practice,
your watercolor skills and confidence will grow.

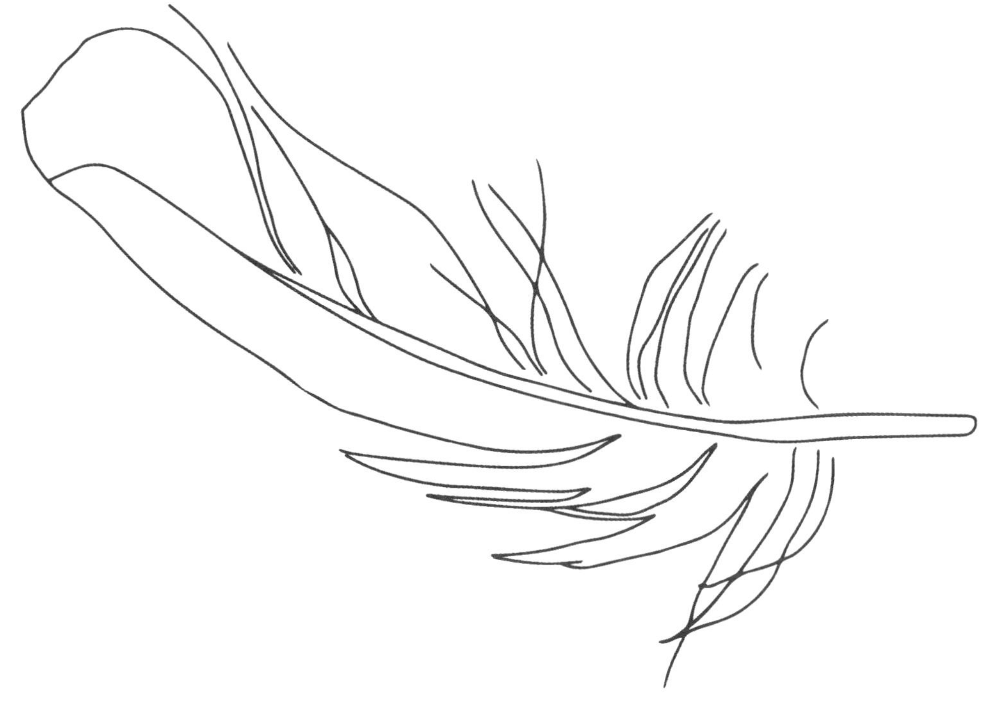

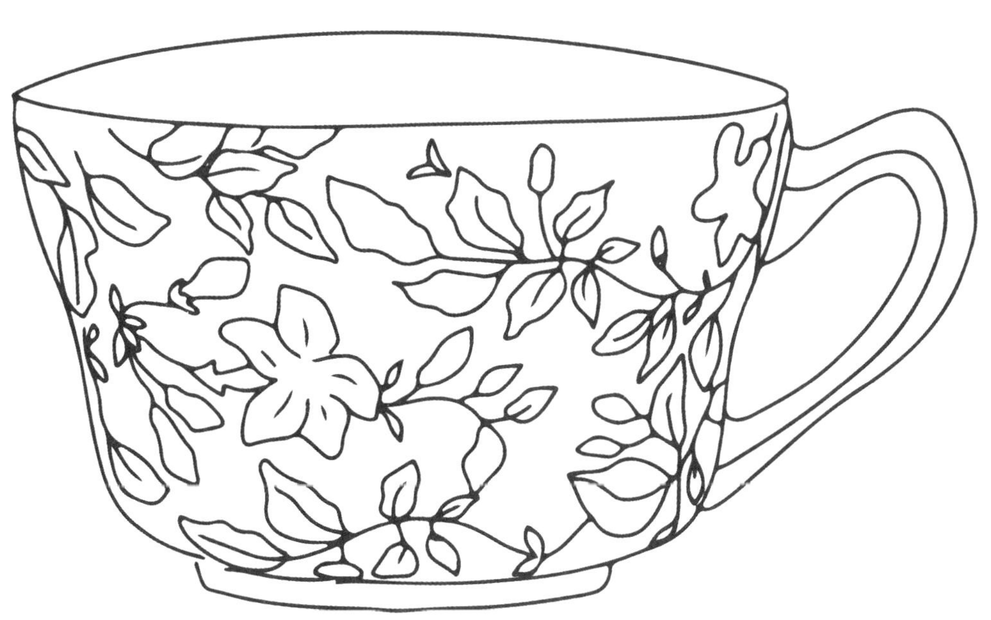

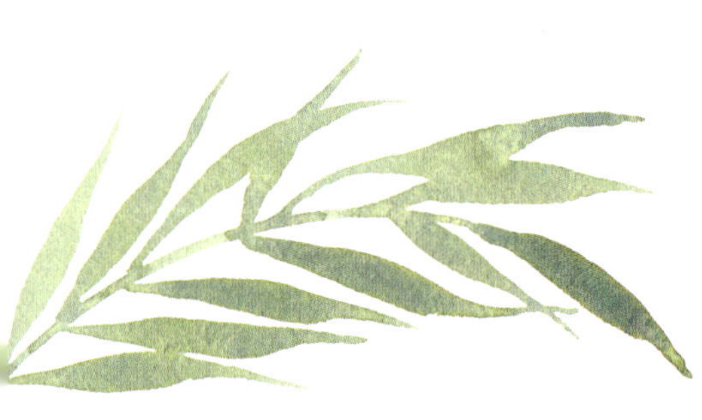

Time painting is time well spent.

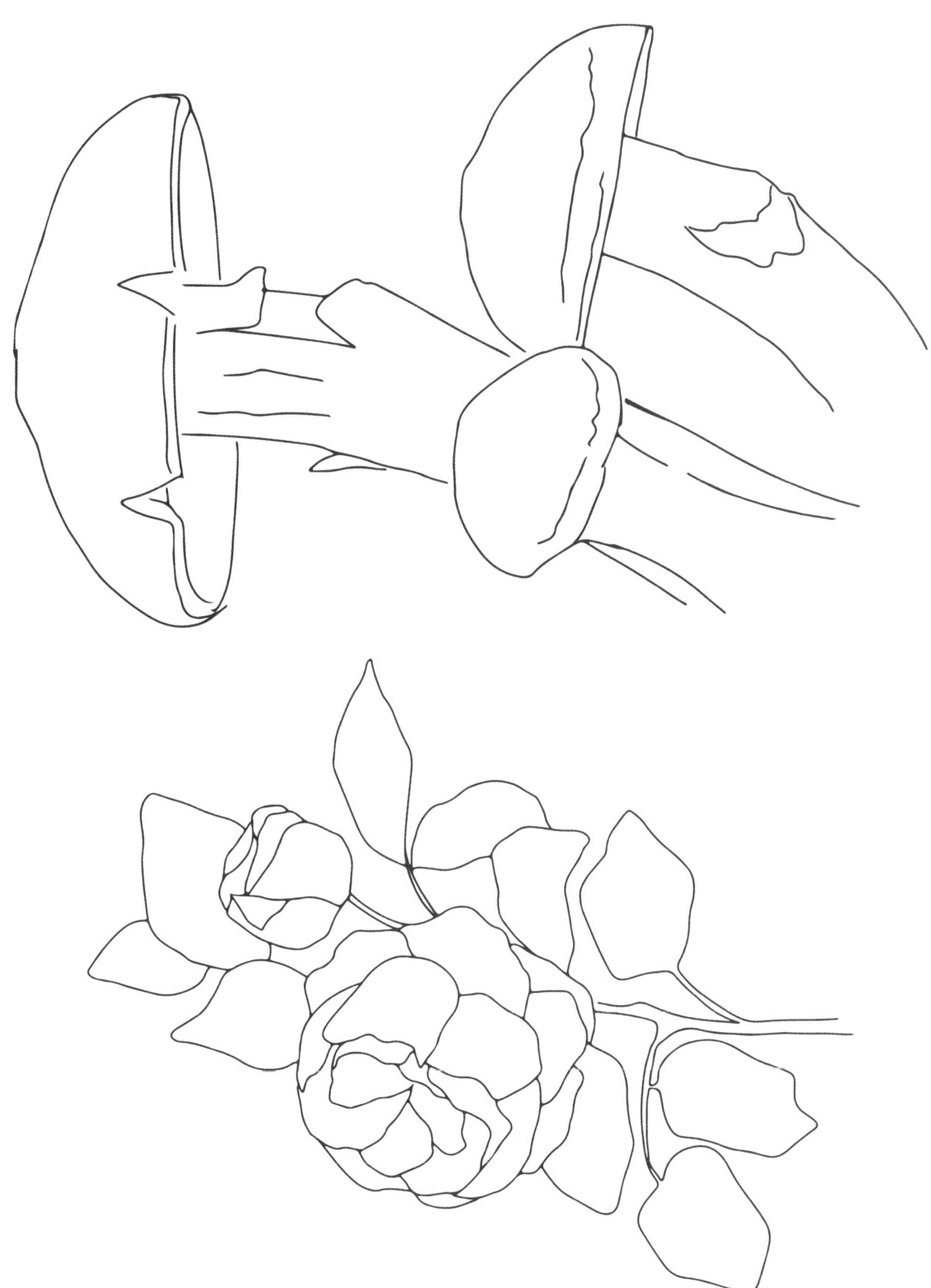

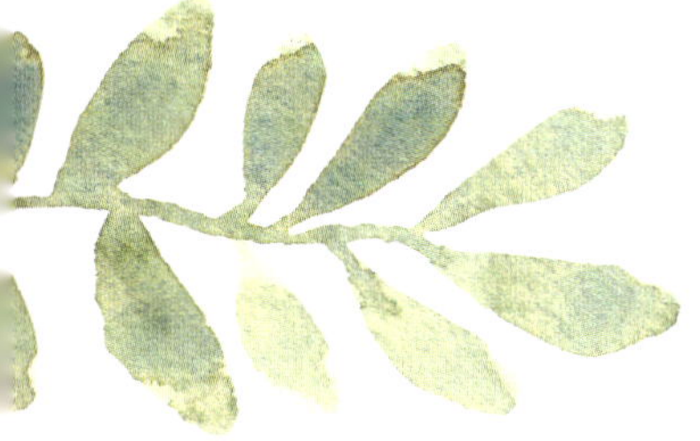

*Create an inspiring space where you will paint,
and enjoy your time creating in that space.*

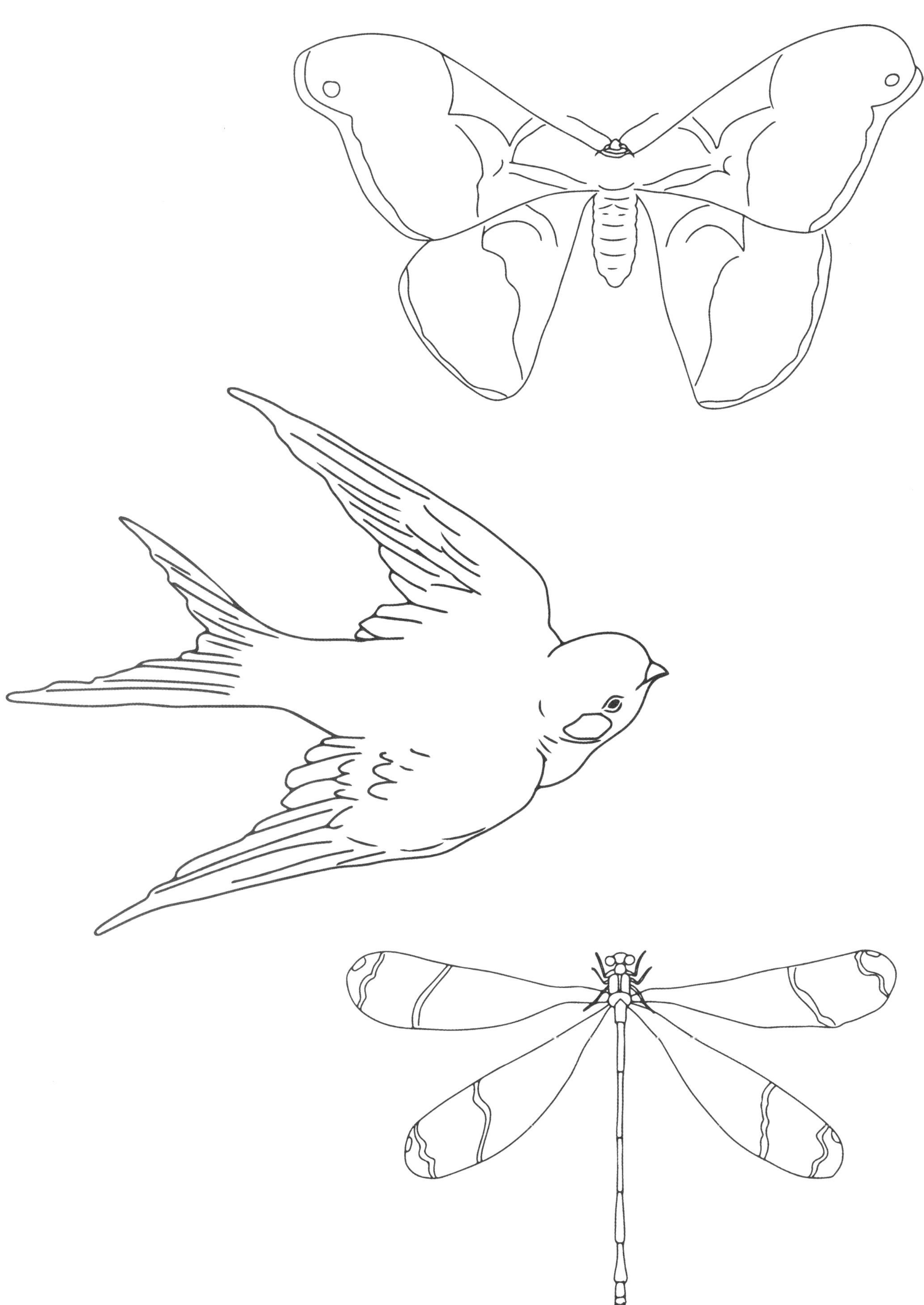

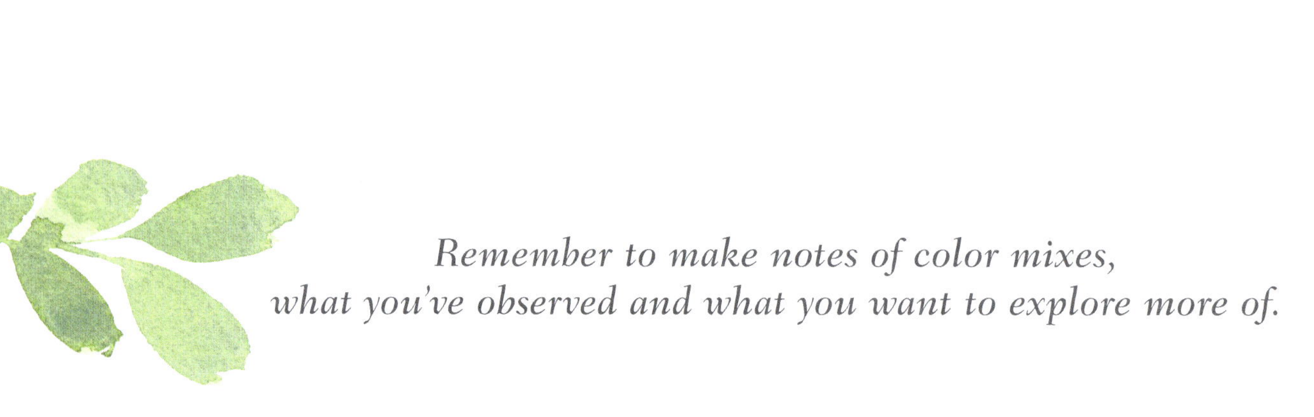

Remember to make notes of color mixes,
what you've observed and what you want to explore more of.

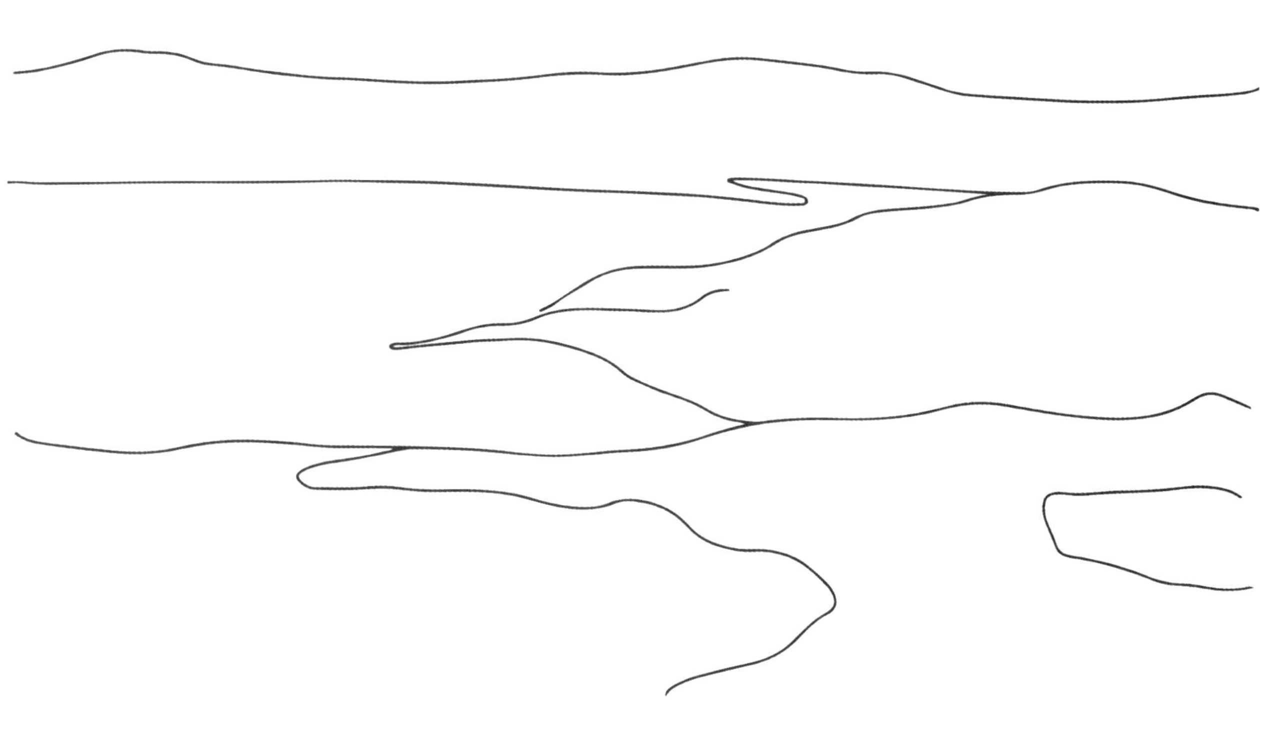

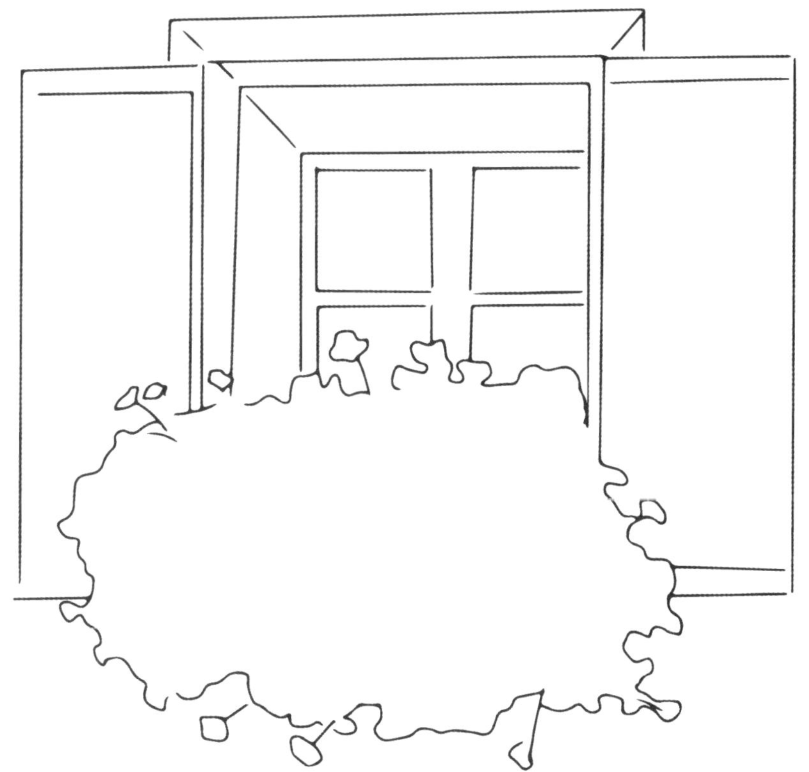

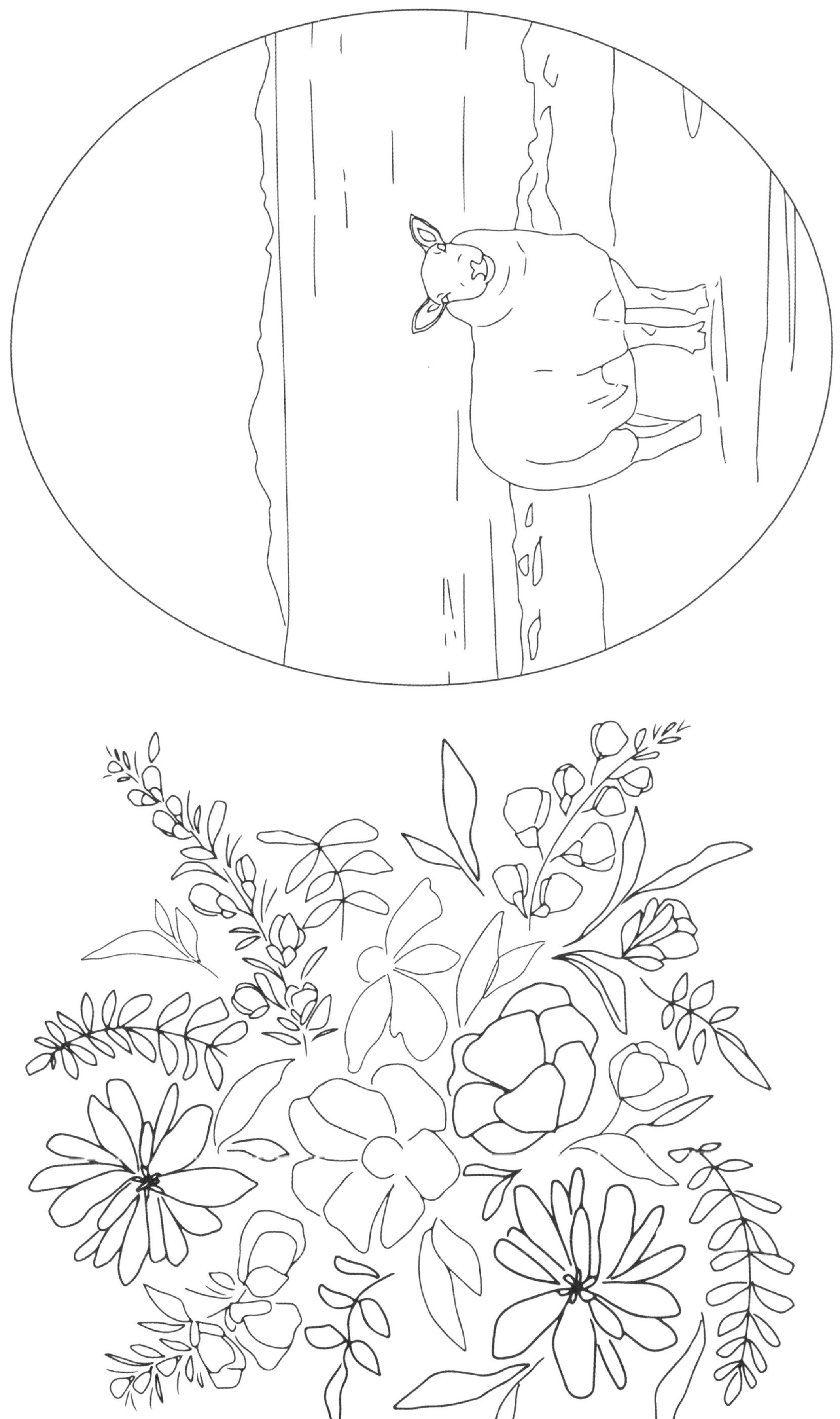

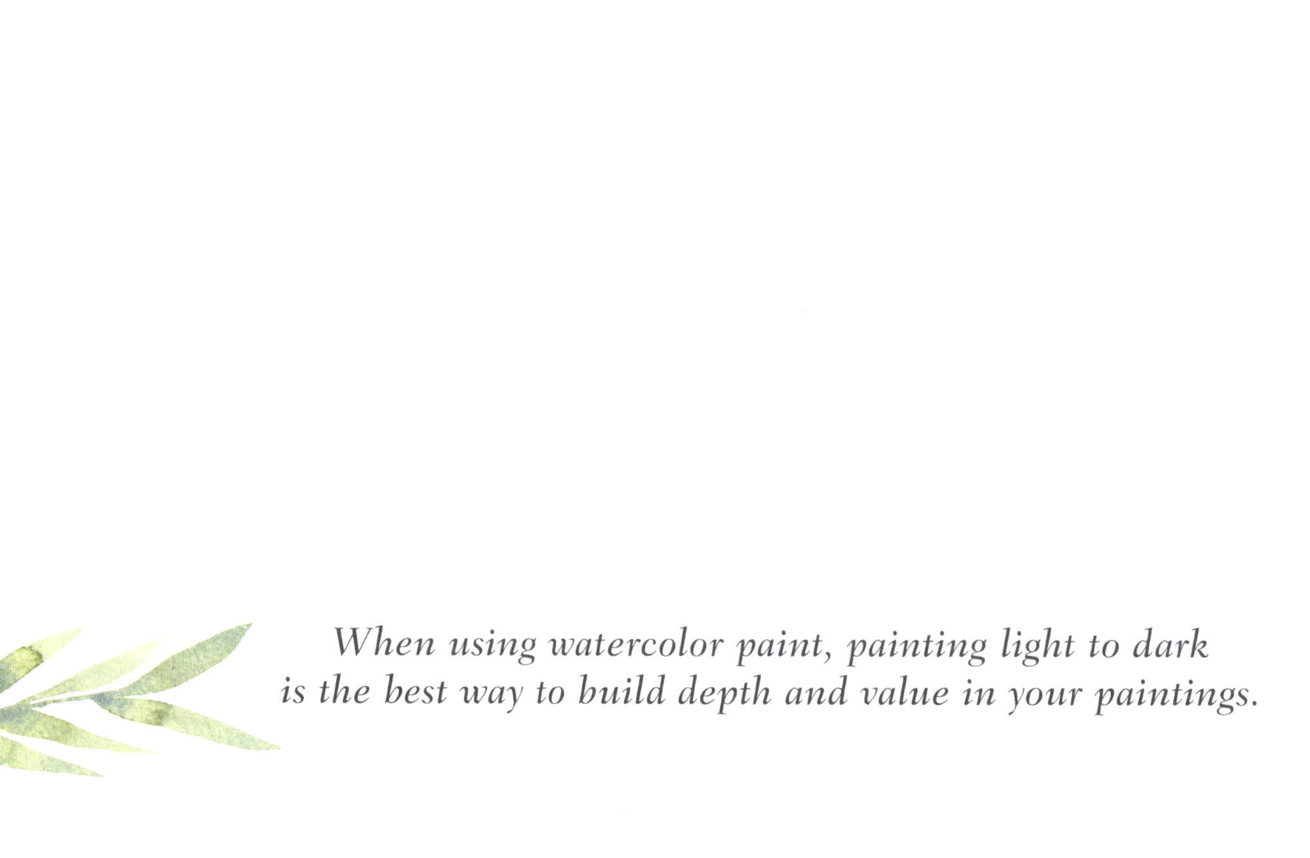

When using watercolor paint, painting light to dark
is the best way to build depth and value in your paintings.

INDEX

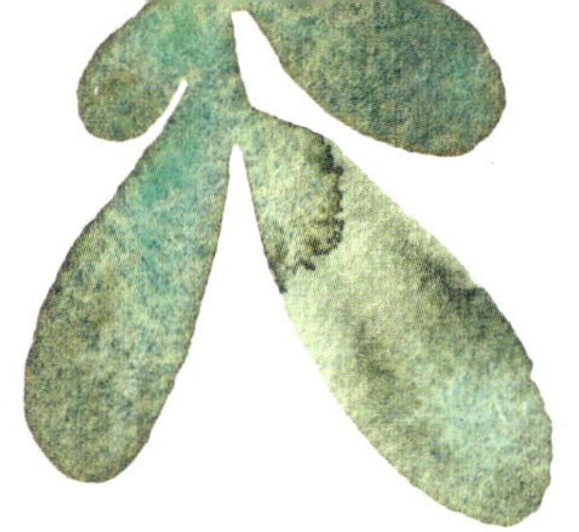

H

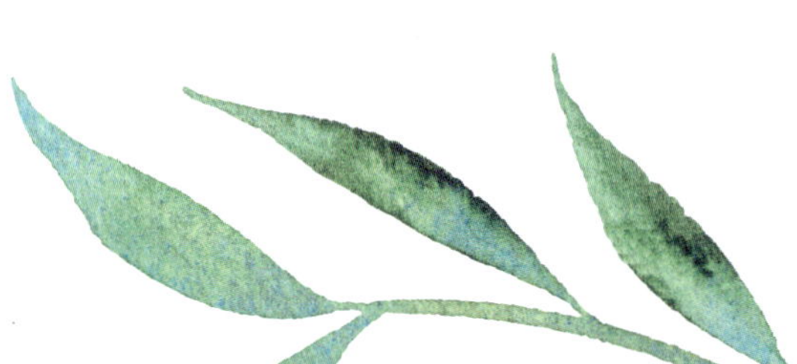

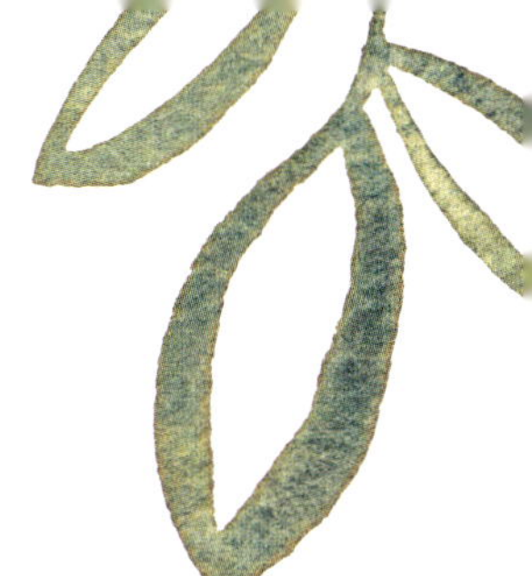

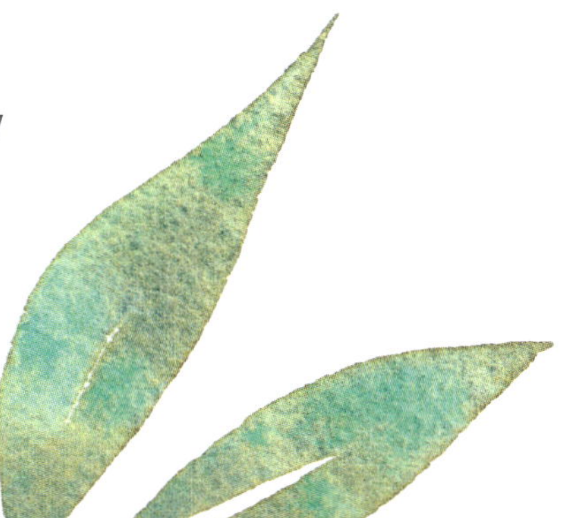

ABOUT THE AUTHOR

Nicki Traikos has been an artist at heart her entire life. The mediums may have changed greatly over the years, but the goal has always been the same—*to have the courage to try, and to find joy in the moments exploring.* Known best for her Watercolors Made Simple online classes, Nicki has a casual and approachable philosophy about making art and inspires other artists to adopt it too. As a mother to two grown kids who are also on creative journeys, Nicki enjoys watching them flourish as they follow their passions and express their art. While traveling with her husband, Nicki also enjoys photography and capturing moments with her phone that will then inspire her next painting, class, and even book.

For more instruction from Nicki and to join her online watercolor classes, visit www.lifeidesign.com. You can also follow Nicki on Instagram @lifeidesign for behind-the-scenes peeks into her home studio and personal art practice.

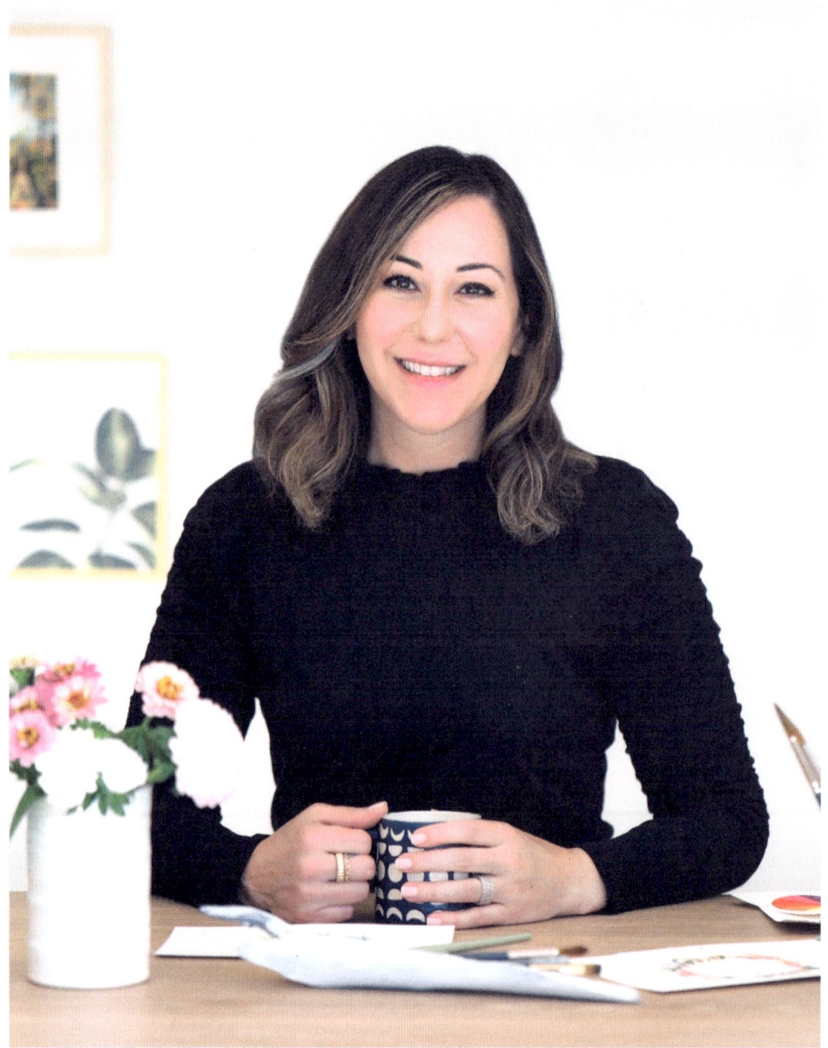

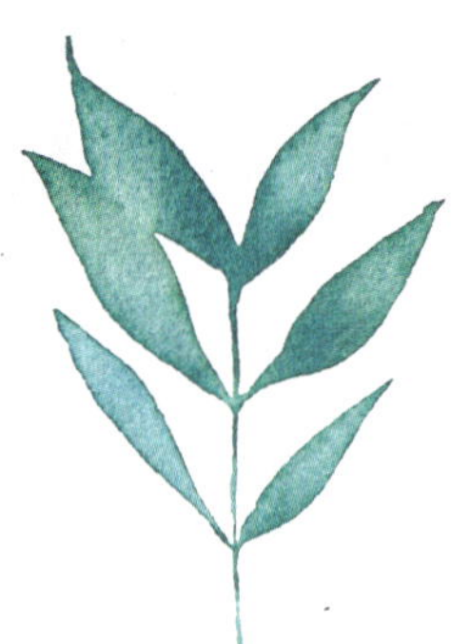

"Paint what you love, using colors you love, and you will love what you paint."